NEGOTIATIONS
WITH
PARADOX

NEGOTIATIONS WITH PARADOX

Narrative Practice and Narrative Form in Bunyan and Defoe

Stuart Sim

HARVESTER
WHEATSHEAF

New York   London   Toronto   Sydney   Tokyo   Singapore

First published 1990 by
Harvester Wheatsheaf
66 Wood Lane End, Hemel Hempstead
Hertfordshire HP2 4RG
A division of
Simon & Schuster International Group

Typeset in 11/12pt Bembo
by Keyboard Services, Luton

Printed and bound in Great Britain by
Billing and Sons Limited, Worcester

British Library Cataloguing in Publication Data

Sim, Stuart, *1943* –
    Negotiations with paradox : narrative practice and
    narrative form in Bunyan and Defoe.
    1. Fiction in English. Bunyan, John, 1628–1688 2.
    Fiction in English. Defoe, Daniel, 1660 or 1–1731
    I. Title
    823'.4

    ISBN 0-7108-1368-6

---

1 2 3 4 5   94 93 92 91 90

TO HELENE

CONTENTS

ACKNOWLEDGEMENTS

THIS work has had a long gestation, reaching back to my time as a postgraduate student at the University of Manchester, 1979–83. Thanks must go to my doctoral supervisor, Damian Grant, for all his help and encouragement during that period. I would also like to thank my colleagues in the Defoe Research Group of the Open University, Walton Hall, for their helpful comments on earlier drafts of Chapters 6 and 7, when these were presented as seminar papers to the group. I have benefited greatly from the advice of my colleague Bob Owens, both inside and outside the Open University's Defoe and Bunyan Research Groups. Shelagh Aston typed the final manuscript with her usual sensitivity and accuracy.

Earlier drafts of parts of some chapters have appeared in article form as follows: '"For some it driveth to dispaire": Calvinist soteriology and character models in Arthur Dent's *Plaine Man's Path-way to Heaven*', *ES*, 69 (1988), 238–48 (Chapter 2); '"Vertuous mediocrity and Fanatick conventicle": pilgrimage styles in Bishop Simon Patrick and John Bunyan', *ES*, 68 (1987), 316–24 (Chapter 3); 'Isolating the reprobate: paradox as a strategy for social critique in Bunyan's *Mr Badman*', *BS*, 1 (1988/9), 30–41 (Chapter 4); 'Bunyan's *Holy War* and the dialectics of long-drawn-outness', *Restoration*, 9 (1985), 93–8 (Chapter 5); 'Interrogating an ideology: Defoe's *Robinson Crusoe*', *BJECS*, 10 (1987), 163–73 (Chapter 6); 'Opposing the unopposable: *Roxana* and the paradox of reprobation', *BJECS*, 8 (1985), 179–86 (Chapter 7).

ABBREVIATIONS

BJECS   *British Journal for Eighteenth-century Studies*
BQ   *Baptist Quarterly*
BS   *Bunyan Studies*
ELH   *Journal of English Literary History*
ELR   *English Literary Renaissance*
ES   *English Studies*
MLN   *Modern Language Notes*
MLR   *Modern Language Review*
MQ   *Modern Quarterly*
PBHRS   *Proceedings of the Bedfordshire Historical Record*
          Society
PR   *Psychological Review*
RES   *Review of English Studies*
SEL   *Studies in English Literature*
SH   *Social History*
TSE   *Texas Studies in English*

Chapter One

INTRODUCTION

THE debt that Bunyan and Defoe owe to the tradition of spiritual autobiography and the Calvinist-influenced predestinarian soteriology that so often accompanied it (particularly amongst sectarian practitioners) has been well documented.[1] Both writers rely heavily on the genre in their major fictions, and texts such as *The Pilgrim's Progress* and *Robinson Crusoe* are recognisably conversion narratives.[2] What has been less well documented is the way that the paradoxes associated with both Calvinism and spiritual autobiography shape narrative in the two writers, as well as how paradox functions ideologically within their fictive discourse. That forms the subject-matter of the present work. The particular bias is to identify Bunyan and Defoe as writers who engage in a very direct, indeed often confrontational, manner with the paradoxes inherent in the genre: those paradoxes, for example, connected with predestination, salvation and reprobation, conversion, and grace. Such paradoxes will be seen to disclose large-scale contradictions in the authors' own belief-system – a belief-system in a counter-cultural relationship with the dominant ideology of the period – and their texts will be treated as highly-charged ideological artefacts: determinate productions that operate within a context of conflict-ridden cultural debate.

The underlying Calvinist theology to be found in Bunyan and Defoe's fiction can be considered to contribute a 'narrative of predestination'; that is, a basic framework and set of

sequences which automatically generate acute personal conflicts, moral dilemmas, and ideological contradictions, within
which an author can proceed to explore, in many ways is *forced*
to explore, wide-ranging problems concerning the individual's sociological and ontological status. Characterisation
practice, narrative form, and ideological subtext in Bunyan
and Defoe are profoundly affected by the paradoxes encoded
within the narrative of predestination. Those paradoxes
surrounding predestination and soteriology cast doubt on the
validity of human action and decision making, thus bringing
to the fore the problem of free will: a phenomenon loaded with
ideological significance in modern European history. In the act
of grappling with the complexities of free will and predeterminism, Bunyan and Defoe are brought up against some of
the most fundamental issues concerning the nature of personal
identity and social existence – again, areas of experience
fraught with ideological implications. They are also forced to
shape their narratives to accommodate these debates, and in
the case of *The Life and Death of Mr Badman*, *The Holy War* and
Roxana, this has resulted in works generally perplexing to the
critics, who have not always paid adequate attention to the
ideology of form involved. My argument would be that,
given their choice of the narrative of predestination as a site of
operations, both authors are required to engage in a constant
process of negotiation with paradox and its effects. It will be in
and around the aporias of Calvinist soteriology that some of
the most crucial decisions concerning the development of the
modern novel will take place, and these decisions resonate
with ideological import, given that both Bunyan and Defoe
are engaged in a sustained critique of contemporary social
values.

Paradox demands decision, both on the part of the author
and his characters, and such decisions dictate the course of
narrative. Robinson Crusoe is simultaneously a free-willed
individual and a pawn in a divine game-plan to which he can
have no access. It is Crusoe's personal decision to break with
his family background ('I would be satisfied with nothing but
going to Sea'[3]), but his 'free' decision is played out against a

divinely-crafted narrative punctuated by providential warnings. Christian, too, has to make a personal decision to flee home and family, but his progress is to be very carefully monitored thereafter by a series of divine agents (one of whom originally planted the seed for the notion of flight in his mind anyway).

Freely arrived at human decisions are seen to shape a journey whose end is already predetermined by divine decree. The pattern applies whatever the individual's nature, and both Mr Badman and Roxana choose to continue as sinners, thereby imposing a certain pattern on their careers, while apparently being predetermined to damnation. Authors and characters are aware, at some level, of being in a constant process of negotiation with their system of belief, and that system of belief in its turn with a dominant establishment ideology. These are fictions which, as Macherey would have it, 'interrogate' ideology;[4] both consciously, as paradox is manipulated by their polemically-minded authors, and unconsciously, as paradox discloses the layers of contradiction buried within that ideology. Narrative must chart the twists and turns of this complex set of negotiations.

All of Bunyan and Defoe's major fictions can be slotted into the tradition of spiritual autobiography, but for the purposes of this study those works which are most marked by paradox are the most interesting. Those I take to be *The Pilgrim's Progress, Mr Badman* and *The Holy War* in Bunyan's case; *Robinson Crusoe, A Journal of the Plague Year, Moll Flanders* and *Roxana* in Defoe's. I briefly consider the specific character of each author's relationship to the tradition of spiritual autobiography and conversion narrative in the second part of this introduction, prior to detailed analysis of the texts above, in terms of paradox, in later chapters. Also prior to the detailed analysis is an examination of Calvinist soteriology, and then of its incorporation into Puritan prose fiction in the work of one of Bunyan's major influences, Arthur Dent, whose *The Plaine Man's Path-way to Heaven* affected both Bunyan's theological and literary development.[5] This act of incorporation has considerable ideological significance. Soteriology rapidly becomes a valuable weapon in the polemical war waged by Puritans and dissenters, allowing them to condemn their opponents as reprobate, hence beyond all possible redemption, and inviting their supporters to identify with the elect élite. The war is fought no less in the field of fiction than of pamphleteering, [6] and Calvin must be rated a major source of influence in Puritan aesthetics. Theology in this period assumes an ideological position, and Calvinistic Puritanism exploits soteriology for all it is worth as a method of interrogating and undermining the currently dominant ideology.

I also consider another key figure in the development of Puritan aesthetics, the sixteenth-century French logician and Calvinist Petrus Ramus, whose importance to the structural aspect of Puritan writing (fiction and non-fiction) is quite crucial. Combine Calvin and Ramus and you have the underlying metaphysics and argument form of Puritan prose fiction: in effect, the ideological subtext. We are then in a position to consider how, almost immediately, as in the fiction of Dent, the form is brought up against paradox. At that point ideologically-implicated negotations ensue, and these are followed on through into the relevant Bunyan and Defoe texts.

Bunyan will be seen to be the more straightforwardly politically-engaged writer of the two, hence the more openly judgemental. His Calvinistic division of mankind into mutually exclusive elect and reprobate categories is sharp and severe, and pertains directly to the position of nonconformists under the Restoration settlement, with Bunyan adroitly manipulating predestinarian soteriology's anti-hierarchical bias as a means of questioning the dominant values of his society. Bunyan would seem to be very much on the side of the poor and the dispossessed, and his is an essentially anti-bourgeois position. [7] The dissenting vision is articulated in fictional form with a distinctively combative element. Parables are being provided for an elect suffering under particularly adverse socio-political conditions. While just as much a product of the Puritan heritage – presbyterian upbringing,

4

Dissenting Academy education[8] – Defoe is not as overtly propagandistic in approach and his targets are, politically speaking, perhaps more diffuse than Bunyan's; although in their own way just as combative and ideologically-sensitive. Both authors' creations confront a hostile world with a body of knowledge rooted in soteriological schemes, and attempt to relate the events of that world, as they impinge on them, to those schemes – with varying degrees of success. Walter J. Ong has referred to the dialectic of 'discourse knowledge' and 'observation knowledge' in the post-Renaissance period, and characterises its mode of operation as a gradual shift from the former to the latter.[9] That would be a good way of describing what is being enacted in Bunyan and Defoe's fictions. Observation knowledge is being processed through discourse knowledge, external events through internalised soteriological doctrines, in a way that insistently challenges, and requires justification of, the characters' and authors' ideological assumptions. Where Bunyan swiftly moves to shore up his own ideology when contradictions come on the scene, Defoe is more prone to highlight the problems of dealing with such contradictions and to pursue them through to their often unpalatable conclusions. Defoe's attitude to ideology – his own and the dominant one of his society – is the more subversive and interrogatory precisely because he does pursue the contradictions through with such honesty, and he is correspondingly more exercised by the gaps he locates. Discourse and observation mesh together less neatly than they do in Bunyan, albeit that the latter's meshing process requires considerable logical sleight of hand.

Despite such differences each author is recognisably operating within the same area of discourse, sharing many of its ideals and wrestling with its common problems. They are conducting a critique of their respective societies from an ideologically-committed position, and they conceive of this critique within the terms of reference of spiritual autobiography. In the process they establish dissent as a major influence in the English novel tradition, bequeathing to that tradition not just dissent's ideals but also its paradoxes and contradictions. Although expressed differently in our time, of course, given the decline of religious belief in the interim, those paradoxes and contradictions are now part of our general cultural heritage and are apparently no less intractable than they were in Bunyan and Defoe's world. To observe the authors locked in dialogue with these phenomena is to observe a fundamental cultural conflict being enacted which still touches us all in some respect in the late twentieth century. It is the debate between free will and determinism that we are witnessing. Determinism has a wider frame of reference than it had in the seventeenth century, and now embraces such varieties as the genetic and the sociological (both of which were subsumed under the theological in Bunyan and Defoe's time), but the impact is much the same. Its claim is that the individual is subject to, or victim of, forces out of his control. Arguments can be put forward that genes leave precious little freedom of choice to the individual, or that the poverty cycle makes a mockery of the idea that anyone is free to choose their position on the social scale; yet the ethical, legal and political codes of Western culture are based on the premisses of free will and individual responsibility for one's actions. The debate is complex, tortuous and far from being resolved. There are few more thoroughgoing engagements with it in literary history than are to be found in the fiction of Bunyan and Defoe.

Schematising the route of argument it goes as follows: Bunyan and Defoe are both critical of the value-system of their times; they both construct fictions to present a counter-cultural case to that value-system; their counter-cultural case, heavily based as it is in Calvinist predestinarian theology, is encoded with paradox; to make their soteriology-reliant critiques work effectively they must engage in negotiation with the assumptions of their own belief-system; and lastly, that such negotiations plunge them into the heart of the free will/determinism debate. Negotiation with paradox: interrogation of an ideology; those will form the principal subjects of this study.

B UNYAN has the less problematic relationship to conversion narrative, as befits an author with such clear-cut
ideological objectives and one who has left us what is arguably
the greatest of seventeenth-century spiritual autobiographies,
Grace Abounding. *Pilgrim's Progress* Parts One and Two and
Holy War all deal with successful pilgrimages through life –
although qualifications have to, and will, be made in respect of
the latter text – while *Badman* maps out an unsuccessful
pilgrimage. Bunyan's other major piece of writing, *Grace
Abounding*, similarly traces an individual's successful progress
to a state of grace and is worth considering briefly before
proceeding to the fictions. The narrative conforms fairly
closely to the standard three-stage division of spiritual autobiography, with Bunyan describing successively his sinful
pre-conversion existence, his process of conversion, and his
post-conversion state of new-found resolution in the face of
spiritual trials. *Grace Abounding* establishes the major themes
and concerns of Bunyan's fiction: the overriding obsession
with salvation; the constraining influence of a predeterminist
theological scheme ('I was bound, but he was free', as Bunyan
notes of his relationship to God (p. 103)); the manic-depressive
pattern of the individual's spiritual development; the sense of a
heroic personal struggle against overwhelming spiritual and
social odds. The sheer intensity of the narrative is its most
striking characteristic, and we are left in no doubt as to the
extent of the emotional upheaval involved in striving to reach
a state of grace through the paradoxes of one's theology:

> Thus, by the strange and unusual assaults of the tempter, was
> my Soul, like a broken Vessel, driven, as with the Winds, and
> tossed sometimes head-long into dispaire . . . Oh, the un-
> thought of imaginations, frights, fears, and terrors that are
> affected by a thorow application of guilt, yielding to despara-
> tion.   (p. 60)

Bunyan the man confronts the paradoxes of predestinarian
theology head on in *Grace Abounding*, and 'I was bound, but he
was free' elegantly and economically sums up the dilemma

facing the sincere candidate for election. It is a dilemma that will form the horizon of Bunyan's fictions. In his personal narrative he must learn to live with the sense of insecurity that such a realisation as 'I was bound, but he was free' brings in its wake: 'God might chuse whether he would give me comfort now, or at the hour of death' (p. 103). The narrative, in other words, must be left incomplete. Such incompleteness is something that Bunyan is usually concerned to overcome in his fiction, and *Pilgrim's Progress* Parts One and Two and *Badman* all counter the incompleteness of spiritual autobiography with their protagonists' death. *Holy War*, however, will leave its protagonist's life incomplete, thus remaining in many ways the closest of Bunyan's fictions to the standard spiritual autobiography pattern.

Pilgrim's Progress Part One is archetypal conversion narrative territory. Christian is discovered by the reader all but overwhelmed by a sense of his own sin and possible damnation. He subsequently risks everything on a pilgrimage to the Celestial City, undergoing a constant series of trials and tribulations – some from external and some from internal forces – on the way. There is an unmistakable conversion experience to be noted ('just as *Christian* came up with the *Cross*, his burden loosed from off his back; and began to tumble'[10]) and ultimately there is the transition to a permanent state of grace in the Celestial City. What we witness in *Pilgrim's Progress*, as we do in *Grace Abounding*, is the slow, painful, but absolutely inexorable progress to grace, in which conversion marks a critically significant break with the subject's past. Christian may in several respects fall short of the pilgrim ideal – he can be led astray, he can lead others astray – but his eventual success seems assured. Having been singled out from his fellows and given the divine seal of approval, he cannot fail to gain the fruits of election. On leaving the world he knew – the world of wife, family, and neighbours in the City of Destruction – he enters a brave, new, and often menacing world of signs, where everything is coded according to the dictates of predestinarian soteriology. Elect and reprobate are to be divided, judged and dealt with

8

accordingly. The conventions of the conversion narrative genre are handled in a practised manner by an author supremely confident in the use of its techniques.

Pilgrim's Progress Part Two covers much the same ground, and fits the conversion narrative model of irresistible progress towards a predestined goal in the case of Christian's wife, children, and their sundry pilgrim acquaintances. While the landscape of election can still appear harsh on occasion, in general it presents a kindlier face to its pilgrims than its Part One counterpart, and there is less sense of individual isolation to be noted. If conversion narrative tends to feature a sense of tension between the justice and mercy sides of Christianity, then in Part Two it is mercy that is in the ascendancy – 'The King, who hath sent for me and my Children, is one that delighteth in *Mercie*' (p. 185) – whereas it was manifestly justice that prevailed in Part One.

Holy War would appear also to fit into the conversion narrative pattern. Mansoul is repeatedly besieged by evil forces, the tirelessly energetic Diabolonians, and just as repeatedly saved by divine intervention. For all the success against invasion, however, Mansoul is not brought through death into the Celestial City by his creator. We leave the scene of soteriological conflict with the issue still unresolved, Bunyan opting for an open-ended narrative on the *Grace Abounding* model in this instance. Mansoul is enjoined by Emmanuel to 'hold fast till I come' in the event of future attack, but not given his ultimate reward of eternal grace as yet. Despite its open-endedness, however, it is clear from all the signs we are given in *Holy War* that Mansoul is of the elect and destined for eternal salvation: '*Remember therefore, O my Mansoul, that thou art beloved of me . . . I command thee to believe that my love is constant to thee*'.[11]

Badman represents the mirror-image to the conversion narrative of *Pilgrim's Progress* and *Holy War*. Here we have a narrative of predestination where conversion is conspicuously lacking and the signs all point towards damnation. Bunyan is just as rigorous in plotting the course of reprobation as he was election, and this is yet another inexorable progress towards a predestined goal that we are being asked to witness: 'I will tell you, that from a Child he was very *bad*: his very beginning was *ominous*, and presaged that no good end, was, in likelyhood, to follow thereupon'.[12] Badman can no more arrest this particular progress by his own efforts than Christian can his elect one, and it is the absence of the expected critical points of the conversion narrative genre – unsolicited doubt, conversion experience, courage in adversity, willingness to heed providential warnings and to engage in doctrinal dispute – that mark this protagonist as doomed in spiritual terms of reference. The coding is firmly against Badman, it is predestined to be so, and he cannot esape the inevitable fate that awaits him.

Bunyan's fictions, therefore, fall fairly unproblematically into the conversion narrative genre, and he employs the genre with identifiably polemical intent. There is a concern to pass judgement on individuals from a very committed, dissenting, ideological position. Which is not to say that there is complete predictability about Bunyan's disposition and distribution of that genre's conventions throughout his narratives. *Holy War* does stand out from the other texts somewhat in its open-endedness and lack of final resolution, which resolution to come has to be taken on trust by the reader rather than being openly visible in its enactment as in *Pilgrim's Progress*. In this sense it is closer to Bunyan's own spiritual autobiography, *Grace Abounding*, than his other fictions. 'God might chuse whether he would give me comfort now, or at the hour of death' but one must continue onwards regardless, despite one's uncertainty as to God's probable conduct. What Bunyan achieves in *Holy War* is to communicate a sense of the continuing struggle that the individual must wage in daily life, where final resolutions must remain in the realm of promise rather than reality. He succeeds brilliantly in capturing the psychology of Calvinism in the process. For all its insistence on predestination, Calvinism tends to promote a perpetual sense of unease in its adherents: a sense of lingering doubt, even after the apparently conclusive conversion experience.[13] It is a state of mind that recalls Samuel Beckett's pithy observation: 'do not despair, one of the thieves was saved; do

not presume, one of the thieves was hanged'.[14] In *Badman*
Bunyan relentlessly pursues his victim, turning all his more
sympathetic character traits, such as his apparent resignation
in the face of death, into doom-laden signals: 'no man can tell
whether a man goes, by *any such* manner of death' (p. 157). Yet
if 'no man can tell' then, viewed from humanity's perspective,
Badman's redemption is theoretically still a possibility and we
enter the realm of paradox. Outward behaviour, so consistently read as an index of spiritual condition in Bunyan,
ultimately reveals itself to be an unreliable sign; as N. H.
Keeble has remarked, 'the experiential fact of uncertainty
is incontrovertible' to the Calvinist.[15] Over the course of
Bunyan's fictions, we are to observe periodic disjunctions of
sign and spiritual fate that belie the inexorability of predestinarian soteriology. In the final analysis man can only *predict*
soteriological status, and a certain note of frustration creeps
into Bunyan's fiction at this realisation. Both *Badman* and *Holy
War* bear witness to this frustration at human limitations.
Bunyan's negotiations with the narrative of predestination
and its inbuilt paradoxes disclose not just the limitations of the
form, but also its immense potential for development. It is as
much in the breakdowns and gaps of Bunyan's handling of
conversion narrative that his continuing fascination as an
author lies, as in his successful adaptation of it to the theme of
fictional pilgrimage. In the meeting of narrative form and
theological imperatives lies Bunyan's greatest struggle, and
his greatest achievement. In his hands conversion narrative
begins to develop into a form with an unparalleled responsiveness to a fundamental human dilemma: the conflict
between free-willed individualism and determinist cultural
system.

Defoe, too, confronts this fundamental dilemma in a
range of fictions that stand in a more self-consciously problematical relationship to spiritual autobiography. In some
cases, *Colonel Jack* and *Captain Singleton* for example, the
conversion narrative content is fairly minimal and handled in a
somewhat perfunctory way, and one wonders just how
seriously the author is taking the spiritual theme. Yet the genre

insistently intrudes itself into Defoe's narratives, and unless we are willing to align ourselves with the Defoe-as-hoaxer kind of reading put forward recently by Laura Curtis,[16] we must accord it more than merely reflex significance. Defoe clearly feels motivated to encompass predestinarian theology in his fiction in some manner. Perfunctory though their spirituality may well be, Colonel Jack's and Captain Singleton's sense of conversion lends depth to what would otherwise be little more than adventure stories. In several of Defoe's texts, of course, spiritual fate *is* a central concern of the protagonist, although in problematic ways, *Robinson Crusoe*, *Moll Flanders*, *A Journal of the Plague Year* and *Roxana* can all be said to have a recurrent spiritual theme. *Crusoe* is most obviously in the tradition of spiritual autobiography, with an easily recognisable conversion experience: 'I threw down the Book, and with my Heart as well as my Hands lifted up to Heaven, in a Kind of Extasy of Joy, I cry'd out aloud, *Jesus, thou Son of* David, *Jesus, thou exalted* Prince and Saviour, give me Repentance!' (p. 96). Crusoe's conversion experience occurs during a bout of illness, where he is seen to be in precisely the state of powerlessness spiritual autobiography requires of the elect: a helpless, passive recipient of divine grace who can accept no credit for what is happening. The irresistible conquers the unresisting in a model example of the election process.

Crusoe is not always such a conventional electee, however, and there is not the same sense of inexorability of progress to grace as is evident in Bunyan's fiction. This is an intensely restless character, driven by his own internal desires, 'that Propension of Nature' (p. 4) as he calls it, who, until the experience of conversion, consistently tempts God and refuses to heed a stream of providential warnings. Crusoe's lapses from grace, the workings of his natural propensity, are of a far more serious kind than those of Christian. The contemptuous attitude to providence displayed by Crusoe often recalls Badman at his worst. Crusoe either misreads or discounts soteriological signs in his pre-conversion phase, and is more than capable of flaunting God's will post-conversion as well. It

is a particularly protracted, sophisticated and unpredictable set
of negotiations that is on view, and Defoe plays with the
conversion narrative form without ever openly disparaging it.
The form deserves respect after all, representing as it does an
entire way of life and system of belief. It is a worthy enemy,
not one to be easily overcome by a single, strong-willed
individual – even one as resourceful as Crusoe proves to be.
Crusoe may test the limits of his system of belief, but he is
nevertheless very aware of having to operate within those
limits.

Moll Flanders too is a strong-willed, resourceful individual who is forced to take on the system in order to survive.
Although she undergoes a conversion experience while under
sentence in Newgate, this comes rather late in a career of
crime, and it is difficult to resist being drawn into Moll's
criminal adventures as an interested and sympathetic party,
rather than the judge-style figure conversion narrative conventionally wants to be. The heroine's tendency to invest the
tales of her criminal jaunts with a definite note of relish, can all
too easily make admirers of us and appear to trivialise the
spiritual content of the narrative. Nevertheless, Moll is prey to
doubts on occasion, and does have a moral streak to her
character:

> I wanted to be plac'd in a settled State of Living, and had I
> happen'd to meet with a sober good Husband, I should have
> been as faithful and true a Wife to him as Virtue it self could have
> form'd: If I had been otherwise, the Vice came in always at the
> Door of Necessity, not at the Door of Inclination.[17]

Yet patriarchal society signally fails to provide her with the
means to pursue this apparently unexceptionable end, and
women appear to be even more at the mercy of necessity than
men in Defoe's world. One might describe Moll as predestined
to suffer by the mere accident of being born into the wrong
sexual category. Neither can she alter the effect of birth on her
economic status. Through no fault of her own, Moll must
seek her spiritual salvation in the midst of a series of pressing

necessities, which precipitate her into actions normally suggestive of damnation. Theft, prostitution and incest, to name
her more blatant indiscretions, present themselves more as
signs of reprobation than election. We must assume Moll to
have progressed to a state of grace – 'we resolve to spend the
Remainder of our Years in sincere Penitence, for the wicked
Lives we have lived' (p. 343), as she claims at the narra--
ive's end – but her election does not carry the conviction of
Christian's.

Journal is riddled with feelings of uncertainty and insecurity, despite the clear hints we are given that the narrator, H.F.,
is of the elect in terms of providential protection from the
plague. He describes himself as being 'supported with a secret
Satisfaction that I should be kept',[18] and survives the plague,
suggesting that the 'secret Satisfaction' was well founded. It
was traditionally argued that the elect would form a very small
part of humanity – Dent suggests they would 'walke very
thinly in the streets'[19] – and of all conversion narratives this is
arguably the most successful in conveying that sense of
élitism, as well as the arbitrariness of election's operation. The
plague is no more a 'respecter of persons' than God is, and
H.F. claims no personal credit for his immunity: 'I was in his
Hands, and it was meet he should do with me as should seem
good to him' (p. 13). H.F.'s apparent resignation to God's will
cannot, however, completely prevent periodic bouts of insecurity (the despair/presume axis at work). No individual can
ever know with absolute certainty what 'should seem good' to
God, and even the devout H.F. acknowledges the problems
that this creates for the individual will when he argues that,
'tho Providence seem'd to direct my Conduct to be otherwise;
yet it is my opinion, and I must leave it as a Prescription, *(viz.)*
that the best Physick against the Plague is to run away from it' (pp.
197–8). As so often in Defoe, there is a sense of conversion
narrative being undermined, although this does not mean that
he explodes the possibility of predetermined fate; rather that
he marks out the terrain of negotiation where the individual
consciousness and the agents of fate are to be locked in
combat. Negotiations in Defoe are precisely about how much

14

room for manoeuvre the individual will can have in the face of necessity. H.F. neatly identifies the paradox involved at this point.

Roxana presents even more intractable problems as regards the conversion narrative genre. This is Defoe's equivalent of *Badman*, but with a subtle twist to the proceedings: over the course of the narrative the heroine exhibits all the doubts, fears and insecurities normally associated with the elect, but apparently without being one of their number. Roxana shows herself to be perfectly sensible of the enormity of her sins and can produce the expected response on demand: 'I had a Terror upon me for my wicked Life past'.[20] Nevertheless, she cannot break out of the vicious cycle of events initiated by necessity: 'Necessity first debauch'd me' (p. 202). There is, therefore, a desire for repentance in the heroine, but it is to be frustrated by the combined efforts of socio-economic, physiological, psychological and metaphysical pressures. The dilemma faced by Moll – how to reconcile morality and poverty – is present in *Roxana* too, but in sharpened form with all its considerable potential for paradox opened up. *Roxana* comes across as a conversion narrative gone sadly wrong; in fact as a failed spiritual autobiography. The heroine stands as a paradigm of the reprobate condition: a character at the mercy of forces outside her control, whose exercise of will merely exacerbates her plight. To resist one's fate is pointless if it is predestined, and necessity certainly presents that way to Roxana. Defoe's achievement is to make us feel the full horror of reprobation through the character's own experience. Roxana engages our sympathy and concern in a way that Badman never could. The text takes the details of Calvinist soteriology absolutely seriously, and then follows through their implications for the reprobate. The heroine is both free *and* determined in her behaviour, a victim of the 'paradox of reprobation', and the text represents one of the most challenging contributions to the free will/determinism debate in the whole of English literary history. Her fate is both an indictment of the ideological system she must live under, and a despairing comment on the metaphysics that operate in her universe.

Roxana demonstrates the hold that predestinarian soteriological theory has on Defoe. Even if he is quite capable of
moving into and out of its conventions he keeps re-engaging
in dialogue with it, and it retains an endless fascination for
him. His other fictions show the traces of conversion narrative
too, if in a more residual way. Colonel Jack, for example,
eventually arrives at a state of spiritual peace: 'I saw clearer
than ever I had done before, how an invisible over-ruling
Power, a Hand influenced from above, Governs all our
Actions of every Kind, limits all our Designs, and orders the
Events of every Thing relating to us.'[21] Given these belated
reflections on the workings of providence, Colonel Jack's
career might just qualify as spiritual autobiography, even if
there is not the same intensity of concern with the spiritual that
informs the texts above. Adventure takes over to a large
extent, but conversion narrative sentiments linger on at the
margins of the text. Similar comments might be made about
The Farther Adventures of Robinson Crusoe. Adventure and
moralisation are here in a state of conflict, with adventure
undoubtedly predominating, and paradox less to the fore; but
conversion narrative maintains a presence under the surface.
Captain Singleton is even heavier on the adventure and lighter
on the moralisation than *The Farther Adventures* or *Colonel
Jack*, but the protagonist eventually feels the need to put a
conversion narrative framework on the details of his life,
while undergoing the ritual late reflections. Perhaps what
comes through most strongly in these narratives is the
individual's desire to impose some kind of spiritually-
significant order on his existence, as well as the reflex power of
the conversion narrative form and the belief-system underpinning it. Defoe's characters invariably, and sometimes rather
desperately, seek a sense of inexorability of progress in their
careers. Whether there is real justification for them doing so is
often open to question, but spiritual salvation would seem to
be dependent on the identification of that inexorability in the
reading of one's life.[22]

Even the most committed argument will not turn
these last three texts into hard-edged conversion narratives,

however, and they must be considered to be fairly low-key examples of the genre, where Defoe displays less interest in negotiating with his belief-system and its paradoxes than in *Crusoe, Moll, Journal* and *Roxana*. It is that act of negotiation that interests me, and I feel that it leads to Defoe's greatest achievements. Those four texts, therefore, are the ones to be treated in this study. What ought to have emerged from this brief survey of Defoe's major fictions is a sense of an author imbued with the ideals of conversion narrative, but uncomfortably aware of the paradoxes generated by its accompanying soteriology. When Defoe brings to the fore those paradoxes and demonstrates their effect on his characters' lives and psychology, then he is at his most stimulating, thought-provoking and ideologically subversive.

The major difference between Bunyan and Defoe's conversion narratives lies in the greater unpredictability in the soteriological coding of the latter's. Signs can mislead in Defoe far more than is acknowledged to be the case in Bunyan. Defoe's characters too, for all their resourcefulness, have the sharper sense of insecurity: providence proving to be a particularly inscrutable phenomenon in Defoe's world. Bunyan is generally content to remain within the rigidities of the conversion narrative form – his ideological imperatives are tightly focused, and his polemic thrives on the sense of remorselessness of judgement that the genre is capable of giving – whereas Defoe restlessly explores its limits. Both authors, though, ultimately find themselves confronted by paradox and that brings them into collision with the assumptions of their belief-system. At that point complex negotiations are called for, and the free will/determinism issue comes to the fore to establish a central place in English literary history. This is a legacy of the predestinarian theology upon which they are drawing. Chapter 2 considers the sources of that theology in order to reconstruct the ideological field of operations within which Bunyan and Defoe's fictions are polemically engaged.

Chapter Two

CALVINISM, PARADOX AND NARRATIVE

ALVIN's conception of predestination and election creates severe problems in the area of free will and determinism. Philosophically speaking, it is extremely difficult to reconcile freedom of action with such deterministically-oriented ideas. Admittedly, recent commentators have been at some pains to deny that this is what these doctrines involve. The editors of the *Commentaries*, for example, claim that although 'it is common to think of predestination as deterministic', that is not necessarily the case:

> Determinism means that one fact arises from one or more others by way of a natural necessity and that one can discover how one situation determines another. But one does not study the conditions of the Christians in this world and arrive at an understanding of predestination . . . Determinism has nothing to do with the mystery of evil. On the contrary, it explains the mystery away. Predestination as Calvin understands it is inseparable from that same mystery and the very ground of courage for living with it.[1]

It will be argued here, however, that despite all such arguments to the contrary, election and predestination do lead to a conflict between freedom of action and determinism: that when it comes to the individual subject's own emotional life, belief in these soteriological doctrines will almost invariably manifest itself in terms of the free will/determinism debate.

18

Francis M. Higman, in an excellent study of Calvin's style, makes a similar point when he argues that, 'the fact that Calvin developed the doctrine of predestination in clearer and firmer terms than did his contemporaries means that the paradox becomes particularly apparent in his case'.[2]

Calvinism was by no means an original theology. One thing that set it apart from its rivals was the stress laid by Calvin on the concepts of election and reprobation, although just how important these are to Calvinism is a matter of some controversy. In the nineteenth century there was a school of thought which saw it as a primary differentiating characteristic – 'an article of faith which did not even need to be verified' in François Wendel's words[3] – but this orthodoxy has since come to be challenged by such scholars as Paul Wernle:

> [I]t cannot be over-emphasized: faith in predestination is a long way from being the centre of Calvinism; much rather it is the last consequence of faith in the grace of Christ in the presence of the enigmas of experience.[4]

More recently, it has been argued that it is not predestination that is central to Calvin's theology, but knowledge of God.[5] The minutiae of this exegetical controversy need not concern us overmuch; the important point for the present enquiry is that election and predestination came to exercise a very strong hold over the English Puritan and sectarian imagination. Dean Ebner has argued that, 'it is only when . . . we regard the central thrust of seventeenth-century Puritanism as a preoccupation with the experience of conversion that the controlling purpose of the vast majority of Puritan treatises, sermons, diaries and autobiographies becomes apparent to us'.[6]

In his major work, *The Institutes of the Christian Religion*, Calvin states that,

> We call predestination God's eternal decree, by which he compacted with himself what he willed to become of each man. For all are not created in equal condition; rather, eternal life is fore-ordained for some, eternal damnation for others.

> Therefore, as any man has been created to one or the other of these ends, we speak of him as predestined to life or to death.[7]

Those predestined to life are the elect, those to death the reprobate. Just why God makes this division of mankind is not to be questioned: 'many, as if they wished to avert a reproach from God, accept election in such terms as to deny that anyone is condemned. But they do this very ignorantly and childishly, since election itself could not stand except as set over against reprobation'. The latter statement is one of the clearest commitments to binarism in Calvinist thought: 'election itself could not stand except as set over against reprobation'. To be elected is to be admitted to eternal grace in heaven; to be reprobated is to be damned to everlasting perdition: 'Therefore, those whom God passes over, he condemns; and this he does for no other reason than that he wills to exclude them from the inheritance which he predestines for his own children' (II, 947). The decree, as Calvin himself readily admits, 'is dreadful indeed', but he holds that 'no one can deny that God foreknew what end man was to have before he created him' (II, 955). So far this is a straightforward, if by twentieth-century standards unpalatable, doctrine; but Calvin proceeds to complicate matters by asserting that the reprobate are responsible for their own actions: 'their perdition depends upon the predestination of God in such a way that the cause and occasion of it are found in themselves . . . man falls according as God's providence ordains, but he falls by his own fault' (II, 957). The issue is then further complicated by the insistence that the mercy of God is open to all: 'God's mercy will always, accordingly go to meet repentance'; although this is coupled with an entirely characteristic qualification that 'all the prophets and all the apostles . . . clearly teach to whom repentance is given' (II, 983). This would appear to create a massive contradiction, with God-given depravity being both cause and effect of divine judgement.

Wendel has referred to the presence of several such paradoxes in Calvinist theology, but defends his subject on the grounds that, 'his writings are not those of a logician, hardly those of a philosopher . . . If we want to speak of a "system" of Calvin, we must do so, with certain reservations, owing to the plurality of themes that imposed themselves simultaneously upon its author's thinking'. Nevertheless, as he points out, 'what have been called the "paradoxes" of Calvin remain'; although it is stressed that there is no question of deliberate deception involved: 'every one of these contradictions was carefully examined by Calvin, with scrupulous fidelity to the Bible. One could even say that his fidelity is proved by the fact that he allowed them to remain'. What this seems to suggest is that, if Calvin leaves it in the text, a contradiction is not really a contradiction, but even Wendel feels compelled 'to admit frankly [that] despite all his fidelity to the Bible, he seems to have been searching the Scriptures more frequently for texts to support a doctrine accepted in advance, than to derive doctrine from the Scriptures'.[8] Higman's gloss on the contradiction problem is that Calvin is such a deeply logocentrist thinker, that he cannot believe biblical contradiction to be other than apparent and superficial. All that is required for resolution is to confront the contradiction with 'other texts of equal status'.[9] If he cannot be accused of deception, therefore, Calvin can at least be taxed with the narrowness of vision so often found in ideologues.

William J. Bouwsma, too, stresses the lack of consistency in Calvin's thought, but is less concerned to rescue his subject from such a charge, or even to regard it as a negative element. It is rather a case of situating Calvin within the context of his turbulent times: 'I do not believe that Calvin even aspired to the construction of a system . . . A systematic Calvin would be an anachronism; there are no "systematic" thinkers of any significance in the sixteenth century'. What we should be admiring in Calvin's work, in Bouwsma's view, is its flexibility and responsiveness to a period of unprecedented social upheaval, where contradictions and paradoxes are an inescapable penalty of polemically-motivated engagement. The presence of paradox can also be read as revealing 'an openness to all the contradictory realities of human experience' on Calvin's part.[10]

Calvin usually gives the impression of evading the issues raised by his paradoxes, and his theology is full of what Wendel has called 'superficial and contrived' resolutions in this respect.[11] Given predestination and election, it is extremely difficult to see how the reprobate can be blamed for their nature, but blamed they are – 'the cause and occasion of it are found in themselves' – and Calvin's usual ploy in such cases is to take refuge in God's innate mysteriousness:

> Let this, therefore, first of all be before our eyes: to seek any other knowledge of predestination than what the Word of God discloses is not less insane than if one should purpose to walk in a pathless waste . . . or to see in darkness. And let us not be ashamed to be ignorant of something in this matter, wherein there is a certain learned ignorance. (II, 923)

Justification for predestination lies solely with God, and 'it is not lawful for mortal men to intrude upon the secrets of God'. God's will provides Calvin with a final answer to literally any problem he is ever likely to encounter: 'whatever he wills, by the very fact that he wills it, must be considered righteous' (II, 949). The divine will functions much like a philosophical ground, and Calvin clearly wants it to communicate a similar sense of self-evidentially justifiable authority such that its mere invocation automatically terminates debate. Assertion does not in any way resolve paradox, however, and it may well be wondered how predestination and election could come to exert such a hold on the Protestant imagination. Both Calvin's logic and his ethics appear highly questionable and can pose considerable problems for modern commentators, who are not always able to suppress a sense of alienation in the face of paradox. The following example demonstrates the point quite graphically. In *English Pulpit Oratory from Andrewes to Tillotson*, W. Fraser Mitchell quotes this passage from a seventeenth-century sermon:

> When we certainly know by the Scriptures & without contro- versie believe, no small part of mankinde, in Gods decree and

eternal purpose, to stand reprobate and rejected from salvation, and all the effects of election, whether in the masse of sin or otherwise, (all is one to the point of this difficultie:) when, I say, it is of all hands yeelded that there be so many reprobates, denied the grace of election, and from all eternitie, prepared, or *finished*, as the Scripture speaketh, to destruction (for what God executes in time he willes in eternity,) what shall wee say to Praier and Thanksgiving for these? or what benefit can either they or we receive thereby?

For Mitchell this is 'one of the bluntest and most revolting statements of the Calvinistic interpretation of faith on record',[12] and while it is not difficult to identify reasons for his distaste – the finality and militancy of the tone, the uncompromisingly exclusivist line of argument – the introduction of twentieth-century ethical sensibility can only cloud the issue. What is being propounded is, in seventeenth-century sectarian terms, a very dynamic doctrine.

Calvinist 'evasions' are not totally sophistical in nature, since within their own terms of reference they represent a genuine attempt to deal with an intractable problem while leaving the original framework of the argument intact. They may fail to meet any of the stringent criteria usually associated with logical consistency, but the committed Calvinist was not likely to be much concerned with such niceties, his goal being proselytisation not philosophical disputation. Far from being a failed system-builder Calvin is to be regarded as a particularly resourceful theologian and politician, who is working tirelessly to synthesise the various intellectual traditions of his time in the cause of reform. It is as a highly-committed theologian that Calvin is addressing us, in which case rhetoric must be considered to take precedence over logic. That is essentially Bouwsma's line and I would endorse it. Faced with a similar problem involving issues of free will, the philosopher would probably question the initial assumptions involved (Are the concepts of free will and determinism, for example, being too rigidly drawn?) whereas the Calvinist theorist would feel more inclined – indeed, obliged – to preserve them.

Hence the need for evasions to neutralise the paradoxes which were bound to arise.

In practice it never was that simple. One has only to look at *Grace Abounding* to see the degree of psychological confusion belief in election and predestination could create within a sensitive individual:

> About this time, I did light on that dreadful story of that miserable mortal, *Francis Spira* . . . especially that sentence of his was frightful to me, *Man knows the beginning of sin, but who bounds the issues thereof?* Then would the former sentence, as the conclusion of all, fall like a hot thunder-bolt again upon my Conscience; *for you know how that afterwards, when he would have inherited the blessing, he was rejected; for he found no place of repentance, though he sought it carefully with tears* . . . Then was I struck into a very great trembling, insomuch that at sometimes I could for whole days together feel my very body as well as my minde to shake and totter under the sence of the dreadful Judgment of God, that should fall on those that have sinned that most fearful and unpardonable sin. I felt also such a clogging and heat at my stomach by reason of this my terrour, that I was, especially at some times, as if my breast-bone would have split in sunder.
>
> (pp. 49–50)

The language here is not that of philosophical or theological disputation but of anxiety-states: 'dreadful', 'frightful', 'rejected', 'trembling'. There is also a strong undercurrent of violent imagery to be noted: hot thunderbolts, bodies bursting asunder. The paradoxes are manifestly being proved upon the pulses in this instance, and a particularly sensitive individual is transmuting philosophy and theology into actual physical suffering.[13] One marked side-effect of paradox-related anxiety was an intensification of the individual's sense of self. The debate on self and identity in Puritan and dissenting prose fiction is to take place very largely within the framework provided by predestinarian theory, a theory at once individuating and isolating; liberating in a personal sense and constricting in a psychological. It is the tension that Calvinist dogma can inspire, and its subsequent expression in literary form, that I focus upon throughout this work. Indeed, it is possible to argue that anxiety is Calvinism's key trait as a theology, and its major legacy to English literary history.[14]

Certain other aspects of Calvinism consequential on belief in predestination deserve mention. 'Grace', 'works' and 'calling', for instance, all have a bearing on the development of narrative structure. The question of grace is one of the most controversial in the Calvinist canon. Calvin's own view is not in question: he is as explicit as he can be on the point. God's grace is offered irrespective of individual merits: 'And he, willing to make himself the free dispenser and judge of this matter, summarily declares that only as it so pleases him will he be merciful to one rather than to another' (II, 939). There would appear to be no way in which anyone could attain to grace by his own actions, Calvin again being quite explicit: 'For we have it from the words of the apostle that the salvation of believers has been founded upon the decision of divine election alone, and that this favor is not earned by works but comes from free calling' (II, 937). This leaves the individual in an impossible position, in that his actions would seem to have no bearing whatsoever on his soteriological status; it being a case of waiting for God to reveal his once and for all decision. One might well think that this would give the elect *carte blanche* to act as they pleased, on the grounds that, being irrevocably elect, nothing could prevent them from achieving their rightful place in heaven (just such a view was expounded by the Ranters[15]). Calvin would not, of course, have agreed with such a reading, and, drawing on St Augustine, he imparts an interesting psychological twist to the argument in his assertion that 'God's grace does not find but makes those fit to be chosen' (II, 943): a view which would appear to be designed expressly to prevent the kind of moral anarchy indulged in by the more extreme of the chiliastic sects.

This did not, however, resolve the issue. There remains a feeling in Calvinist circles that works are intimately connected with election, and that good works are obviously preferable to bad, moral to immoral. It is but a short step to believing that the connection is a necessary and not a contingent one, and a Calvinist might well come to consider commercial prosperity as objective proof of God's grace. God's free calling could then be read off from economic success and the works that led up to that success invested with spiritual significance. Success in the individual's own calling implied the presence of God's free calling. By Defoe's time, such connections are natural enough ones to make (given the dissenting concentration on trade and commerce in the wake of political exclusion), and the almost obsessive concern shown by his characters for the economic consequences of their actions is evidence of the tendency to treat the economic sign as simultaneously a spiritual one. The gulf between Bunyan and Defoe on matters economic is wide, and it does seem that the socio-economic ideal being espoused in Bunyan's fiction is old-fashioned, even by the standards of the author's day. It is, in fact, essentially medieval in character (as John McVeagh has remarked, when it comes to economics, Bunyan 'is a throwback'[16]). Defoe's flexibility and modernity *vis-à-vis* Bunyan on economic issues is mirrored in his narratological practice, and his personal dialogue with Calvinist theory is to be considerably the more complex.

Calvinism's adversarial quality held obvious attractions for a reform movement like Puritanism, which found similar qualities in the work of Petrus Ramus, whose systems of logic and rhetoric came to have a profound effect on English intellectual life of the sixteenth and seventeenth centuries.[17] Ramism is something of a historical curiosity these days: a system of logic no longer taken very seriously by philosophers (it merits only the briefest of mentions in any recent history of logic); a method of argument which grew up in the tradition of Renaissance humanism, yet had its greatest impact in English intellectual circles on a movement which it seems justifiable to describe overall as anti-humanist.[18] Ramus, a Regius Professor at the University of Paris in the mid-sixteenth century, devised systems of logic and rhetoric which were anti-Aristotelian and anti-scholastic in intent. Ramus's own philosophical bias was Platonic, and indeed the transition from

Aristotelian to Platonic metaphysics is characteristic of Renaissance humanism in general.[19] Ramist logic has long since ceased to exercise any influence in the philosophical world, where it is now regarded as having historical interest only. Miller and Johnson neatly pinpoint the reason for its decline: 'it was intended not so much for proof and analysis as for assertion'.[20] Modern logics tend to be concerned primarily with the notion of proof, which indeed provides the fundamental motivation for the entire exercise. Ong, too, can be fairly scathing about Ramism's philosophical pretensions: 'Its central element is a logic or dialectic which cannot be taken very seriously by any competent logician'.[21] Ashworth, in the act of damning Ramist logic with faint praise, manages to suggest some reasons for the extraordinary success of the *Dialectica*:

> Despite all its glaring faults, it is not difficult to see why this rather messy little book became as popular as it did. If logic had to be learned at school or university, far better from the student's point of view to learn it from a book written in a lively manner with a minimum of technical jargon and indeed, a minimum of logic. Moreover, it was a book which by its very simplification and reliance on self-evident axioms seemed to promise a short cut to the mastery of argumentation.[22]

Ramism is not, therefore, to be completely rejected for its failings on the score of proof-technique. Its nature may well be assertional rather than deductive, but it does have a proof-technique of sorts – those 'self-evident axioms' that Ashworth refers to – if a suspect one as far as the modern logician is concerned.

Despite its apparently iconoclastic nature, Ramism has a long intellectual history. Ong traces it back through medieval suppositional theory to the thirteenth-century logician Peter of Spain, whose *Summulae Logicales* anticipates the Ramist scheme in certain ways. In the final analysis, however, Ramism is essentially the product of Renaissance humanism; although it is worth noting that Ramus himself was reputedly suspicious of Italian humanism for what he took to be its excessively rhetorical bias. Ramus was first and foremost a teacher, and all his work is designed for pedagogical ends. He stands in that humanist educational tradition which is developing in reaction to the prevailing neo-scholastic orthodoxy: 'In terms of the established pattern, humanism forced a crisis by proposing a program which in effect challenged the primacy of dialectic and, in so doing, impugned the whole curricular organization and the teaching profession as such, and thereby threatened the intelligibility of the whole universe'.[23] Ramus's primary objective, therefore, is to break the stranglehold exercised in the educational world of his time by 'arts scholasticism'.[24]

Ramist logic is a system marked by a stress on method – 'the arrangement of many good arguments' in its author's words[25] – and is heavily dependent on the notion of dichotomy for its proof-technique; the argument moving relentlessly on by way of antithesis. The emphasis on method is crucial since 'Ramus lived in an age when there was no word in ordinary usage which clearly expressed what we mean today by method'.[26] The argument is that Aristotelian logic, the scholastic orthodoxy, is deficient in methodological terms. Miller suggests that Ramus's aim was 'to arrange concepts in ordered rubrics, so that at the portal of logic would not stand a nondescript array of catchwords'.[27] The most detailed formulation of Ramus's conception of method can be found in the 1569 edition of the *Dialectica*:

> Method is disposition by which, out of many homogeneous enunciations, each known by means of a judgement proper to itself (i.e., the way an axiom is known, without dependence on syllogisms) or by the judgement of syllogism, that enunciation is placed first which is first in the absolute order of knowledge, that next which is next, and so on: and thus there is an unbroken progression from universals to singulars.[28]

The Ramist approach is to break down any given argument into divisions, each of which is thereafter reducible to a dichotomy.[29] Miller has outlined what this could mean in practical terms:

> To expound the relation of inward to outward covenant, the Congregational theorist resorted, as with every vexing question, to the logic of Petrus Ramus. He found a satisfactory solution to any problem as soon as he could define the nature of the relationship; once he could show that the terms were in disagreement with each other, he had demonstrated a law of God no less than when he proved them in agreement. Once all forms of connection are specified and named and then ranged in schematic series, man has a logical transcript of the wisdom of God in so far as that is manifested in creation . . . Disjunction is as much a law of God as harmony.[30]

The procedure is highly schematic, and indeed highly visual, in approach. It involves constructing arguments in the form of elaborate tree-like structures, through a process of internal dichotomization of the argument points. This could be done by the use of either 'artificial' or 'inartificial' arguments; the former being directly perceived, the latter being taken on trust. Regardless of how the divisions were produced, however, the procedure remained essentially the same: firstly, the invention of individual arguments; secondly, the disposition of one argument with another to form an axiom; thirdly, the disposition of one axiom with another in a syllogism to form a conclusion; finally, the assembling of conclusions into the correct order to create a piece of discourse.[31]

For the Ramist, therefore, discourse consists of aggregates of arguments, and the passage from one to the next is supposed to be effected exclusively by means of definition and division. Such aggregates are strung together to form ever-longer sequences, the method being simple to master and easily extensible in practice. This method is held to apply to *any* form of connected discourse, to a poem no less than an oration. When reduced to its essential elements each discourse will prove to be nothing more than 'a string of definitions and divisions somehow or other operating through syllogisms'.[32]

A variety of objections can be levelled against Ramus's system. The major criticism would have to be that the method involved is philosophically simplistic and somewhat facile: a logic for 'those who wished to attain intellectual eminence fast'.[33] If it has no great philosophical status, the case is very different in the literary field. Ramism comes to exert a very considerable influence in the latter, not least in that highly specialised form of literary activity, the Puritan sermon:

> Get his definitions and distributions into your mind and memory . . . He that is ready in those of P. Ramus, may refer all things to them. And he may know where again to fetch any thing that he hath judiciously referred; for there is not one axiom of truth ever uttered, that doth not fall under some special rule of art.[34]

For the committed adherent like Leonard Hoar above, Ramist logic would seem to have had the status of an all-purpose panacea. Through the sermon theoretics of William Perkins it will come to have a profound effect on the argument form of Puritan prose fiction, where debate between characters is conspicuously Ramist in style in its persistent utilisation of division.

It is method and dichotomy which lie at the heart of Ramist thought and of its appeal to the Puritan temperament (if Puritanism is anything, it is an antagonistic position within a discourse, and dichotomy naturally complements antagonism). The advantages of these concepts to a movement of such unashamedly didactic orientation are only too obvious. They enable the Puritan sermon writer, for example, to structure his argument according to principles easily assimilable by both author and audience: 'The Puritan parson did not need to argue every doctrine from A to B to C, but could preach in straightforward propositions, each doctrine followed by its reasons, the reasons by their uses, exhortations, and the pertinent applications'.[35] Puritan prose fiction writers will peform in a similar way when presenting their debates on election and reprobation. Given that it had originally been developed to meet pedagogical exigencies, it is not surprising that Ramist logic could prove to be an extremely functional device for the Puritan author, committed as he was to reaching the widest possible audience to the greatest possible effect.

Ramus's employment of dichotomy is as revolutionary a demand as his insistence on methodical procedures in the construction of arguments. It encourages the reader to see the world as consisting of a set of binary relations. Ramus's anti-Aristotelianism is very much in evidence in this respect in that binary relations are being substituted for hierarchical, the latter being the Aristotelian and medieval scholastic ideal. This commitment to the disjunctive led to a manifest over-simplification of argument form, but it is not difficult to imagine the nature of its probable hold on minds attuned to conflict in the cultural arena: here the 'messy little book' very much came into its own. In this sense it could even be argued that Ramism provided a *necessary* simplification. Dichotomization was, after all, to prove a valuable tool in the process of assertion through argument which formed such a crucial part of the growth-mechanism of sectarianism in England. It had, in other words, overtly propagandistic applications.

Ramism is to be seen, therefore, as an expression of a changing world-view, in which the notion of a conflict-oriented relationship between the individual and the world eventually comes to the fore. Ramist theory, with its emphasis on the binary and dialectical progress of argument, would certainly reinforce such an attitude. We are to observe Ramist principles being assimilated into Puritan literature, with its penchant for argument between ideologically-motivated individuals.

Argument between ideologically-motivated individuals is precisely what is to be found in Arthur Dent's *Pathway*, one of the most important of pre-Bunyan prose fictions. Dent's text is worth dwelling on in order to show how, from the start, soteriology-debate fiction is brought up against the fact of paradox. Published in 1601, *Pathway* effectively ushers in the era of seventeenth-century Puritan prose fiction, establishing as it does so a pattern that is to be extremely influential,

Bunyan himself freely acknowledging the work's appeal in *Grace Abounding*. *Pathway* will be seen to contain within its pages the prototype of the Puritan pilgrim figure: that figure later to reach its classic formulation in Christian; as well as a prototype reprobate for Mr Badman. It is to Bunyan's credit that he can, so to speak, 'tease out' two masterpieces from the one source-work; but we might also praise Dent for the density of significance, ideological as well as literary, that he contrives to pack into *Pathway*.

Dent has attracted only minimal critical attention in modern times, living on in literary history primarily as a footnote to Bunyan.[36] There is also disagreement amongst historians as to Dent's exact position in theological terms. We can find him being variously described as an 'ardent Puritan', a 'moderate Puritan', and a 'High Calvinist'.[37] When we refer ourselves to *Pathway* for pointers as to the nature of Dent's Puritanism, we come up against the thorny problem of predestination and its role in Calvinist theology. Horton Davies has rightly stressed that predestination 'is not an Anglican, Puritan, or even a Protestant doctrine; it is a Christian doctrine'.[38] What cannot be ignored, however, is the increasing degree of emphasis that Calvinist theorists came to place upon the doctrine of election as compared to their counterparts in other Christian sects. Election would appear to be the crux of the problem, since it is the constitution of the elect – to be more specific, the conditions of entry involved in its constitution – rather than its actual existence that is the point at dispute. Calvinism played a prominent role in the growth of Puritanism in England, and election served as a natural focus for reform-minded Puritan propaganda. Election gave Puritan writers a basic structure within which the life of an individual could be formulated in ideologically-paradigmatic fashion. In *Pathway* the doctrine is to determine the narrative's shape, and the result is a pattern satisfying enough to provide succeeding generations of Puritan (and Puritan-influenced) fiction writers with a model for narrative strategy, particularly in terms of the dialectic between free will and determinism. Dent himself conceived of soteriology as a

battle between the individual free will and divine predeterminism; as he noted in another of his texts, *The Opening of Heaven
Gates*: 'let a man enter into himselfe, and consider whether it
be compulsion, that doth cause him to sinne, or his own
voluntary will, and I doubt not but he shall soon perceive the
whole fault in his own freewill'.[39]

Pathway's narrative form is quite simple: an encounter
between two sets of friends, Theologus and Philagathus on the
one hand, Asunetos and Antilegon on the other (divine,
honest man, ignorant man, and caviller, as the author's
marginal notes have it (p. 1)); a debate lasting several hours on
religious matters; conclusion of debate and separation of
parties as nightfall approaches. The task Theologus and
Philagathus set themselves is to examine Asunetos and
Antilegon as to their conduct, and to establish the likelihood of
their being candidates for election. Their objective will be to
divide the two neighbours – Asunetos the merely ignorant
from Antilegon the dangerously cavilling – and to place the
former, the 'plain man' of the title, on the 'pathway to
heaven'. The fascination of the work is derived from observing the strategies adopted to clarify Asunetos's status as a
member of the elect and Antilegon's as one of the reprobate. It
becomes the duty of Dent's Puritans to explain who shall be
saved, and why. ('Puritan' is no longer regarded as a precise
term, but in the context of Dent's lifetime its use can be
justified. 'Dissenter' or 'nonconformist' will more usually be
substituted when referring to the later seventeenth century.)
They set out to explain the reasons behind God's closure of
heaven to the reprobate: a closure whose severity the lay
person, untutored in the use of Ramist logic to bypass the
paradoxes of Calvinist theology, tends to find alienating: 'I can
forbeare no longer, my conscience urgeth me to speake: for
methinkes you goe too farre, you goe beyond your learning in
this, that you condemne good neighbours, and good Townes-
men' (p. 19).

In the opening dialogues Asunetos already presents as the
more righteous of the two neighbours, contributing comments which are almost as moralistic in tone as those of

Theologus. Antilegon's views tend to be worldly-wise: 'we see all men have their imperfections'; whereas Theologus is openly critical of such pragmatism: 'you speak prophanely and wickedly' (p. 63). Puritan theology confronts the saved and the damned and in approved Ramist fashion separates them, bringing each to a consciousness of his position in the Calvinist soteriological scheme of things. The division made is severe and the possibility of reconciliation is not explored. Justice, not mercy, is at work. Antilegon is to stand condemned as doctrinally unsound, having been skilfully outmanoeuvred by the combined intellectual and emotional forces of the Puritans bent on dividing him from Calvinist doctrine. The author's strategy soon becomes transparent. It is to reveal the progressive hardening of Antilegon's heart under questioning, until he condemns himself in his own words as a reprobate. He is to be isolated and the ranks of Puritanism closed against him.

The character traits which most clearly signal Antilegon's reprobate nature are his pragmatism and his scepticism regarding biblical authority. The former implies a worldliness that Puritans, whose major concern in life is to find evidence of God's grace manifesting itself in their actions, cannot accept. 'There is no man but he hath his faults: and the best of us all may be amended' (p. 186), argues Antilegon, therefore it matters not if a man becomes drunk, lies, or swears on occasion, since 'it is the custom to sweare'. Nothing could be more calculated to arouse a Puritan's ire than the argument from custom; this being a theology which demands such intense concentration on the minutiae of personal conduct in the search for signs of grace, that uncritical reliance on custom and practice as justification for individual behaviour cannot be countenanced. It may be the custom, but 'it is nevertheless a wicked and divellish custome' (p. 164). Pragmatism, for all that it can appear an attractive doctrine ('there is no man but he hath his faults' could even be given a Christian gloss, on the lines of 'let him who is without sin cast the first stone') is to be regarded as running counter to the requirements of Puritan reform, which dictates very high standards of personal behaviour.[40] Neither custom nor pragmatism can ever serve to excuse immoral conduct in Puritan eyes. The individual is instead to be held accountable for all his actions: 'God doeth allowe none to live idely: but all both great and small, are to be imployed one way or another, either for the benefite of the Church, or Commonwealth' (p. 192).

For all its debate-closing nature Puritanism, most likely as a result of its Ramist bias, can still present a dynamic face in disputation. The ever-branching form of the Ramist-influenced sermon requires constant redefinition of one's concepts and postpones resolution momentarily, if not indefinitely. As is the case in structuralist analysis (Roland Barthes' practice particularly comes to mind) codes can be uncovered within codes in what might appear to be an endless process of refinement. Refinement of this kind is a notable feature of Dent's narrative practice in *Pathway*. New and improved lists branch out into more new and improved lists, each of which generates its table of contraries. Eight 'signes of damnation' become nine 'signes of condemnation'. Nine 'signes of condemnation' become nine 'foresignes of wrath' (p. 234). Nine 'foresignes of wrath' generate contrary signs of 'the found soule' (p. 257). On the objection that 'some of them may be in the reprobate', nine signs of 'the found soule' become 'St Peter's signes': 'Faith; Vertue; Knowledge; Temperance; Patience; Godlines; Brotherly Kindnes; Love' (p. 258). Even these, it seems may deceive on occasion, and yet another set is derived from them:

> Assured faith in the promises. ACT. 16.31.
> Sinceritie of heart. JOB. 1.47.
> The spirit of adoption. RO. 8.14.15.
> Sound regeneration and Sanctification. JOB. 3.31. THESS. 4.3.
> Inward peace. ROM. 5.1.
> Groundednesse in the truth. COLL. 1.23.
> Continuance to the end. MATH. 24.13. JOB. 8.3.

> (p. 259)

The exact reason for this latter selection being more acceptable to the Puritan conscience is unclear (unless it is a case of its being harder to counterfeit such inward concerns by outward sign than such dubious things as 'industry'), but it closes off this particular line of enquiry: 'in my judgement none of these can be found truly in any reprobate. Therefore I think no Divine can take exception against any of these' (pp. 259–60). Revealingly enough, given Puritanism's obsession with scriptural grounding, the list in question is the only one of the sequence to include biblical references: another triumph for the Word in what is a conspicuously logocentrist theology.

If evidence were needed as to why 'precisianist' became an alternative term for Puritan in the Elizabethan period, this particular exchange alone would probably suffice. One can see in it the intellectual rigour as well as the meticulous logic-chopping of the Calvinist theological tradition. It is at once admirable and tedious. No wonder Puritans so often reduced their opponents to a state bordering on exasperation, as Theologus and Philagathus do here with respect to the unfortunate Antilegon. Precision of this kind is needed to contest the argument on election, that being the goal to which the entire narrative is directed. Dent's treatment of the subject plunges us into the ultimately baffling paradoxes of Calvinist hermeneutics; baffling, that is, if one assumes that they must be logically resolved – as poor Antilegon does. Exclusiveness is the hallmark of the doctrine, as Dent's blunt wording invariably reveals:

> Therefore saieth Christ: Because I have called, and ye refused, I have stretched out my hande, but none would regard: ye have hated knowledge, and despised all my counsell. Therefore I will laugh at your destruction, and mocke when your feare commeth upon you like sudden defoliation, and your destruction like a whirlewinde. Then shall they call upon me, but I will not answere. (p. 148)

The chilling certainty of the tone (assertiveness to the fore yet again) is noteworthy, and indeed much of the debate revolves around the certainty of our knowledge as regards election. In typically paradoxical style, the Calvinist considers doubt a sign of election and certainty a sign of reprobation – at the pre-conversion stage, that is. At the post-conversion stage, certainty is transformed into a positive sign. Asunetos can venture to suggest that 'for all that, a man cannot be certaine'; Theologus will insist that he can. There are, it seems, 'certaine testimonies' (p. 265) in the individual's own conscience as to the notion of election; although *absolute* certainty is not one of them, and Antilegon's claim that 'for mine own part, I make no question of it' must be rejected: 'you are perswaded before you knowe' (p. 273). At the very least a discreet modicum of doubt seems to be a necessary part of the proceedings.

The argument will be that 'our salvation is laid in Gods eternal election'; in which case 'it standeth most firme in respect of God, and his eternall, and immutable decree' (p. 267). It is even claimed that 'to doubt thereof in respect of Gods truth, is blasphemous against the immutabilitie of his truth' (p. 268). Yet if the grounds of argument are not up for discussion then dialogue is hardly possible, and discourse will inevitably be reduced, Ramist fashion, to assertion, or what Maurice Hussey (referring to Dent's mentor William Perkins) has called the 'emphatic dogmatism' of the English Calvinists.[41] Pressed as to whether there are not 'some doubts at sometimes even in the very elect', Theologus will admit that 'he that never doubted, never beleeved' (p. 268), an admission which only succeeds in generating an entirely characteristic Calvinist paradox: the individual can be sure of the fact of salvation, but not his own personal share of it. This would appear to leave the said individual in a state of chronic indecision concerning the destination of his soul, although Puritans consistently denied this to the extent that Theologus can be made to criticise 'the doctrine of the Papists, which would have men alwaies doubt and feare in a servile sort' (p. 271). Exactly how Calvinist election contrives to avoid this condition is mysterious. Once again we are compelled to confront the peculiarities of the Calvinist psyche, with its ability to create paradoxes and then ignore their existence when it suits its polemical purpose to do so. Small wonder that Antilegon can complain at one point, 'you would make a man madde' (p. 280).

A major source of paradox in Calvinist theory is the relationship between works and faith, and it admits of no easy solution, no matter how clear-cut the original formulation may seem in Calvin: faith from free calling not works. The subtlety of Puritan thinking on the topic is revealed in Dent's treatment of it in Antilegon's case. The latter's claim that 'we must be saved by mercy, and not by merit' (p. 276), ostensibly has the weight of scriptural evidence on its side. It is objected, however, that to invoke mercy in this instance is to make 'Christ a cloake for sinnes'. The ambiguous status of that word 'mercy' rapidly becomes apparent, and indeed the quality of mercy can be more than a little strained in Puritan thought. No Christian is going to deny its presence (and importance) in his theology, but to *rely* on it is, in Calvinist eyes, to misread the nature of faith. In a very real sense it must be worked for; as Theologus makes clear when he reminds Antilegon that 'he must bee zealous of good workes' (p. 278). Works would, therefore, appear to be both necessary and unnecessary elements of salvation: quite typically, Calvinistically, paradoxical. The despair/presume axis is very much in operation at such points.

The radical quality of Calvinist soteriology comes most sharply into prominence when the author outlines why the 'number of Gods elect upon the face of the earth, are very fewe in comparison' to the reprobate. It appears to be necessary to weed out certain sections of the populace; to wit: Papists, Atheists, heretickes, swearers, drunkards, whoremongers, worldlings, deceivers, coseners, proud men, rioters, gamesters, hypocrites, carnall protestants, vaine professors, backsliders, decliners, and cold Christians. One wonders just who would survive such an operation, and indeed Theologus wryly points out that the elect 'would walke very thinly in the streets' (p. 287). The crucial part of this particular debate concerns God's purpose in creating the saved and the damned. Theologus is able to withdraw behind Calvinism's barriers at such points, arguing a belief in the inscrutability of God: 'it is as possible for us to comprehend the ocean sea in a little dish: as to comprehend the reason of God's counsell in this behalfe' (p. 308). Antilegon's indignant response, 'what reason, justice, or equitie is there, that sentence of death should be passed upon men before they be borne, or before they have done good, or evill' (p. 309), seems an entirely reasonable reaction to the bland assertion that we must accept such doctrines without question; yet it only succeeds in damning him even more irrevocably.

Perhaps it is difficult for the twentieth-century sensibility to appreciate the import of Antilegon's statement. It is not so much the sentiment itself that is wrong, but rather the fact of its utterance. That he can even voice it is proof of Antilegon's reprobate status. If he had shown a proper sense of humility and expressed amazement at *anyone* being saved in face of man's corrupt nature, he would have displayed the existence of a matrix for grace. He chooses instead to question God's will: a bad sign for Puritans of Dent's stamp, who might well admit to the doctrine of election being unreasonable, unjust and inequitable, but only by man's standards not God's. These must not be confused; man's are knowable, God's are not. Even Antilegon's questioning as to why 'if God hath decreed mens destruction, what can he doo withall? who can resist his will?' (p. 310), logical though it too seems, and more illustrative of humility, simply succeeds in revealing his damned nature to an even greater degree. One 'must live not after the lusts of men, but after the will of God' (p. 278). The key tenet to be observed is that one must not question God's will. One must work from the Bible, the received word of God, and realise that all references on this issue are at base descriptive rather than prescriptive. One may search for signs of grace, one is in fact obliged to, but one must *never* question. Antilegon does question, and therefore stands condemned out of his own mouth, although the paradox must surely remain as to his guilt in all this since 'God hath decreed mens destruction' beforehand.

In the hands of a Puritan preacher, paradox can be an extremely powerful disputational weapon. An argument from faith can coexist with an argument from works, an argument from doubt with an argument from certainty, an argument from justice with an argument from mercy, an argument from inscrutability of purpose with an argument from revealed truth. All very bewildering to the poor layman.

In order to suggest active compliance with the will of God, Dent must imply a change of consciousness in Asunetos which proceeds from an internal realisation of the truth of the Word as delivered by Theologus. The process can best be described as a coming to one's senses, a gradual growth of awareness of what has in fact always been the case: 'I doo now see that which I never sawe: and feel that which I never felt'. Added to such a realisation, however, is the subtle suggestion that what has always been the case might be reversible by man's exercise of free will: 'I do plaine see, that if I had died in that state wherein I have lived al my life, I should certainly have bene condemned, and should have perished for ever in my sinne and ignorance'. 'Sinne and ignorance' form an interestingly paradoxical conjunction. 'Sinne' implies free will acting in the face of evidence to the contrary, 'ignorance' lack of knowledge as to evidence to the contrary; in other words a simultaneity of knowledge and absence of knowledge about the facts of soteriology within an individual: fertile ground for the despair/presume axis.

Throughout the conversion sequence the reactions of Asunetos and Antilegon are carefully contrasted to give us at the last clearly delineated pathways to salvation and damnation respectively. The detailed exposition of the facts of predestination which has been offered to both characters prompts vastly different responses. From Asunetos we have gratitude and humility: 'I am the better for you Sir, I thank God. I never knew what sinne ment till this day . . . I am greatly distressed in my conscience to think what I have bene' (p. 429). From Antilegon on the other hand there is anger and frustration: 'I think the preaching and publishing of this doctrine of predestination hath done much hurt: and it had bene good it had never bin knowne to the people, but utterly concealed: for some it driveth to dispaire: and others it maketh more secure and carelesse' (p. 320). Once again it is the mere fact of his voicing the sentiment that serves to condemn Antilegon. He is to provide a model of reprobation against which the conduct of Asunetos can be measured. What is very notable is that it is the candidate for election who continues to manifest the greater sense of anxiety ('I feel great terrour in my conscience, I am afraid I shall be damned'), and the reprobate the more balanced outlook ('what speak you of damning . . . if you should be damned, I know not who shal be saved' (p. 429)). The trick would seem to be to despair where one might presume, but never the opposite. Presumption is to remain a ghostly presence which can hardly be articulated and certainly never claimed, its efficacy apparently dependent on its non-evocation. Paradox has now become a subversive element within the epistemological processes of the individual.

Once division of the elect and the reprobate has been effected, it is noticeable that Asunetos in his turn falls back on all the Calvinist tricks of the trade in dealing with the reprobate, offering assertion as proof and expressing unde-viating commitment to biblical authority: 'I regard not your flatteries. I beleeve God. I beleeve his word. I beleeve those things which M. Theologus hath alledged out of the holy scriptures' (p. 407). 'Alledge' effectively equals 'assert' here, and an ideologically-motivated resolution has been accom-plished. Not one, however, with quite the contradiction-disguising power of that to be found later in the work of such Anglican apologists as Simon Patrick (*The Parable of the Pilgrim* (1664)) where a consolatory tone masks an even more authoritarian ideology than the Calvinist espouses: at least as far as individual development, that notably subversive aspect of the period, is concerned. What is being suggested is that for all its authoritarianism, soteriological resolution in Dent never *quite* succeeds in hiding the contradictions of Calvinistic Puritanism, particularly with regard to the paradoxes sur-rounding predestination. Engagement with, and foreground-ing of, these latter paradoxes – processes which Calvinism effectively commits its followers to – means that the sem-blance of choice must be there in the text. It must at least *appear* to be the case that the individual can will his own damnation, and since will is held to be in all men and 'alwaies free unto evill',[42] it is at least implied that it is involved in salvation – if only in the sense of what we might call the will-to-suspend-one's-will.

The effect of all this on characterisation is quite momentous. Free will is seen to be a major factor in human life, even if it is disapproved of by the Calvinist, and a phenomenon in a constant state of conflict with divine predeterminism. Dent's dialogue with ideology's judgements does not inhibit debate therefore, and debate involves considerable concentration on the role of free will in human affairs. Free will is an inherently subversive concept in ideological terms since it posits the existence of an alternative source of power to the collective will, and as such can be regarded as threatening by the social system in question. Yet it must be brought into the salvation debate, and it carries with it the possibility of a far more radical individualism than Puritanism is probably willing to envisage. That such individualism will be seen to be logically derivable from Calvinist principles, will be simply one more paradox to add to the many we encounter in engagement with this system of belief and its narrative of predestination.

Dent's model of conversion narrative fiction can only achieve its primary intention – the strict categorial division of elect and reprobate – by the foregrounding of paradox, since the paradoxes in question are inscribed in the very Word; as such it might be said to contain the seeds of its own destruction in a dialectical sense. The theory is based on internal contradictions; its articulation brings the contradictions to light; exposure of the contradictions creates the need for concealment of them to protect the power of the theory; concealment can only be done, disputationally, by vigorous assertion of those same contradictions as if they were *not* contradictions; resolution is effected, to the satisfaction of the Calvinist at any rate, but only at the expense of simultaneously acknowledging and refusing to acknowledge those contradictions. A better recipe for individual anxiety than this despair/presume stalemate can scarcely be imagined, nor for the eventual act of seeing through all this. Step by step, in subversive fashion, the 'driven to dispaire' reprobate of Puritan prose fiction comes to do just this, with *Roxana* being an excellent example of the process in its more advanced stages.

Chapter Three

PARADOX AND PROGRESS I
The Pilgrim's Progress

FOR all its apparently authoritarian manner, Calvinism can still be a fairly radical system of belief which ultimately encourages self-reliance in its Puritan and then later its dissenting adherents. *Pilgrim's Progress* amply bears out this observation, and its subversive connotations within the context of Restoration culture are considerable, as both Keeble and Hill have vigorously argued.[1] Paradox has a key role to play in this process of subversion, and it is a process that can be better understood when comparison is made between Bunyan's narrative practice and that of one of his eminent contemporaries, the Anglican bishop Simon Patrick. Patrick's best known work is *The Parable of the Pilgrim*, thought by some to have had certain influence on the writing of *Pilgrim's Progress*, although others have been more sceptical.[2] The question of influence is not, however, pursued here. The study is instead directed towards the representative roles of the two authors as articulators of opposed ideological positions – establishment versus nonconformity. To read *Pilgrim's Progress* through *Parable* is to reveal the counter-discourse that inspired Bunyan's literary intervention in Restoration culture, and to observe ideological subtexts in competition.

Patrick was noted for his moderation, and in 1662 he is to be found praising 'that vertuous mediocrity which our Church observes between the meretricious gaudiness of the Church of Rome and the squalid sluttery of Fanatick conventicles'.[3] The ideological implications of the contrasting pilgrimage styles

44

found in the two works above can be explored by analysing the respective narrative strategies adopted in the cause of 'vertuous mediocrity' and 'Fanatick conventicles'. It is only when we examine texts like *Parable* that we can come to appreciate fully the ideological force of Bunyan's negotiations with paradox, and of that characteristically Calvinist anxiety they promote in his pilgrims. It may be that, as with Calvinism, anxiety is arguably Bunyan's most important legacy to literary history. (On that score I would take issue with McKeon's otherwise persuasive reading of Bunyan as the voice of a 'new Christian' capitalism, where *Pilgrim's Progress* becomes 'a model of how the average, earnest, modern Protestant may pursue his calling somewhere within the antithetical extremes of utter selfishness and utter selflessness'.[4] This is considerably to underrate the emotional plight of the individual within the confines of a theology like Calvinism.)

Restoration Anglicanism and nonconformity divide sharply over the value of individualism, the one seeking to create a sense of dependence, the other of independence. Comparison of the opening sequences of *Pilgrim's Progress* and *Parable* reveals quite clearly the radical differences in attitude that this involves. In the case of Patrick's hero, Philotheus, individualism has brought scant benefits in the search for salvation:

> Many strange countries there were which he visited in pursuance of this purpose; many steep hills he climbed, and many dangerous praecipices he narrowly escaped; he committed himself not once or twice to the anger of the Sea, expecting to be brought to the Port which he so much wished: But still he was as far from the accomplishment of his desires, as when he first launched out.

Individualism eventually reduces the character to a state of 'deep melancholy, and . . . great heaviness of mind'.[5] Such torpor contrasts sharply with Christian's vividly realised anxiety state:

> Now, I saw upon a time, when he was walking in the fields, that he was (as he was wont) reading in his book, and greatly distressed in his mind; and as he read, he burst out, as he had done before, crying, *What shall I do to be saved?*

The search for salvation leads away from individualism in Philotheus's case to the protective influence of a spiritual director, who will guide him through the many perils of life's pilgrimage. With Christian it is to be otherwise, and we note a sharpening of his sense of identity in relation to the community:

> sometimes they would deride, sometimes they would chide, and sometimes they would quite neglect him: wherefore he began to retire himself to his Chamber to pray for, and pity them; and also to condole his own misery: he would also walk solitarily in the Fields, sometimes reading, and sometimes praying. (p. 9)

Christian is frequently placed in a position of having to 'walk solitarily' (in Tawney's apt phrase, he is like 'a soldier in hostile territory'[6]), whereas the entire thrust of the Patrick text is directed against such expressions of individuality. The latter's is ostensibly the more comforting message and encourages a modest optimism to counter Calvinist despair. A high price is exacted for this comfort, however, and that is no less than the surrender of individual autonomy. In Patrick, paradox is discreetly removed from the electee's field of experience, but so too is personal growth through paradox.

Anti-individualism is an essentially repressive doctrine within the context of post-Commonwealth culture (individualism being identified with sectarianism[7]), and if Restoration Anglicanism is to present an attractive image it will need to be disguised in some way. *Parable*'s narrative strategies are designed to that end. Throughout the text, Philotheus is subjected to a series of deferrals and denials of experience of the type that would foster individual initiative. The aim is to establish a childlike dependence on his spiritual director.

Pilgrimage becomes a case in point. Although it is introduced as a goal at an early stage in the proceedings it is delayed until the second half of the narrative, as if the author desired to stave off action involving the individual (and possibly putting him at risk) for as long as possible. Bunyan's practice in *Pilgrim's Progress* constitutes a notable contrast. A few pages of scene-setting is concluded by the injunction to '*Fly from the wrath to come*', which induces a particularly active response: 'the Man began to run' (p. 10), at which point we are off on what Sutherland has called 'simple, earnest, and *continuous* narrative'.[8] Identity is to be forged by exposure to a continuously unfolding stream of events (much in the Ramist pattern of progress by disjunction[9]), whereas in *Parable* such events are postponed while the character is invited to reflect, in a noticeably non-urgent manner, on 'a journey wherein there are so many hardships, and so many cross paths. A journey which is so tedious also, and wherein I cannot promise you security from frights, theeves, beatings, and such ill usages' (p. 19). Lack of security would hardly deter the Calvinist pilgrim – he would most likely regard it as the normal state of affairs, since even the elect must 'admit some ignorance where God's wisdom rises to its height' (*Institutes*, II, 982) – but Patrick will continue to be very concerned with the elimination of this identity-enhancing factor from the experience of salvation, and to this end will spend more time on the preparations for pilgrimage than on the actual pilgrimage itself. The objective would seem to be an evasion of those experiences which provoke psychological crisis – an inherently subversive phenomenon to the Restoration Anglican mind. Sutherland's remark about the 'perfunctory and discontinuous'[10] use of the journey-through-life motif in *Parable* is a pertinent one, but the ideological implications of discontinuity of this sort do need to be stressed lest we read it as a simple failure of narrative technique. The didacticism of the work is in fact very carefully gauged.[11]

The desire to create a tension-free environment for pilgrimage is also evident in Patrick's attitude to doctrinal controversy. Philotheus is distracted by the competing claims of the 'no less than twenty (and some say many more) very different parties that contended sharply with each other' (p. 8). Not only is there sharp contention between sects, but also in the actual experience of pilgrimage at the individual level:

> it did quite astonish him to see that so many men did dream that the way to *The Vision of Peace* lay through the field of strife and war; and that we must come to live together in endless love hereafter, by living in perpetual frays and brawls in the world where we now are. (p. 11)

Bunyan is later to fashion one of the most enduring of modern myths out of an individual's involvement in just such 'perpetual frays and brawls', but Patrick wants to exclude conflict from the process of salvation, substituting patriarchal protection in its stead. 'Vertuous mediocrity' is designed to be the remedy for the enthusiastic autonomy of mid-century sectarianism, which had led, in Anglican eyes, to social breakdown.

The positive side of Patrick's Anglicanism is that it is a non-exclusivist doctrine which provides a lifeline for all the Antilegons of this world: figures who in twentieth-century terms seem worth the saving. Not every temperament is attracted by ontological insecurity or extremes of individuality, in which case the Church of England can exert a considerable appeal. As Froude has noted of the possessor of such a temperament as the latter, 'if he is quiet and reasonable, he finds in it all that he desires'. Froude's pro-Bunyan preference is for 'enthusiastic ages and enthusiastical temperaments',[12] but this amounts to social divisiveness on the English Revolution model, which again is unlikely to prove a popular doctrine, especially in the aftermath of an 'enthusiastic age'. Patrick's ontology is, in any case, of a markedly non-individualistic cast: '*If we look on men in general, they do not seem so much a great many several entire bodyes, as so many divided parts which Society reunites*' (p. 321). This quasi-Aristotelian view of social existence is in sharp contrast to the ontological landscape of Bunyan's world, in which essentially isolated and internally divided beings progress through a

48

series of conflict-ridden encounters, continuously unfolding like the dichotomies of a Ramist argument, to an individual salvation. Talon has neatly summed up Bunyan's philosophy of life as follows: 'Whatever share other people have in our interior lives, ultimately we have to carry our burdens and the responsibility for our choice alone'.[13] As far as Patrick is concerned this is simply not true, and our burdens and responsibilities can be taken over by the Church and its directors. All that is required of the individual is 'quiet and reasonable' behaviour:

> Follow your affairs like other folk, but take heed and beware of covetousness, and watch that you be not overtaken with surfeiting and drunkenness, or the cares of this life. Let the World understand that you can see it every day, and not fall in love with it: that you can deal and traffique with it if need be, and yet not be unrighteous: that you can behold all its honours and not be ambitious: that you need not hide your eyes from its beauties, and yet retain your own and live in purity of heart.   (pp. 109–10)

This is the polar opposite of enthusiasm and it can easily be imagined what a Theologus would make of such sentiments, but there seems no point in denying its popular appeal in post-Commonwealth England.

The less savoury side to Restoration Anglicanism can be seen in Patrick's paean to authority, which cunningly conflates secular and spiritual concerns:

> For my part I cannot see less reason to believe, that our Lord was miraculously conceived, ushered into the World by a Star and the shouts of the Heavenly hosts, anointed with the Holy Ghost at his Baptism, transfigured on the holy Mount, confessed by Devils, acknowledged by Angels, justified by Miracles, raised from the Dead, and taken up to Glory; then our children will have to believe that our present Soveraign after a long banishment was suddenly restored to his Throne, that he entred his Royal City on such a day with the joyful acclamations of all his people; that he rode in Triumph and was solemnly Crowned the

year following; and that the Book containing a description of the
Magnificent Ceremonies of that day, gives a true and just
account of them. (p. 326)

The submission to authority being demanded at this point is
even more insidious than that found in Calvinist doctrine
because it allows no scope for individual reflection on the truth
of the holy writings. If these are to be guaranteed by externals
such as the mere *existence* of the monarchy then no exegesis is
required. Passivity becomes the order of the day as the
Church/State power bloc assumes all responsibility for soteriological matters. It amounts to a victory of the quiet and
reasonable over the 'enthusiastical', but it involves the greater
closure of the individual psychology and its capacity to effect
ideological confrontation, since it encourages the populace to
remain in a perpetual state of innocence as regards the burning
issues of contemporary theology. Thought-provoking experience of any kind is actively to be discouraged, and to the
enthusiastical temperament this would represent a far more
inhibiting factor to personal development than engagement
with all the paradoxes of Calvinist soteriology. In the case of
the latter, submission to the will of God can only be achieved
after a period of intense personal struggle with the mysteries
and contradictions of the Word. Patrick's concern is to prevent
the individual from reaching this state of dynamic participation, and *Parable* is, quite deliberately, a very undynamic text.
Gordon Rupp has suggested that Puritan theology 'over-
stressed the will of God',[14] and while there is undoubtedly a
great deal of truth in this, it can also be argued that this tendency
had liberating qualities in comparison to Anglicanism's stress
on the will of secular authority. The passivity demanded by one
doctrine and the activity by the other have very definite
ideological connotations therefore, and their effect on narrative structure is very carefully calculated by the authors in
question. Adventure has many pains, but lack of it few
pleasures in terms of psychological development.

   Adventure and psychological development take high
priority in Bunyan. *Pilgrim's Progress* is a severely goal-

directed work; the aim being to map the route from the City of
Destruction to the Celestial City, at which point the ultimate
Calvinist spiritual division will be made: Christian, the
successful pilgrim, will be met by *'ministring Spirits, sent forth to
minister for those that shall be Heirs of Salvation'* (p. 158), while
Ignorance, the reprobate, will be thrust down into Hell, 'even
from the Gates of Heaven' (p. 163).[15] The contrast in fates is
stark and suggests just how far from Anglican mediocrity we
shall be in this instance. Mediators no longer just shield,
sometimes they sentence. In the face of such severity, modern
commentators are wont to become uneasy, often to the
extent of feeling the need to rescue Bunyan in some way.
Newey, for example, argues that although 'Ignorance is
damned on theoretical and moral grounds he is redeemed by
art'. This is ingenious, and we do have to allow for the
possibility of the text undermining itself in unwittingly
promoting sympathy for the unfortunate Ignorance, but it
bypasses the ideology issue rather too conveniently. The
desire to redeem not just Ignorance but Bunyan too, leads
Newey to claim that the former's 'damnation is neither
something relished nor something regretted'; but surely
Bunyan was more militant and less liberal than this?[16]
Bunyan's ideological objectives are extremely clear and uncompromising when it comes to Ignorance's fate, and as such,
in the best tradition of Calvinist thought, they are to bring him
into collision with the paradoxes of predestination. It is part of
the paradoxes of Calvinism that ignorance can be a virtue as
well as a vice, as the following dialogue between Prudence and
Matthew from *Pilgrim's Progress* Part Two would seem to
suggest:

PRU. *What do you think of the Bible?*
MAT. It is the Holy Word of God.
PRU. *Is there nothing Written therein, but what you understand?*
MAT. Yes, a great deal.
PRU. *What do you do when you meet with such places therein, that
you do not understand?*
MAT. I think God is wiser then I. I pray also that he will please

> to let me know all therein that he knows will be for my
> good.
>
> (p. 226)

The message would seem to be that a little ignorance is a good thing, perhaps even to be read as evidence of elected status. Some subtle distinction (no doubt of the type that would 'make a man madde') is being implied between elect and reprobate ignorance, but its nature would be hard to define.

In *Pilgrim's Progress* the paradoxes of predestination are very much concerned with the individual will, and in terms of the free will/determinism debate it proves to be a classic example of the radically subversive yet authoritarian text in which Calvinism specialises. On the one hand, total subordination to a higher will is demanded, to the extent that instances of free will, such as deliberate digressions from the straight and narrow path, can be very severely punished by God's representatives:

> he commanded them to *lie down*; which when they did, he chastized them sore, to teach them the good way wherein they should walk; and as he chastized them, he said, *As many as I love, I rebuke and chasten; be zealous therefore, and repent.* This done, he bids them go on their way, and take good heed to the other directions of the Shepherds. (p. 134)

By such means is the individual brought into line and taught to subjugate his will and desires to a superior authority. On the other hand, the solitary nature of so many of Christian's trials tends to encourage self-reliance and a sense of one's own individuality.[17] Periodic assistance from divine agents – which so often comes after the event in *Pilgrim's Progress*, and performs an essentially corrective function – does not alter the necessity for psychologically-disturbing experiences, such as the walk through the Valley of the Shadow of Death or the pitched battle with Apollyon, to be undergone alone. Authoritarianism of the Calvinist kind ultimately must come from within, not be imposed from without as in the Anglican version, and can only be achieved by the operation of that radicalising phenomenon, self-censorship of the will. The more Christian seeks to bind himself the more he succeeds in individualising himself, which is an implicitly anti-authoritarian move. We have not only a spiritual quest in the work, but also what one psychologist has called 'a quest for individuation'.[18]

Inscribed in *Pilgrim's Progress*, therefore, is a conflict between the imperatives of conformism and individualism in which the progress towards a predetermined end is constantly being undermined by the sheer dynamism of the progress towards individuation (on which basis it would seem justified to oppose Kaufmann's reading of the narrative as static and lacking in sense of drama: 'The linear development, then, is a program of implementation answering the question "How?" rather than a course involving emergence of true novelty answering the question "What?" '[19]). Will is one of the focal points of this conflict. The central paradox of Calvinist predestination demands that the elect can take no credit for their own conversion, but that the reprobate must carry the blame for their own damnation. Christian's works, and the will that inspires their performance, are to be discounted as a factor in the attainment of grace – which is prevenient in nature anyway – except in the sense that 'if we be truly willing to have it, he will bestow it upon us freely' (p. 14). Such a state of willingness, although it may sound as if it contains an active element, cannot be brought about by the self, however, and must also be granted by God. Its mere outward appearance (as in the case of Talkative) is not evidence enough of the state, as the author's marginal gloss makes abundantly clear: '*To cry out against sin, no sign of Grace*' (p. 81). The paradox is effectively brought to the fore in the contradiction of a desire for grace being both a sign of grace's presence and its absence; proof of the abdication of the individual will that election requires, and the provocative assertion of it said to mark out reprobation.

There is what amounts to an ambivalent attitude towards will in *Pilgrim's Progress* which manifests itself in the contradictions just mentioned. The subtext of the hero's progress towards individuation involves an implicit acknowledgement of the value of wilful action. Nothing could be more wilful than Christian's original flight from his home city, taken in the face of concerted opposition by neighbours and relatives; an act which, Keeble argues, in its singularity of purpose, is 'noble though it appears ignoble'.[20] Independence of action can hardly go much further than desertion, noble or otherwise, of one's wife and children, whose entreaties will be answered by a stopping of one's ears: a particularly graphic illustration of the closure-oriented nature of ideology. The conscious assertion of individual autonomy in this episode is very strong indeed and it seems very much an act of will that is involved, as it does at many other points in the narrative when all that Christian has to fall back on in trouble is what Richard Baxter called the 'meer promise' of salvation.[21] On other occasions the will is allowed to have similarly beneficial effects in terms of spiritual development:

PRU. *Do you not yet bear away with you some of the things that then you were conversant withal?*

CHR. Yes but greatly against my will; especially my inward and carnal cogitations; with which all my Country-men, as well as my self, were delighted; but now all those things are my grief: and might I but chuse mine own things, I would chuse never to think of those things more; but when I would be doing of that which is best, that which is worst is with me.

(p. 50)

Will, in this instance, is pictured as a positive feature which functions as a barrier against evil thoughts and actions. What Christian seems to be asking for is a stiffening of the will, not any restriction of it. Presumably some sort of fine balance requires to be struck between surrender of the will that leads to a Philotheus-style passivity, and its reckless 'alwaies unto evill' assertion that argues reprobate tendencies. Will can be on the side of the angels too under certain circumstances. What has to be developed is a 'Good Will' that will sustain one when needed: 'As to the burden, be content to bear it, until thou comest to the place of Deliverance; for there it will fall from thy back it self' (p. 28).[22] (Interestingly enough, the language is made to enact just such a stiffening of resolve at a slightly later point in the exchange:

> when I think what I saw at the Cross, that will do it; and when I look upon my Broidered Coat, that will do it; also when I look into the Roll that I carry in my bosom, that will do it; and when my thoughts wax warm about whither I am going, that will do it.   (p. 50)

The repetition of 'will' seems to be an attempt to supply precisely what Christian's character is lacking at this point in the narrative.)

The reprobate characters in *Pilgrim's Progress* fail to exhibit any such fine balance of will, being either wilfully passive or wilfully assertive. What is crucially missing is the will-to-anxiety that will help one to chart a course between the extremes of despair and presumption that salvation is necessarily held to involve. The reprobates prove to be either under-despairing or over-presumptive. The argument is that they are operating self-reprobation on themselves, since the myth has to be adhered to, for doctrinal purposes, that God's grace is open to all who are 'truly willing to have it'; as Good Will is to insist when receiving pilgrims, 'We make no objections against any, notwithstanding all that they have done before they come hither, *they in no wise are cast out*' (p. 27). When confronted by such as Simple, Sloth and Presumption, Christian must interpret their actions as wilful refusals to heed God's word: 'Yet was he troubled to think, That men in that danger should so little esteem the kindness of him that so freely offered to help them; both by awakening of them, counselling of them, and proffering to help them off with their Irons'. The accompanying marginal note points up the paradox that lies behind this 'rejection' of freely-offered help: '*There is no perswasion will do, if God openeth not the eyes*' (p. 39). Wilful refusal to see and predetermined blindness are being made to coexist, although logically speaking they are totally incompatible. Somewhere in that gap, between the body of the text and the marginal commentary, a proof is being assumed.

The typographical layout can be considered to constitute a faithful reflection of Calvinist reasoning on the problems of predestination. There so often *is* a gap in the argument when we pass from God's will to man's responsibility. What we are usually offered at such points is a contiguity of propositions rather than any necessary connection between them.[23] Whereas conviction can help one to bridge this gap, when it ebbs – as it is all too likely to do periodically in the case of sensitive individuals like Christian or his creator – the gap can come to appear unbridgeable. At such points, feelings of extreme anxiety and ontological insecurity begin to reveal themselves. Bunyan was much exercised by the idea of there being an unbridgeable gap between himself and God, as *Grace Abounding* so frequently reveals:

> Sometimes I would tell my condition to the people of God; which when they heard, they would pity me, and would tell me of the Promises; but they had as good have told me that I must reach the Sun with my finger, as have bidden me receive or relie upon the Promise. (p. 26)

Coping with the uncertainties of such 'proof gaps' is a necessary attribute of an elect nature, and failure to display any signs of anxiety and insecurity effectively becomes an index of its reprobate opposite number. There are *some* certainties in the pilgrim's field of experience, but these concern the operation of God's will rather than his own spiritual status. To assume any sense of certainty about the latter is to cross the line that separates the elect few from the reprobate many. When Formalist and Hypocrisy argue that 'so be we get into the way, what's matter which way we get in? if we are in, we are in', they are assuming that their own freely-executed actions ('we are also in the way that came tumbling over the wall') can create certainty of salvation: in Calvinist terms a gross piece of over-presumption. Christian divides them from the elect by calling on the greater certainty of God's will:

> I walk by the Rule of my Master, you walk by the rude working of your fancies. You are counted thieves already, by the Lord of the way; therefore I doubt you will not be found true men at the end of the way. You come in by your selves without his direction, and shall go out by your selves without his mercy. (p. 40)

One kind of certainty is made to unmask another in the subtlest of divisions. The only certainty that the Calvinist can countenance as regards individual consciousness of salvation, is the certainty of its *un*certainty. The wilfulness that presumes to resist this fact of existence calls down upon itself the ultimate sanction available to the God of predestination.

While it is perhaps not too difficult to see why a Formalist or Hypocrisy would merit such sanction, the case of a character like Ignorance is more problematical. He seems a harmless enough creature for a reprobate, lacking in the cunning or aggression that distinguishes so many of his fellows in *Pilgrim's Progress*:

> I know my Lords will, and I have been a good Liver, I pay every man his own; I Pray, Fast, pay Tithes, and give Alms, and have left my Countrey, for whither I am going . . . be content to follow the Religion of your Countrey, and I will follow the Religion of mine. I hope all will be well. (pp. 123–4)

Guileless sentiments such as these would undoubtedly win the approval of *Parable*'s spiritual director, with his advice to 'follow your affairs like other folk'. It represents a counsel of social conformism as far as Bunyan is concerned however, and his elect characters must reject it in the name of a yet higher authority that demands anxious behaviour from its adherents on the assumption that, as we are informed in Part Two, 'No fears, no Grace' (p. 254). That individualism should be instrumental in helping to effect the transition from one form of authoritarianism to another, is entirely in keeping with Calvinism's paradoxical nature as a social philosophy.

Greater paradoxes are to be found in the dialogues between Christian and Ignorance. Like Antilegon before him, Ignorance signals his reprobation as much by his failure to observe the contradictions of Calvinist soteriology as anything else (as David Seed has pointed out, 'skill at debate is directly correlated to . . . spiritual stature' in the work[24]). In the dialogue on salvation, for example, Ignorance's simple faith is confounded by Calvinist deviousness of reasoning. What sounds like an election-affirming argument from faith, 'My heart tells me so', is summarily dismissed by Christian on the grounds that 'He that trusts his own heart is a fool'; although the tradition that Christian springs from, spiritual autobiography, invariably saw conversion as involving a sense of inner revelation. Faith would appear to be a deceptive state of mind: '*Ask my fellow if I be a Thief: Thy heart tells thee so!*' The argument from faith being disposed of, the argument from works is attempted by Ignorance: 'But is it not a good heart that hath good thoughts? And is not that a good life, that is according to Gods Commandments?' No comfort is forthcoming here either: '*Yes, that is a good heart that hath good thoughts, and that is a good life that is according to Gods Commandments: But it is one thing indeed to have these, and another thing only to think so*' (p. 145). Presumably one must *know* one has these things before claiming proof of election, but this is precisely the kind of presumption that Calvinists are always warning against: in which case 'hoping' or 'thinking' all will be well would appear to have much to recommend them – yet here they are being roundly criticised. We are back with the paradox noted in *Pathway*: that it is wrong to be persuaded before you know, and wrong to know that you are persuaded. It seems either can be used in evidence against you. Ignorance, like Antilegon, gives up the battle: '*You go so fast, I cannot keep pace with you; do you go on before, I must stay a while behind*' (p. 149).

Eventually it becomes a case of arguments from faith and arguments from works being relegated to a subsidiary position behind arguments from the Word: '*Except the word of God beareth witness in this matter, other Testimony is of no value*' (p. 145). It is, in fact, the Word which usually fills in those worrying gaps in the argument for the Calvinist (that logocentricity noted by Higman), and the inability to come up with a despair-inducing biblical quotation at times of presumption, and vice versa, suggests that one is a candidate for reprobation. Ignorance's blend of under-despairing and over-presumption involves a state of psychological equilibrium foreign to the Calvinist mind. Engagement with the paradoxes demands that awareness of the contradictories to one's present psychological condition must always impinge, such that presumption becomes merely a prelude to the inevitable onset of despair, and despair to presumption, in an endless series of bewildering transitions; the result being what Royce, in an analysis of Bunyan's psychology, has called the 'chaos of motor processes' in the author.[25] The chaos in question is well illustrated in the following passage from *Grace Abounding*: 'so my soul did hang as in a pair of Scales again, sometimes up, and sometimes down, now in peace, and anon again in terror' (p. 65).

The inscription of this chaos into *Holy War* will lead to that narrative's endlessly-recurring cycles of conflict and its modern, open-ended appearance. In *Pilgrim's Progress* a more determinate form of chaos is at work, and it is repeatedly made clear throughout the work that the journey undertaken is finite: 'I come from the City of *Destruction*, but am going to Mount *Zion*, that I may be delivered from the wrath to come' (p. 25). In this goal-directed pilgrimage all resolution-deferring digressions are to be monitored, and a network of divine agents stands ready to correct Christian and encourage adherence to the path of soteriological determinism: 'there are many ways *Butt* down upon this; and they are Crooked, and Wide: But *thus* thou may'st distinguish the right from the wrong, *That* only being straight and narrow' (pp. 27–8). A determinate journey in which the resolution of death is actively sought ('Why not willing to die? since this life is attended with so many evils?' (p. 10)) is cunningly coupled with the death-denying properties of the salvation state: 'There is an endless Kingdom to be Inhabited, and everlasting life to be given us; that we may Inhabit that Kingdom for ever' (p. 13). Remaining true to this counter-culture to the Restoration establishment holds out the hope of an escape into a realm of endlessness, where there will be freedom from the repressive attentions of reprobates and mediators alike. Anxiety seems to have its rewards.

Salvation is reached through individual experience, individual experience is reached through pilgrimage, pilgrimage is reached through a deliberate break with the socially-conformist community. The progression is given the appearance of both inevitability and freedom of choice; an inevitability which takes no account of individual actions ('thou hast forsaken the way that is good, to tread in forbidden paths: yet will the man at the Gate receive thee' (p. 24)), and a freedom to evince willingness to be the recipient of grace ('if we be truly willing to have it, he will bestow it upon us freely'). The fact that such willingness can be unsuccessful, as it is in Ignorance's case, and that freedom to choose is a God-given attribute anyway, can be glossed over by the strategic use of emphasis (emphasise mercy with Christian, justice with Ignorance) such that the repressive side of Calvinist doctrine is to a large extent concealed. That such a repressive side does exist becomes apparent when we examine the imagery suggesting enclosure in the work. One of the most powerful of these images is '*Despair like an Iron Cage*' (p. 34) in the House of the Interpreter:

> God hath denied me repentance; his Word gives me no encouragement to believe; yea, himself hath shut me up in this Iron Cage: nor can all the men in the World let me out. O Eternity! Eternity! how shall I grapple with the misery that I must meet with in Eternity? (p. 35)

A different kind of infinity from the heavenly variety is to be noted here: the infinity of a despair inculcated in man by God ('himself hath shut me up'), but directly attributable to the prisoner's freely chosen courses of action:

> I left off to watch, and be sober; I laid the reins upon the neck of my lusts; I sinned against the light of the Word, and the goodness of God: I have grieved the Spirit, and he is gone; I tempted the Devil, and he is come to me; I have provoked God to anger, and he has left me; I have so hardened my heart, that I *cannot* repent. (p. 34)

Denial of repentance by God is not enough to absolve the individual reprobate of responsibility for his own unwillingness to receive what is not, in this case at least, being freely offered.

In similar instances of enclosure involving the elect, ways of escape can be engineered, as the emphasis shifts from justice to mercy. Christian's confinement in a cage at Vanity Fair is temporary, as is his imprisonment in the dungeon of Castle-Doubting. The paradox that such discriminatory treatment declares, can perhaps best be summed up by the following exchange:

> CHR.   *Is the way safe, or dangerous?*
> SHEP.   Safe for those for whom it is to be safe.
>
> (p. 119)

Deciding whether one fits into that latter category is where the creative use of anxiety comes in; as Hopeful is made to remark at a later point in the text: 'I do believe as you say, that fear tends much to Mens good' (p. 150). To structure a pilgrimage on such an idea is to confront the dominant ideology of one's time, with its bias towards mediation and the reduction of spiritual insecurity. In this respect the man in the iron cage is an untypical example of the reprobate in Bunyan, since he too patently is experiencing feelings of anxiety and ontological insecurity. The shift is a significant one, but Bunyan does not choose to explore the possibilities inherent in over-despairing in any detail, being content to deal with the easier targets of under-despairing and over-presumptive reprobates.

In the case of both elect and reprobate, therefore, divinely-generated inevitability and freedom of choice appear to be involved, although in practice Calvinist doctrine is loaded for or against any given individual. Greater stress is placed on free will with regard to the reprobate, and their sense of individualism derives from this; with the elect, individualism is a by-product of anxiety: the anxiety that comes from engagement with the paradoxes of Calvinism. The ideal in the latter case is an uncompromising self-censorship; the ability to put one's fingers in one's ears as an act of assertion against the will of the conformist community. The commitment, then, is to a spiritual fate which works through, and at least in some sense requires the co-operation of, the individual, rather than one that is imposed on him from without as happens in *Parable*.

By the time pilgrimage is brought under way in *Parable* the individualistic nature of the enterprise has been undercut by a series of discourses delivered by Philotheus' spiritual director. The state of 'profound stillness' (p. 177) these tend to induce in the protagonist is a revealing comment on the author's social philosophy: authority is to be active, targets of authority passive. The goal of pilgrimage comes to seem not so much personal salvation at the expense of one's reprobate fellows, as conformity to an establishment (the Church/State power bloc of the Restoration period) anxious to promote the virtues of 'profound stillness' over socially divisive enthusiasm: a case of 'follow your affairs like other folk' rather than 'fly from the wrath to come'. Wharey has complained that 'there are almost no incidents' in the work,[26] and while he has a point we do need to bear in mind the ideological implications of this authorial decision. A life lacking in incident is a life lacking in threat to those in power. Sheer absence of incident is, in fact, an asset in the Anglican scheme of things at this historical juncture. The less individual initiative the better as far as figures like Patrick are concerned. When pilgrimage proper begins, Philotheus does, it is true, set out alone, although the author is careful to remove all sense of tension from this particular condition of solitude:

A Fine Sunshine-morning it was when he first went out of doors; The Air was perfumed with the Sweet Odors which the

Sun exhaled from the flowers, the birds whistled and sung their Hymns to him that made glorious Light; and there was no hedge that he passed by, but it welcomed him with some new Songs and pleasures, nor any Traveller he met, but wished Good speed.   (p. 281)

There could hardly be a more marked contrast with the 'soldier in hostile territory' school of writing than this gentle saunter through an Arcadian landscape; but then, Anglicanism in the 1660s is not trying to strike terror into the hearts of the populace. It is more concerned with reconciling the warring factions in the country and presenting itself as the true inheritor of the ancient Christian Church. The absence of any sense of menace in the scene and the suggestion of harmony between the pilgrim and his environment, effectively neutralises the subversive implications of individual action. What Sharrock has described as *Pilgrim's Progress*'s 'persistent general idea of striving towards a goal across a difficult and dangerous terrain',[27] is conspicuously missing in *Parable*, where lack of incident is the more desired state.

Philotheus' spell of solitude is very brief and his spiritual director eventually returns as a permanent presence: 'Let this be our Wedding-day: and from henceforth take me for your inseparable Companion' (p. 317). Inseparability is a comforting but dependent state which enables the author to screen the electee from all disturbing experience. There will be none of the terrors of Calvinist pilgrimage, none of the 'frights, theeves, beatings, and ill-usages' met with by Christian. Neither will there be any of the dynamism of a Calvinist pilgrimage, in which victories over adversaries such as Apollyon promote new levels of understanding and personal independence in the electee. In exchange for the disorienting, but ultimately rewarding, swings of manic-depressive psychology there is peace of mind, emotional stability – and constant policing by authority.

Philotheus is consistently denied any of the dramatic encounters by which Christian's faith is put to the test. His inseparable companion smooths over all the problems that arise and explains away life's terrors before they can have any significant effect on his charge. Patrick's unemotional style works against the notion of catharsis so that any potentially dramatic situation is defused:

> I remember, that one day as they went through a certain place, which was more like a Garden than an High-way; He askt him if he was not afraid of those strange Beasts in green skins, and those armed men with weapons of the same colour in their hands. At which he smiling said; though you have been conscious too much of my weakness, yet I have so much courage, as not to be affrighted at the Images of things which I see cut in hedges. You shall see how confidently I will walk naked by that Lyon and that the Bear in the other thicket shall strike no terrour unto me. (p. 348)

It is characteristic of Patrick's method that mediation serves to render all such problematical experiences harmless, whereas Bunyan is invariably concerned with striking terror into the heart of his pilgrim in order to heighten his sense of anxiety. *Pilgrim's Progress*'s lions are substantial, block the path, and cause Mistrust and Timorous to retreat because 'we could not think, if we came within reach, but they would presently pull us in pieces' (p. 43). The assurance of the porter at the lodge that he need 'fear not the Lions, for they are Chained; and are placed there for trial of faith where it is; and for discovery of those that have none' (pp. 45–6), provides some consolation, but does not remove the necessity for Christian to undergo the trial 'solitarily': which he does 'trembling' in the best manner of one balancing despair and presumption. Such trials of faith are hardly to be found in *Parable*, and nothing there will rival the pitched battle between Christian and Apollyon, full of 'hideous roaring . . . sighs and groans' (p. 60). Philotheus will never be required to stand and fight for his beliefs in such a dramatic manner as this, being protected at every turn by his mediator. Even when there is a trial of faith in *Parable* – as in the Valley of the Shadow of Death scene in the brief interlude between the beginning of pilgrimage and the onset of election

– it is not used in a dynamic way. In this instance it merely points up the character's inadequacies when left to his own devices. A string of rhetorical exclamations – 'O what a Wilderness am I faln into where I can find no water! What Desarts are these, in which all Comfort forsakes my soul! Into what strange regions am I wandred' (p. 298), and so on – are made to substitute for dynamic individual action. Christian's dogged progress through a landscape of 'blood, bones, ashes, and mangled bodies of men' (p. 65) represents the Calvinist answer to psychological blocks, and it promotes independence of spirit. In Patrick's world, trials of faith merely prove the need for dependence on authority, as well as the futility of personal autonomy.

Despite its orientation towards individually-repressive resolution, *Parable* contrives to be an open-ended narrative in its way, since it concludes with the pilgrimage still in progress: 'I cannot say, for the present, what the ensuing part of their travels were, my own observation here having an end' (p. 518). It may well be that deferral here simply points to a greater concern with this life than the after-life amongst Anglicans, as opposed to the Calvinist scheme of things where, as Weber noted, 'the after-life was not only more important, but in many ways also more certain than all the interests of life in this world'.[28] Bunyan opts for the latter kind of certainty in his pilgrimage, with Christian welcomed into a vividly-described Celestial City which 'shone like the Sun' (p. 162) after his passage across the River of Death, much in the manner of a conquering military hero. The whole episode suggests a triumphant vindication of individual endeavour against the forces of evil. In *Parable* we remain in this world under the guidance of a spiritual director, with such triumphs of individuality deferred. The future, it would seem, belongs to the forces of worldly authority, who have not yet relinquished control of the individual's destiny. The argument here is that 'vertuous mediocrity' has its sinister side and that it represents a greater challenge to free will than Calvinist predestinarian theory, for all the latter's commitment to divine predeterminism. Whereas will is a live issue in predestinarian theory –

something to be juggled with as one shuttles back and forth between despair and optimism – it is hidden from sight in 'vertuous mediocrity' by the surrender of personal autonomy to a superior, whose brief is to restrict his charge's range of experience. Lack of incident replaces progress.

The dialogue with ideological closure in Bunyan ultimately works against such repression, although he flirts with 'vertuous mediocrity' in *Pilgrim's Progress* Part Two. Part Two is an altogether less severe work than its predecessor, or indeed any other in the Bunyan canon. It is, in Sharrock's words, 'a more humdrum world, but a gracious and good-humoured one'[29] (Keeble, on the other hand, has made a strong case for it as having an innate sense of thematic continuity with Part One, in many ways completing its vision[30]). The narrative is indeed far less harsh in tone, and although it is still Calvinist in orientation, it steers clear of the system's more controversial aspects and seems weighted more towards the mercy than the justice side of Christianity; as Christiana insists, 'the King, who hath sent for me and my Children, is one that delighteth in *Mercie*' (p. 185). Throughout the greater part of the pilgrimage, much more of a social affair this time around, a guide is in attendance. This guide, Great-heart, undertakes most of the company's battles:

> the Women and Children did nothing but sigh and cry all the time that the Battle did last . . . the *Giant* began to faint, and could hold up his Club no longer. Then Mr. *Great-heart* seconded his blow, and smit the head of the *Giant* from his shoulders. Then the Women and Children rejoyced, and Mr. *Great-heart* also praised God, for the deliverance he had wrought. (p. 245)

The scene forms a notable contrast to Christian's solitary battle with Apollyon, and suggests a shifting of trial-by-faith on to a mediator: a significant move considering the author's commitment to individual action elsewhere in his fiction. The reason for the shift is that in Part Two we are dealing with women, who cannot, Bunyan feels, be expected to have the strength of character of the other sex.[31] Their first champion in distress, Reliever, notes that '*I marvelled much when you was entertained at the Gate above, being ye knew that ye were but weak Women, that you petitioned not the Lord there for a Conductor: Then might you have avoided these Troubles, and Dangers: For he would have granted you one*'. Even 'weak Women', however, may benefit from facing hardship unprotected: '*Had my Lord granted you a Conductor, you would not neither so have bewailed that oversight of yours in not asking for one, as now you have occasion to do. So all things work for good, and tend to make you more wary*' (p. 196). Adversity promotes character development, in other words: not a sentiment to be met with in *Parable*, where stillness and lack of incident become life's most desired qualities for the common man and woman. In any Bunyan pilgrimage there has to be a certain amount of fear: 'no fears, no Grace', as one of Christiana's children succinctly puts it. Fear played an important part in Bunyan's theology, and Talon has commented on his sermons conforming to a pattern of 'fear, then love'. Bunyan 'aroused terror in his listeners only so that they could better savour the peace of love'.[32] ('Work out your salvation with fear', as he advised in *A Treatise of the Fear of God*; adding, with the characteristic sting in the tail of Calvinist paradox, 'not that work is meritorious, or such that can purchase eternal life'.)[33]

Pilgrim's Progress Part Two is as close to 'vertuous mediocrity' as Bunyan will allow himself to come, and there are weak men as well as weak women to be catered for. Mr Fearing, Mr Feeble-mind, Mr Despondency, and Mr Ready-to-halt, characters whose names suggest reprobation more than election, all reach the Celestial City in an unprecedented act of clemency on the author's part. Nevertheless, all the work's electees will be given some experience of adversity, along the lines of Mr Fearing's initiation into pilgrimage '*in Solitariness, with Fears and Cries*' (p. 172). Mediocrity never *quite* circumscribes individuality. Even in the case of the meek the author will insist that 'Nothing teaches like Experience' (p. 263). The Puritan/sectarian commitment to what Ong called observation knowledge is much in evidence at such points.

We might also speak of a nonconformist commitment to adventure which is in direct opposition to the commitment to lack of incident in Anglicanism. There is a truly epic quality to be noted in Bunyan's fiction, where the individual electee is cast in the role of hero rather than being a mere 'divided part' requiring to be absorbed back into an experience-restricting collective, as Patrick would have it. The difference involved mimics that between childhood innocence and adulthood experience, with the Anglican extolling the virtues of the former and the nonconformist insisting on the necessity of the latter if God's purposes are to be realised. Innocence is a seductive state and Patrick makes the most of the fact, painting a rosy picture of life under Anglican mediocrity: no fears, no crises and no insecurity. It has all the drawbacks of childhood too: minimal control over your environment, continual dependence on the will of another, and a sense of being excluded from the events of a more exciting world by the powers-that-be. As a member of those powers-that-be, Patrick has a vested interest in maintaining the exclusivity of the bloc, and hymning the joys of dependent status is a particularly subtle and effective way of doing just that. Bunyan, on the other hand, makes a virtue out of insecurity – 'no fears, no Grace' – and even here, in his most mediocrity-conscious text, it puts in a significant appearance. The commitment to adventure may be qualified somewhat in *Pilgrim's Progress* Part Two, but it is still a force to be reckoned with. In comparison with Patrick, the work has a heroic dimension.

Bunyan's commitment to heroic progress is never in doubt. Patrick denies this experience of individual progress to his hero in the name of an authoritarianism more subtle, and more effective, than that of Calvinism. Opt for Anglicanism and you can dispense with the burden of responsibility which radical Protestantism will place on your back; but you must also forego all those moments of release when burdens are lifted and the sense of one's own identity becomes intensely life-enhancing: 'then *Christian* gave three leaps for joy, and went on singing' (p. 38). Nothing comparable will be found in

Patrick's anti-enthusiastic world, where election is a matter of surrendering personal autonomy to a dominant authority figure, who will screen the pilgrim from all potentially individuating experience by means of 'vertuous mediocrity'. Within the terms of reference of the Restoration it is a message with powerful appeal, but the fear-based pilgrimage of the alienated nonconformist provides a subversive counterpoint, whose ideological import is only too clear to the 'Fanatick conventicles' whose aspirations it articulates. In each text, narrative structure is heavily encoded with ideological assumptions. Taken together, *Parable* and *Pilgrim's Progress* are like a microcosm of Restoration culture, with their contrasting pilgrimage styles bearing witness to its deep social divisions.

In *Pilgrim's Progress* Bunyan is conducting negotiations with paradox in the sense that his ideology requires him to acquiesce in certain closures of experience, and also to effect them himself; to accept concealment of contradictions, and to engage enthusiastically in the practice of concealing. Ideology, author and fictional individual must all conspire to ensure the required closures, and they take many different forms. Thus soteriology presents itself as a set of possible experiences enclosed within the boundaries of election and reprobation, and the electee simply treats these boundaries as part of the human condition. Bunyan is operating within various other enclosing sets in the course of his fiction, such as determinism/free will, despair/presumption and justice/mercy. These sets represent limits of experience for the individual, and although movement occurs within them (to some extent they may be treated as sliding scales), movement from inside to outside does not. (McKeon has referred to 'the psychological fluidity that is characteristic of Calvinist doctrine',[34] but it should be stressed that it is fluidity within very precise limits.) The degree of movement varies considerably. As far as the election/reprobation set goes, it might seem to be more a case of irreversible progression from mid-point (pilgrimage beginning) to either end. On the one side, the pathway to heaven, on the other, the pathway to hell; neither apparently permitting the individual to retrace his steps. In psychological terms it does not work that way, however, and the electee at least can never completely convince himself that backsliding is not a real and ever-present possibility. His 'chaos of motor processes' movement back and forth between despair and presumption bears witness to his lack of certainty in this regard.

In the determinism/free will set, chaotic movement is acknowledged as a permanent possibility given man's 'alwaies free unto evill' tendencies. These work against God's determining powers in an apparently inwardly-generated resistance to divine closure, with the paradox-related qualification that they owe their existence *to* God's determining powers. No escape is possible from this set either; although Calvinist ingenuity of reasoning enables an author like Bunyan to argue that it is in fact the individual who is indulging in closure of experience, by allowing his will to close off access to God's freely-offered help.

Adroit deployment of paradox also enables Bunyan to slide back and forth along the scale between justice and mercy as ideological needs dictate. The individual has no say in whether God chooses to make him a target for one or other of these dispositions, and the author can use this fact to give soteriology a harsh or gentle face as he pleases. It can excuse mass clemency at the end of *Pilgrim's Progress* Part Two, or violent exclusion of an unassuming candidate for election at the end of Part One. In the conspiracy between ideology, author and fictional individual, paradox, with its impeccable biblical connotations, provides all the justification that is required for such judgemental divisions. It can stand as proof, evidence, or received authority as needed.

Chapter Four

PARADOX AND PROGRESS II
The Life and Death of Mr Badman

PREDESTINATION demands that the elect can take no credit for their salvation, whereas the reprobate, although similarly predetermined as to ultimate fate, must carry the blame for their own damnation. Bunyan confronts this paradox head on in *Badman*, his reworking of the *Pathway* narrative, where a reprobate progress is outlined in all its unsavoury detail. *Badman* has proved to be one of Bunyan's more problematic fictions. Grudging (in some cases *very* grudging) admiration has tended to be the dominant critical response; 'a remarkable, if an offensive book' as Venables once put it. Froude has some complimentary things to say about it, 'a natural story' with a sense of 'grave solemnity' to its ending he felt, and Sutherland has claimed it as 'a brilliant transfer of English middle-class life in the seventeenth century'.[1] But these are fairly isolated instances of praise: generally speaking this is a text which has received a bad press in the last century or so, with such heavyweight Bunyan scholars as Wharey, Talon and Sharrock expressing severe reservations about the work.[2] The paradoxes associated with Calvinist soteriological theory are, perhaps, mainly to blame for this reception, and if the work is to be resurrected then that is where the focus has to be directed. The work's 'offensiveness' is in fact a carefully calculated exercise in social critique on the author's part to which paradox holds the key. Bunyan is engaged in subverting Restoration society and its values – '*O Debauchery, Debauchery, what hast thou done in* England' as he feelingly declaims in *Badman*'s preface (p. 7) – and the person of Mr Badman is made to bear the brunt of his considerable ideological displeasure.

Mr Badman is built up into an image of all the vices that the sectarian of Bunyan's time has come to despise; vices such as hypocrisy, greed and latitudinarianism. His personality is derived from the Antilegon figure of *Pathway*, but this is an Antilegon who has declined from pragmatism into outright immorality and blatantly unethical behaviour. The text comes to represent Bunyan's judgement on Restoration society; a society in which nonconformists are forced to register their ideological criticisms in an oblique manner such as prose fiction affords.[3] Mr Badman is to symbolise the rotten elements of his society as Christian so manifestly did the righteous: 'England *shakes and totters already, by reason of the burden* Mr Badman *and his friends have wickedly laid upon it*' (p. 2). When a Bunyan character comments with regard to the times, '*I fear they'l be worse before they be better*' (p. 14), the observation can be considered to have greater depth than its clichéd form might at first suggest. *Badman* is designed to provide a message of hope for those caught within a context of overt cultural repression, where 'Mr Badman *has left many of his Relations behind him; yea, the very World is overspread with his Kindred*' (p. 1). If Badman himself can be separated from the elect and punished for his part in creating a hostile cultural climate based on corrupt values, then Bunyan's act of critique will have fulfilled its ideological objective.

The outcome is an uncompromising work concerned to leave its opponents no room for manoeuvre. Bunyan takes no chances. *Badman* opens with the brute facts of its protagonist's death and damnation in what looks very much like a case of ideological over-determination: 'He died that he might die, he went from Life to Death, and then from Death to Death, from Death Natural to Death Eternal' (p. 14). Little attempt is made to sugar the bitter pill of reprobation, and severity remains the keynote of a text which is invariably unfavourably compared to *Pilgrim's Progress*. Talon has observed that, 'by an act unconsciously imitative of the arbitrary decrees of his God,

Bunyan has predestined his character before he was so much as born in the pages of his manuscript'.[4] The point is relevant and well-taken, but it could be justifiably read as an instance of *conscious* rather than unconscious imitation. Bunyan's concern is to isolate the reprobate so that he can function as a symbol of his culture's corruption to the narrative's nonconformist audience. Paradox is the key tactical device in this process of isolation, operating as follows. Since paradox sets up a logical contradiction (characters being seen, for example, to be simultaneously free and predetermined in their actions) it permits the author to emphasise whichever side of the contradiction he wishes in order to achieve his ideological objectives. If free will works tactically to damn your character then stress free will; if predestination seems more appropriate to the situation then stress predestination. Soteriological theory gives you that extremely useful option in that free-willed actions presuppose predestination, and predestination, at least in the case of the reprobate, presupposes the existence of free-willed actions. The author can be selective according to the local circumstances of the narrative.

If this sounds a somewhat cynical practice for an author to adopt, it is worth pointing out that there are modern equivalents in the free will/determinism debate as currently constituted. Despite the arguments – some of them very powerful[5] – of, for example, genetic and sociological determinists, there is still widespread belief in, and commitment to, free will, and the advocates of the respective positions can be fairly selective in their manipulation of the evidence. Again, this is not infrequently for ideological reasons, 'free' being one of the most emotive of words.[6]

Bunyan's selectivity and severity are made clear from the beginning of the narration of his subject's life, when we are assured that 'from a Child he was very bad'. It is insisted that the fault was Badman's own, and already we enter the world of paradox:

> he was, as you say, polluted, very much polluted with Original Corruption. For to speak my mind freely, I do confess, that it is mine

73

opinion, that Children come polluted with sin into the World, and that oft-times the sins of their youth, especially while they are very young, are rather by vertue of Indwelling sin, than by examples that are set before them by others. Not but that they learn to sin by example too, but Example is not the root, but rather the Temptation unto wickedness. The root is sin within; for from within, out of the heart of man proceedeth sin. (p. 17)

Here we reach the heart of this particular Calvinist soteriological paradox; the sin is 'indwelling' but the individual is at fault. It is judgemental severity of this kind that has alienated recent generations of Bunyan critics, whose uneasiness about the narrative has perhaps best been summed up by Sharrock, who has argued that although 'neither the narrative nor the moral interest of *Pilgrim's Progress* is stultified by the doctrine of predestination', those of *Badman* are.

Sharrock's comparison of these two works is worth analysing in a little more detail in order to show the kind of critical block to be dealt with. He claims that predestination presents no real problem to the appreciation of *Pilgrim's Progress* because 'the point of reference is in the mind of Christian and for him the issue is always in doubt'. In *Badman*, on the other hand, the author 'makes no attempt to enter the mind of his central character: judgement is passed on him at the start, and his life is studied from the outside'. This is described as a 'technical lapse' deriving from the fact that:

> For Bunyan, fiction has to be filtered through theology, and the characters he describes with intimate knowledge have to think as theologians; Christian and Hopeful hope for salvation, but Badman does not believe he is going to be damned: his own estimation of his life is in terms which fall quite outside the Puritan scheme.[7]

The clear implication is that 'filtering through theology' can only be to the detriment of narrative development. *Pilgrim's Progress* under this form of analysis is a masterpiece *despite* its ideological content, whereas *Badman* unfortunately succumbs

74

to the stultifying effects of deterministic theology. Wharey had earlier made similar objections to *Badman*:

> The weakness of *The Life and Death of Mr Badman* is found in the many long discussions of the sins to which Mr Badman is addicted. So long as Bunyan sticks to the story proper, just so long does he hold the individual attention of his reader; interest lags when he begins to preach. This same weakness is found in *The Pilgrim's Progress*, but not to the same degree as in the later story.[8]

To adopt such an attitude is to miss, or at the very least significantly to underestimate, the didactic import of Bunyan's fiction and his ideologically-motivated desire to articulate certain culturally sensitive signifying practices, notably election and reprobation, in narrative form. Culturally sensitive, because they can be applied in a subversively-minded, non-hierarchical manner which takes no account of social or economic position: neither God nor a nonconformist author being any 'respecter of persons'. Bunyan is first and foremost a polemical author, and what might look like stultification from a twentieth-century viewpoint was, for a reader brought up in the Puritan tradition – where, Sharrock notwithstanding, the ordinary person very often could indeed 'think like a theologian' – the very core of the narrative enterprise. 'The many long discussions' are precisely what that reader will be absorbed by. We do Bunyan a disservice if we do not allow the possibility of a distinct shift in 'the story proper' between his time and ours, and if we are to resurrect the discourse of this text then this is just what we must allow.

Since our concern here is precisely *with* the narratological effect of Calvinist doctrine, our perspective is rather different. It is the manner in which a narrative like *Badman* is 'filtered through theology', as well as the ideological implications of such filtering, that are the focus of attention. Attention is directed to the interplay between ideology and narrative structure in the text, and an examination is made of the moral dilemmas and authorial manoeuvres that this interplay engenders. The concern is to reconstruct the text's ideological field of operations. Where Sharrock sees a life 'studied from the outside', and Wharey 'many long discussions', I would see a superbly well orchestrated process of isolation where paradox is deployed as a literary figure to ultimately devastating social–critical effect.

'Filtering through theology' often equals 'filtering through paradox' in the Puritan prose fiction tradition, and there is consistent engagement with Calvinist doctrinal contradictions throughout *Badman*. Reference has already been made to the God's will/reprobate's fault paradox being applied to the infant Badman, and Bunyan holds firmly to this line through the narrative, as in Attentive's remarks on the soul:

> *if a man had no Soul, if his was not truely Immortal, the matter would not be so much; but for a man to be so disposed of by his Maker, as to be appointed a sensible being for ever, and for him too to fall into the hands of revenging Justice, that will be always, to the utmost extremity that his sin deserveth, punishing of him in the dismal dungeon of Hell, this must needs be unutterably sad, and lamentable.*

Since Calvinist theory insists that it is God who has predetermined who is to be a candidate for 'revenging Justice', this would appear to absolve the individual reprobate from all blame as to his sins; but for Calvinists this was not the whole story. Wiseman is to go on to state that even the damned 'have *sense* and *reason* too' (p. 15). It is, in short, their own fault that they sin, and they are held to be fully aware of this fact. The fault is 'found in themselves' as Calvin defiantly proclaimed.

The recurrent appearance of the God's will/reprobate's fault paradox is evidence of the strong Calvinist line that Bunyan is taking on predestination in *Badman*. Judgement is repeatedly effected by means of paradox, in the sense that paradox allows one to substitute assertion for proof. One simply asserts the locally appropriate part of the logical contradiction in an authoritative manner, as Bunyan's spokesmen so confidently do, and conclusive proof is assumed. The aggressively dogmatic tone that this practice produces in the text is heightened by the absence of a dissenting voice. This double-filtering process (by God and by man) robs the work of the sheer sense of drama of *Pathway*, where reprobation was unfolded before us step by step; but the synoptic narrative nevertheless has its virtues, not the least of which from the Calvinist's point of view is that it imposes a more coherent pattern on the material. It imposes inevitability on the reprobate's career, thus bringing the fact of soteriological closure even more forcefully before its audience. Judgement of this kind operates more subtly than the 'judgement by debate' format of *Pilgrim's Progress* because it is more difficult to identify. It is based on a 'lack' rather than a 'presence'. There is a certain irony in Sharrock's reference to *Badman*'s 'central character' because the work in many ways *lacks* a central character; he has been comprehensively filtered out of the narrative situation by death and damnation, and exists only in a shadowy, second-order sense. Badman is to be denied even those limited opportunities to elicit audience sympathy granted to such as Antilegon and Ignorance. Bunyan will make extensive use of all the paraphernalia of Puritan herme-neutics (that 'union between exegesis and homiletics' as Kaufmann has described it[9]) – checklists of signs of reproba-tion, division technique, strategic deployment of the Word, arguments from paradox, for example – but it is all directed against this 'lack' and as such constitutes a bid for an even more total sense of exclusivist judgement than is to be found in *Pilgrim's Progress*. Badman stands revealed as the antithesis to dissenting rectitude, and therefore as a target for ideologically-motivated narrative strategies. Paradox, an endlessly-available local tactical device, allows you to operate a pincer movement on your target: to argue that his sins are both predestined *and* premeditated.

This paraphernalia of Puritan hermeneutics provides the basis for narrative structure in *Badman*, and the text is organised around a series of checklists designed to prove beyond any possible doubt Badman's reprobate nature. Strong stress is laid on the premeditated quality of Badman's conduct. As a child, we are informed, 'he would invent, tell, and stand to the Lyes that he invented and told' as if to *'force his own heart unto it'*. Such premeditation, for the Calvinist, argues the deliberate exertion of a will 'alwaies free unto evill'. It also enhances, in a particularly subtle way, the text's argument for summary judgement against Badman. A character who sets out *'to harden himself in sin betimes'* (p. 18) is effectively bringing about his own ultimate punishment. To bring the intention to the fore is very cleverly to draw the audience's attention away from the character's innatist inheritance of 'Original Corruption'. The generally unsympathetic tone adopted towards reprobates in soteriology-debate fiction is based on precisely this premiss of deliberate hardening. The mercy/merit paradox we met with in Dent becomes transformed, by the subtlest of logical transpositions, into 'no mercy if you show no merit'. From earliest childhood Badman follows an anti-merit path, therefore he can expect no mercy from God or nonconformist: to Bunyan and those of like mind, end of the argument.

Having established a basic nature in which free will predominates, the author traces his reprobate's progress through the sequence of spiritually-damning sins, treating the resultant catalogue much in the manner of a semiotic system.[10] Great store is placed on the importance of recognising signs, and in terms of Badman's character his sins are the diachronic elements which are to confirm his basic, synchronic nature. They act as semiotic reminders to the elect in the audience that his personality has been reprobationally determined in advance, such that the dynamics of his life can be considered subservient to an overall narrative scheme. For the Puritan, and the dissenter after him, the reprobate's life is a narrative to be read off against the wider narrative of divine predestination, with acts of free will serving to justify predetermined verdicts. Given an unshakeable belief in the power of the Word of God as revealed in the Bible, human life itself becomes a book to be read for edificatory purposes.

Badman's development is to bear out his unpromising start in that it transcribes an unbroken progression on the pathway to hell. The process is seen to be both inevitable and irreversible: one long, continuous decline into reprobation marked out by appropriate checklists and divisions. This relentless concern to amass evidence informs the whole text, and Wiseman systematically works his way through Badman's catalogue of sins, the approach being very much that of the Puritan preacher skilled in the use of division to make polemical points.[11] The motivation behind this is to build up an overwhelming case against its silent victim; to isolate him from the elect in order to reveal his reprobate nature: that fatal conjunction of the predestined and the premeditated. To go to such lengths to expose your subject is almost to accord his values a certain credibility, and Bunyan is careful to incorporate periodic closures of such gestures towards debate: 'what need I thus talk of the particular actions, or rather prodigious sins of Mr *Badman*, when his whole Life and all his actions, went as it were to the making up one massie body of sin' (p. 127). Guilt, like the truth of the Word, is ultimately unquestionable; buried in the very texture of the subject's life. Badman is simply beyond redemption: 'an *angry, wrathfull, envious* man, a man that knew not what meekness or gentleness meant, nor did he desire to learn' (p. 129); 'knew not' signalling predestination to the reader, and 'nor did' free will. Compulsion and deliberation combined together like this spell out reprobation to a predestination-sensitive readership.

The truth of the Word is rigorously insisted upon, with constant reference being made by Wiseman and Attentive to the scriptures. Such references again have a debate-closing function – paradoxes are not pursued very far when scripture comes on the scene. A prime example of this can be found in Wiseman's handling of the 'indwelling sin' paradox:

> I am glad to hear you are of this opinion, and to confirm what you have said by a few hints from the Word. Man in his birth is compared to an Ass, (an unclean Beast) and to a wretched Infant in its blood: besides, all the first-born of old that were offered unto the Lord, were to be redeemed at the age of a month, and that was before they were sinners by imitation. The Scripture

79

> also affirmeth, that by the sin of one, Judgement came upon all;
> and renders this reason, for that all *have* sinned. (p. 17)

Those 'few hints' serve to dissolve paradox to the Calvinist, although closer inspection reveals this piece of 'proof' to be little more than a series of assertions awaiting a debate that is never really allowed to occur, except in the following cunningly-loaded manner: 'nor is that Objection worth a rush, That Christ by his death hath taken away Original Sin. First, Because it is Scriptureless. Secondly, Because it makes them incapable of Salvation by Christ; for none but those that in their own Persons are sinners, are to have Salvation by him' (pp. 17–18). Faith in the Word can hardly go further than the invocation of the absence of scripture as a criterion of argument validity. This is logocentricity taken to its limits. The system does not just produce meaning, in effect it *is* meaning, and its adherents have what amounts to privileged access to it which they can capitalise on at any time by mere assertion of the Word and its confirming 'hints'. It is always the case that 'Many other things might be added', as Wiseman so confidently, and perhaps also somewhat sinisterly, puts it.

The neatness of the logic at this point has to be applauded. You can only be damned if you are a sinner; but if you are not a sinner you cannot be saved, because you can only be saved if you are a sinner too. Given an Antilegon figure to argue the point and so keep the paradox in the foreground, a debate between free will and determinism could be maintained (and audience identification with a beleaguered Antilegon is always a distinct possibility). In the deliberately engineered absence of such a central character, though, predestinarian determinism is thereby rendered all the more powerful. The paradoxes still have to be articulated, however, which means that the dialectic is floating around somewhere in the text – and in the text of 'life', as Wiseman concedes in referring to the need for Word-based arguments for 'when an Antagonist comes to deal with us about this matter' (p. 18). Nevertheless, the fact that the paradoxes are not brought to the fore in *Badman* constitutes an attempt to mask them as much as possible, and when objections can be countered by both presence and absence of scriptures then the movement towards total closure of debate becomes extremely difficult to arrest. Yet another pincer movement is to be observed successfully in operation.

The Word effectively forms a safety net for any problems encountered in the deployment of paradox. Indeed, one of the reasons that Bunyan can use paradox with such confidence is that he has this higher-level criterion to appeal to in times of difficulty. And times of difficulty do occur, as in the case of Badman's marriage. This union of the believer and the unbeliever almost constitutes a paradox in itself since there is, as Wiseman notes, 'a prohibition, plainly forbidding' it in the scriptures (p. 74). An unfortunate by-product of the marriage is that the offspring are denied access to the Word, hence they are placed in a position of peril as regards salvation. Yet it must always be remembered that we are not born free. This is a state we can only attain when we come to activate that latent disposition towards evil in the individual will; therefore such children must be considered to be predetermined to election or reprobation anyway, as their father has been in his turn. Bunyan, however, seems to allow some exceptions to this rule. Some of Badman's children are described as 'mungrel Professors, not so *bad* as their Father, nor so *good* as their Mother, but were betwixt them both. They had their Mothers *Notions*, and their fathers *Actions*' (pp. 75–6). There would seem to be a suggestion at this point that these particular offspring (in marked opposition to their brothers and sisters who rapidly divide themselves, in approved binary fashion, into elect and reprobate types) could have gone either way in the spiritual scale, thus intimating that works *could* affect salvation. We are to go no further than intimation, however, since the said 'mungrels' eventually 'look out a people that were Hypocrites like themselves, and with them they matcht, and lived and died' (pp. 76–7): and presumably also discovered that salvation did not come with either works or the appearance of works.

This is not perhaps the most incisive of solutions to this problem. Precisely why did actions win out over notions?

Why did notions, surely God-granted entities, have so little determining power? What its somewhat strained argument suggests is that Bunyan is being taxed to the limit by this particular paradox, which is generating complex moral dilemmas for him. His severity seems momentarily to waver, whereas Calvinism, Ramism, and Perkins-style division technique all demand that he be much more incisive. Experience of life might well have taught Bunyan that black-and-white solutions are not always the rule, and this knowledge could co-exist only uneasily with a commitment to strict binarism in theological matters. Yet the answer to such dilemmas invariably seems to be, when in doubt push the paradox as hard as you can – that is, take full advantage of its assertorial quality – and make its pincer function work for you. Concoct an act of free will ('look out' having that active connotation) and you can then claim your victims that are both responsible *and* predetermined: precisely the combination that you need to place them beyond all hope of redemption.

Having brought in paradox tactically, Bunyan can now proceed to resolve the works/faith dilemma that has been created by the case of Badman's children. When we come to reflect on the fate of those children, '*we must say nothing, because this also is the soveraign Will of God*'. Nevertheless, subtle distinctions are possible as to the character of our silence: 'We may not by any means object against God: yet we may talk of the advantages, and disadvantages that Children have by having for their Parents such as are either Godly, or the contrary' (p. 77). One wonders why we may talk of such things, since the nature of predestination being what it is it cannot in any way materially affect the outcome to debate the issue. In effect, this can be no more than a consciousness-raising exercise for the participants involved because the decision has already been made. Badman, after all, managed to turn out as he did *despite* having godly parents concerned for his spiritual welfare. The argument proceeds with all the tortuous logic we have come to expect from the Calvinist mind when it is forced to reconcile some ostensibly irreconcilable positions:

1. The children of Godly Parents are the children of many Prayers: they are prayed for before, and Prayed for after they are born, and the Prayer of a godly Father and godly Mother doth much.

2. They have the advantage of what restraint is possible, from what evils their Parents see them inclinable to, and that is a second mercy.

3. They have the advantage of Godly instruction, and of being told which be, and which not be the right ways of the Lord.

4. They have also those ways commended unto them, and spoken well of in their hearing, that are good.

5. Such are also, what may be, kept out of evil company, from evil Books, and from being taught the way of Swearing, Lying, and the like, as Sabbath-breaking, and mocking at good men, and good things, and this is a very great mercy.

6. They have also the benefit of a godly life set before them doctrinally by their Parents, and that doctrine backt by a godly and holy example and all these are very great advantages. (pp. 77–8)

It is the notions/actions dialectic in operation again, but with notions apparently taking on a determining role where godly parents are concerned. Ungodly parents, on the other hand, 'commend not to their children an holy life, nor set a good example before their eyes. No, they do in all things contrary: Estranging of their children what they can, from the love of God and all good men, so soon as they are born'. We would imagine that such treatment would make no great difference, until Wiseman delivers the *coup-de-grâce*: 'Therefore it is a very great Judgment of God upon children to be the Offspring of base and ungodly men' (p. 78). With Job 30.8 included for good measure as the biblical seal of approval, we have as cunning a piece of reasoning as any Calvinist could wish for. Judgement is being made on the basis of a fault in man, which fault manifests itself in the form of free will, which free will seems to function as both cause and symptom of the original judgement. How anyone could escape from such a vicious circle it is hard to imagine. Predestination dogmatism reasserts itself with a vengeance at this point, closing off entry into the charmed circle of those elected to uphold old-style Puritan virtues through the dark days of Restoration culture. Financial and theological deviousness may well be the new cultural norms, as Badman's conduct clearly suggests, but they will bring no spiritual rewards. Paradox is being very effectively manipulated to isolate the 'one massie body of sin' from the ranks of the righteous elect.

Grace is another notable source of paradox, and one that exercises Bunyan considerably. It counts against Badman, for example, that although he experiences 'trouble of mind' (p. 131) while suffering physical affliction, 'when his pain was gone, and he had got hopes of mending, even before he could go abroad, he cast off prayer, and began his old game; to wit, to be as bad as he was before' (p. 132). In Calvinist terms this behaviour amounts to a rejection of grace, and hence a further sign of reprobation; but this must be seen as paradoxical, since the extension of grace to the individual sinner has been decided upon long before this point in Badman's career. Indeed, we could go so far as to say (and supralapsarians did), that his reprobation has been the case, and will be the case, for all time.[12] Yet even here in *Badman*, an apparently rigidly predeterministic work in which the didactic imperative would seem to be of paramount importance, the possibility of a disjunction between the signs associated with reprobation and a character's ultimate spiritual fate cannot be totally ruled out: paradoxical though that may seem in the twentieth century. Badman's 'trouble of mind' just *might* conceivably turn out to be what Dent called that 'strife which is in the very mind of the elect' (*Pathway*, p. 270). Bunyan is exploiting just that sense of insecurity apparently intrinsic to Calvinism when in *Badman*'s preface he writes: '*thou mayest, as in a Glass, behold with thine own eyes, the steps that take hold of Hell; and also discern, while thou are reading of Mr* Badmans *Death, whether thou thy self art treading in his path thereto*' (p. 1). As long as there is room for doubt and indecision on such matters, there is scope for personal anxiety; and to admit the anxiety is to undercut the charge of stultification to some extent.

Without such indecision there could be no palpable sense of conflict between man's and God's will in the text, and it is in fact crucial to the author's purpose that such a conflict be enacted, even if the free will in Badman's case has the behaviourally-predictable quality of the return of '*the Dog to his vomit*' (p. 140), in Wiseman's graphic and entirely unsympathetic phrase. In theory at least, two courses of action must always be open to Badman, for the author's argument that 'he could not but know' his chosen one was against God's will to have any real force. This consciousness of sin on the character's part, and what amounts to a wilful disregarding of sin's spiritual implications, is stressed throughout the narrative:

> he knew he lyed, he knew he dissembled; yea, he knew that he made use of the name of God, of Religion, good Men, and good Books, but as a stalking-Horse, thereby the better to catch his game. In all this his glorious pretense of Religion, he was but a glorious painted Hypocrite, and hypocrisie is the highest sin that a poor carnal wretch can attain unto. (p. 68)

The reiteration of that assertive 'knew' conjures up a picture of a character applying division technique to his life, but according to the wrong principles: those of his own free will rather than God's will. Such 'daring' argues a will to damnation even stronger than Antilegon's, since it involves a deliberately calculated rejection of all evidence to the contrary. Badman 'knows' whereas Antilegon often simply 'cannot see'. 'He knew' is one of the most damning indictments the Calvinist can make concerning the reprobate. The suggestion is that, left to its own devices, free will moves inexorably down an anti-God path, displaying as it does so that intriguing mixture of freedom and reflex behaviour the Calvinist feels resistance to the divine will involves. The dog has no option but to return to his vomit, but he does so wilfully. Pity is therefore a misplaced response under the circumstances to someone of Bunyan's ideological outlook.

The finality of decision as regards free will has to co-exist with the indecision regarding the judgements of God's will noted earlier, in a way that can only heighten the work's sense of paradox, thus creating potential sign-reading problems. Badman's end is a case in point. As he approaches it he does not take refuge in death-bed repentance, which refusal is read as evidence of chronic 'hardness of heart' (an attribute brought about by human free will, but also constituting another 'very great Judgment of God' against the reprobate). Had Badman indulged himself, however, Wiseman and Attentive would in all probability have discounted the action's significance. '*Sick-bed Repentance is seldom good for any thing*', we are assured (p. 139). It would seem to be a case of 'damned if you do, and damned if you don't' as paradox is called into play to disguise the contradiction. There would appear to be little scope for free will for the individual subject in such an all-pervasive form of predeterminism, yet he is still to be held responsible for his actions: '*one may see, by this, the desperateness of mans heart*' (p. 140). In characteristic Calvinist fashion the assertion must suffice for proof.

Paradox is also present at Badman's death. He goes 'as quietly as a Lamb', a promising sign of resignation to God's will perhaps – but not to the hard-to-please Wiseman (whose approach in general, as Kaufmann has noted, 'is to make a virtue of necessity'[13]):

> There is no Judgment to be made by a quiet death, of the Eternal state of him that so dieth. Suppose one man should die quietly, another should die suddenly, and a third should die under great consternation of spirit; no man can Judge of their eternall condition by the manner of any of these kinds of deaths. He that dies quietly, suddenly, or under consternation of spirit, may goe to Heaven, or may goe to Hell; no man can tell whether a man goes, by *any such* manner of death.[14]   (p. 157)

It might well be objected that if a quiet death is no proof of salvation, neither is it conclusive proof of reprobation if indeed 'no man can tell whether a man goes'. To miss – or perhaps deliberately refuse to see – such a subtle point is typical of the narrowness of vision so often to be noted in Calvinist thought, but it also provides evidence for the presence of narrative tension in Bunyan, again helping to rescue him from the charge of stultification. Clearly, if manner of death is an imperfect guide to election or reprobation then at least the illusion of dynamism will always be present in literature of this kind, even if only in a subliminal sense. What the passage graphically reveals is the permanent sense of insecurity of the Calvinist: an insecurity so well caught in the pages of *Grace Abounding*. Even after Bunyan feels himself to have been saved, he is still prey to the attentions of demonic forces. One senses that Bunyan never did find complete peace of mind. Perhaps this was an inescapable conclusion of commitment to a theological system based on the 'meer promise' of election, and in which free will was always disposing the individual 'unto evill'.

Despite the carefully constructed sense of narrative tension there seems little doubt as to Badman's fate – 'from Death to Death, from Death Natural to Death Eternal'; nor what he is designed to represent: 'Mr Badman *has left many of his Relations behind him*'. From first to last the text is a ruthless dissection of Restoration culture by an author totally out of sympathy with its aims and values: *'wickedness like a flood is like to drown our English world'* (p. 7). That culture, to which nonconformism stands opposed as a watchful counter-culture ('wise' and 'attentive') is clearly the product of reprobation, and no amount of repression of the Puritan and sectarian traditions can alter that fact for a Bunyan striving to adjust to the adverse conditions of post-Commonwealth existence. Trapped within these adverse conditions with the bleak outlook they provide for the dissenting conscience – '*I fear they'l be worse before they be better*' – Bunyan can still find cause for hope. The worse the times, the worse the behaviour of the Restoration establishment – that 'one massie body of sin' – the better the prospect, spiritually speaking, for nonconformists. Being in possession of predestinarian doctrine allows Bunyan to draw the boundary between the two sides with unmistakable ideological intent, and it is paradox which enables him to make the requisite value-judgements regardless of external appearances; to reveal the 'one massie body of sin' to be that fatal conjunction, both innately *and* wilfully reprobate.

There seems little doubt about the lasting impression that Dent made on Bunyan's authorial practice, although all the evidence seems to suggest a much tougher line being taken on predestination in the latter's case: a toughness which is inscribed in *Badman's* formal structure. Austerity of ideological message is not however matched by austerity of style. Bunyan's is considerably the more varied and vital, with its mastery of colloquialism, and drawings on popular literature to spice the scriptural and theological material and so enhance his style's general appeal. Each author is committed to closure of debate and stresses its necessity and inevitability through a repeated assertion of the power of the Word: 'the question is not what men do believe concerning their sin, but what Gods Word says of it' (p. 32). Such logocentrist fundamentalism can only be defended by reference to paradox, which simply highlights the contradictions inherent in the entire system of belief. It then becomes a question of concealing these in order to ensure the acceptance of soteriological closure. Dent approaches the task by the most careful and systematic application of division technique to two initially uncategorised beings, with the result that contrasting patterns of behaviour are allowed to emerge, each with its own clearly articulated significance in terms of the semiotics of predestinarian soteriology. A damning body of evidence is painstakingly built up against a character, who assists in his own gradual revelation as reprobate by the extent to which he opposes his own will to God's and God's agents. The reprobate increasingly comes to be the focus of the text's argument, and free will the main obstacle to a closure which paradox can never quite guarantee.

Even greater evidence of free will is to be noted in Badman's case, but it takes place within a more loaded context of argument: Bunyan eschewing revelation by debate for double closure as if to emasculate the subversive element of free will at source. The various narrative strategies in the text, such as those significant 'lacks' (debate, central character) are deployed to reinforce the judgemental power of Calvinist soteriological theory. Paradox ultimately prevents this bid for total closure of the discourse to reprobate outsiders from being completely successful, and once again the reader is left with the impression of an author unable to explain away the contradictions of his system of belief, no matter how much he may load the argument against them. Free will, even the free will of a somewhat abstract concept like Badman, continues to be an inherently subversive concept in terms of Calvinist theory, and one which tends to call forth its most repressive features as a countering device.

Badman represents the most detailed analysis of the reprobate personality in Bunyan's work, and creates more problems for him than does the treatment of election since free will is less of a factor in the latter context. Nevertheless, it is still closure and exclusion that is being sought in election's case, and paradox is still required in its articulation: to the point that the author's electees can manifest a very high level of anxiety, inasmuch as they are aware of the very delicate balance of despairing and presuming their condition necessarily involves.

Chapter Five

SELF UNDER SIEGE
The Holy War

BUNYAN is very much the Calvinist in conceiving of salvation as a state of conflict and anxiety, and he maximises this element in what is probably his most dramatic, and certainly his most ambitious text, *The Holy War*: 'a people's Paradise Lost and Paradise Regained in one', in Froude's apt phrase.[1] Despite its drama and ambitious scale the text has traditionally been regarded as the least successful of Bunyan's fictions, and has tended to inspire even less enthusiasm amongst critics than *Badman*. Talon may be considered to sum up the general tenor of the critical heritage on the work when he dismisses *Holy War* as 'too long-drawn-out and overweighted and obscure to add very much to Bunyan's literary glory'.[2] Possibly the only modern critic to accept the text without reservation has been Alick West, in an article treating *Holy War* and *Pilgrim's Progress* as parables of the class struggle, where the narratives are held to illustrate 'that there can be no progress without conflict'.[3] Bunyan himself gives the broadest of hints in *Holy War*'s preface that the work is to be read through the political and theological conflicts of the time:

> But, *Readers I have somewhat else to do,*
> *Than with vain stories thus to trouble you;*
> *What here I say, some men do know so well,*
> *They can with tears and joy the story tell.*

The Town of Mansoul *is well known to many,*
Nor are her troubles doubted of by any
That are acquainted with those Histories
That Mansoul, and her Wars Anatomise.

(p. 1)

West, however, is to push the 'Restoration political allegory'
reading to the point where he comes to query the importance
of the Christian elements in the text, even managing to
suggest that predestination is no more than peripheral to the
author's real narrative objective. That objective is taken to be
the exposition of the class struggle.

This is a provocative view, although it would find a
certain echo in the work of Hill. If it slides further over into
fundamentalist Marxism than I would wish to go, the reading
does have the virtue of focusing our attention on the ideological subtext, where *Holy War*'s true significance lies. West is
somewhat unusual in being able to turn a blind eye to
soteriology's inscription in the narrative. Twentieth-century
commentators are all too prone to see predestination as having
an adverse effect on narrative development and tend to classify
Holy War, therefore, as a 'failure', whether of the 'compara-
tive' (Tindall) or 'magnificent' (Sharrock) variety.[4] The
conclusion would seem to be that theology and narrative
tension are mutually exclusive, and that given too much of the
former it becomes reasonable to speak of a narrative failure.
Even that great Bunyan enthusiast Hill sadly concludes that in
Holy War 'the theology got in the way'.[5]

Nevertheless, it is odd that the 'narrative failure' view has
been quite so predominant in the critical literature, since *Holy
War* is probably Bunyan's most interesting work in formal
terms. It is the least 'closed' of his fictions, and, significantly,
the only one not to include the death of its protagonist (thus
reproducing the 'incompleteness' of *Grace Abounding*). Determinism and deferral are in a fascinating state of tension in *Holy
War*. The cycle of despair and optimism being traced in the
text has not yet run its course when the narrative is terminated,
with Mansoul being enjoined by Emmanuel at that point to

'hold fast till I come' (p. 250) when the next outbreak of despair (triggered by Diabolonian invasion) occurs. The work is deeply imbued with Calvinist soteriological assumptions, but it substitutes for the hard-line message of texts like *Pilgrim's Progress* and *Badman*, with their clear-cut resolutions, an apparently unending dialectical conflict between good and evil, free will and necessity, which imparts a notably dynamic quality to individual experience. This dynamic quality persists even though it is conceived within a rigidly predeterminist soteriological scheme. '*For yet a little while, O my* Mansoul' (p. 247) must Diabolonian attacks be borne before divine agents will be sent to '*convey, conduct, and bring you to that, when your eyes see more, that will be your desired haven*' (p. 248). In the meantime Mansoul must, personal anxiety and ontological insecurity notwithstanding, be brought to accept the fact of predetermined fate: '*I command thee to believe that my love is constant to thee. O my* Mansoul, *how have I set my heart, my love upon thee*' (p. 250).

This is the self under siege, forced to experience the psychological swings of Calvinist soteriology in terms of military invasion, with its integrity seemingly permanently on the verge of compromise. There appears even less reason than usual to speak of any stultification of the narrative by predestinarian concerns in what is essentially an open-ended text, where the author significantly extends his range as regards the construction of narrative from theological materials. We are in the presence of what Keeble has described as a 'complex allegory [which] implicitly appeals to the cultivated taste of a more sophisticated élite'.[6] Wherever he received the Miltonic echoes from,[7] Bunyan is clearly aiming higher, both in terms of narrative structure and audience, than hitherto. The work is certainly given an epic scale: 'that famous *Continent* of *Universe*; a very large and spacious Countrey', within which 'a *fair* and *delicate Town*, a Corporation, called *Mansoul*' (p. 7) lies poised 'between the two worlds' (p. 8) – that delicate balance of pessimism and optimism again. Within this theatre the drama of salvation will be enacted, and the stirring battle which subsequently occurs, with its huge cast, cannot fail to put one in mind of *Paradise Lost*.

The 'works/faith' issue constitutes the main problem area in any text on election written from the predestinarian position. If grace is bestowed rather than won, how can the individual be said to be involved? Bunyan's answer in *Holy War* is to counterpoint repeated assurances of election (*'Let all men know who are concerned, That the Son of Shaddai the great King, is ingaged by Covenant to his Father, to bring his Mansoul to him again'* (p. 29)) with repeated lapses from grace ('having got possession of this stately Palace, or Castle' Diabolus proceeds to 'make it a Garrison for himself, and strengthens and fortifies it with all sorts of provision' (p. 18)) such that stability is never established, and the individual is pictured as being caught between the 'two worlds' of despair and presumption in a way that can only encourage anxiety to grow. *Holy War*'s electee is never allowed to presume too much, remaining prey to the many divisions of 'doubters' as the narrative draws to its close: 'the *Election-doubters*, the *Vocation-doubters*, the *Grace-doubters*, the *Perseverance-doubters*, the *Resurrection-doubters*, the *Salvation-doubters*, and the *Glory-doubters*' (p. 226) – an extremely resilient army of creatures with the ability to regroup after every defeat in what looks like a perpetual anti-closure movement. The ultimate paradox of Calvinist soteriology is that whereas reprobation can be read with certainty, election cannot, which explains the permanent presence of anxiety in the electee's life.

The narrative traces a cycle of four Diabolonian campaigns against Mansoul. Embedded in this sequence of events is a trial scene which, since it cannot prevent the return of the 'election doubters' afterwards, does not resolve the issue with any great sense of finality. It must be assumed that the author does not *want* so to resolve it – hence that 'hold fast' at the narrative's end – and that we might postulate a fifth, sixth, or *n*th Diabolonian campaign as 'life in sin' succeeds 'temptation' succeeds 'repentance' in the inevitable progression of the medieval morality play scheme.[8] Narrative becomes almost infinitely extensible under such circumstances, as it traces what might be called the 'pre-established disharmony' of Calvinist universal history, where conflict is assumed to be the norm up to the point of Judgement Day. *Holy War* is like the ultimate Ramist structure, with divisions remorselessly spilling out into the future towards an impossibly remote goal. The only possible closure to such a sequence is death, an option that the author does not exercise in this case. He chooses instead to stress the never-ending quality of the conflict between good and evil – its long-drawn-outness as it were – in which at any one point Mansoul is subject to renewed attack, and any given Diabolonian defeat merely prompts a '*great consultation, how they might get the Town of* Mansoul *again*' (p. 134). Narrative interest is no longer a question of 'why' or 'how' but 'when', and if 'when' can mean Judgement Day this ensures that a certain degree of tension can be maintained in the text, predestinarian objectives notwithstanding. This lack of resolution, contrasting so sharply as it does with the author's practice in *Pilgrim's Progress* and *Badman*, gives *Holy War* a very modern feeling. Bunyan is, after all, articulating what has since become a literary commonplace – the unending repetition of life (and narrative) cycles: Nietzsche's 'eternal recurrence', with all its attendant existential implications. It is as if the conversion experience must be repeated continually in the face of fresh onslaughts, and anxiety and fear endlessly reproduce themselves in the individual caught up within this impersonal, indeed inhuman, process:

> Must not all things that *can* run have already run along this lane? Must not all things that *can* happen *have* already happened, been done, run past? . . . and must we not return and run down that other lane out before us, down that long, terrible lane – must we not return eternally?[9]

This is closer to Camus or Beckett territory than we might ever expect an artist like Bunyan to be, and closer yet perhaps to Ionesco. *The Bald Prima Donna*, for example, could, at least in theory, be repeated *ad infinitum*, as the closing stage direction ('*Repeat of start of first scene*') clearly implies.[10] So too could *Holy War*. Yet another Diabolonian campaign can always be postulated. Bunyan would not, of course, have accepted the metaphysical assumptions on which such works as the above are based. These imply a certain non-determinism and in this sense Bunyan is no existentialist in the twentieth-century sense of the term. For a Camus, Beckett or Ionesco, human existence is an arbitrary, hence absurd, phenomenon; whereas for Bunyan, the firm believer in predestination, nothing is arbitrary or meaningless and universal history proceeds according to a divine master plan. Bunyan perceives teleology where a modern existentialist perceives blind chance. The experience of alienation in Bunyan relates solely to the question of relative soteriological status (saved or damned), and not to more general problems on the nature of existence. The Bunyans of this world know *why* they are here: their anxiety derives from the fact that this particular 'why' has two possible answers, election or reprobation. Doubts are contained within a rigid metaphysical scheme therefore, but the sense of ontological insecurity that they involve is in its sheer intensity comparable to that of the twentieth-century existentialist experience, such that it seems perfectly reasonable to argue for a certain modernity in Bunyan's work. Keeble argues that the text maps out the route to 'resolute patience'[11] on the electee's part, but we must never lose sight of the existential edge that Calvinist soteriology consistently imparts to such a journey, particularly here in *Holy War* where patience has to be contextualised within perpetually recurring cycles of violent conflict.

The text features an internal dialectic, therefore, between its predestination-oriented message and narrative strategies which work to resist resolution. In a doctrinal sense Bunyan is as severe as ever in his theology, as the following speech by the chillingly-named Captain Execution would seem to reveal:

What wilt thou do? wilt thou turn? or shall I smite? If I fetch my blow *Mansoul*, down you go: For I have Commission to lay my Ax *at*, as well as *to* thy roots, nor will any thing, but yielding to our King, prevent doing of *Execution*. What art thou fit for O

Mansoul, if mercy preventeth not, but to be hewn down, and
cast into the fire and burned? (p. 47)

The repressive features of Calvinist predestinarian theory are
well to the fore at times like these. The threatening tone, the
demand for total subjugation of the individual personality
before the divine will, the concern for justice rather than
mercy, it all adds up to a rather depressing picture of the
human condition, bringing to mind *Badman* at its harshest.
Even when divine love is promised in *Holy War* it comes, as
we have just seen, in the form of an order: '*I command thee to
believe that my love is constant to thee*'. Working against this
authoritarian imperative in the text, however, is the persistent
delaying of permanent resolution whenever the narrative
presents this opportunity in the form of a triumph over the
evil principle:

> we do not know but that to this day many *Diabolonians* may yet
> be lurking in the Town of *Mansoul*, and they will betray us when
> thou shalt leave us, into the hand of *Diabolus* again; and who
> knows what designs, plots, or contrivances have passed betwixt
> them about these things already; loth we are to fall again into his
> horrible hands. (pp. 111–12)

Clearly, such victories as Mansoul achieves are somewhat less
than decisive, merely serving as preludes to further lapses
from grace as each thesis repeatedly succumbs to its 'lurking'
antithesis in a process of continual evasion.

It is over this question of resolution that, in the opinion of
many critics, Bunyan the literary artist and Bunyan the
ideologue begin to come into conflict – much to the detriment
of *Holy War* as a piece of fiction, it is usually held. Froude,
from where we can probably date modern Bunyan criticism,
is an instructive case in point. He argues that the narrative is
prolonged well beyond its natural ending – an event marked
by the second defeat of the Diabolonian forces for this critic –
and speaks of a reader taking up 'the continuation of the "Holy
War" with a certain weariness'. It is plain that he dislikes the

narrative's open-ended quality with its implication of an endless reiteration of the Diabolus–Shaddai struggle, since this means that 'the reader whose desire it is that good shall triumph and evil be put to shame and overthrown remains but partially satisfied'. Given the existence of this ostensibly perpetually recurring figure, 'to attempt to represent it, therefore, as a work of art, with a beginning, a middle, and an end, is necessarily a failure'.[12] Talon's complaint about a long-drawn-out book suggests similar, perhaps also neo-Aristotelian, misgivings about *Holy War*'s structure.

We reach a critical impasse at such points because its being long-drawn-out is precisely what Bunyan, the ideologically-committed author, is trying to evoke in his narrative: the long-drawn-out battle between good and evil, and of the struggle towards election. Individual solutions can, it is true, be found to these problems – a Christian can reach heaven, a Badman hell – but they transcend mere individuality, and in a sense the desire for soteriological resolution too. The latter must take account of the sequence involving mankind and not just any one man. This longer sequence will describe a perpetually recurring figure throughout history, in which individual solutions are simply isolated points in a long-drawn-out dialectic which has happened before, and will happen over and over again until God chooses to implement his ultimate solution of the Day of Judgement. The drive towards election and the perpetually recurring figure, the historical and the transhistorical, are in a state of fruitful dialectical tension in the text, enabling the author to suggest that election is enormously significant to the individual but that individual election is relatively insignificant in terms of the larger, universe-wide conflict. We have another despair/presume balancing act on our hands, with the long-drawn-out condition functioning as a critical semiotic element. Partial satisfaction is all that the individual can hope for under such circumstances, and is in fact a necessary part of the experience of election. To go any further than this is to assume a certainty that, paradoxically enough, is never quite open to the electee, no matter how committed he may be to the deterministic imperatives of Calvinist-style predestination.

The commitment to determinism in the text is certainly strong and deep, and within each cycle of the recurring figure, rival authorities – one might say rival determinisms – are to be observed competing for control of the individual, whose search for partial satisfaction must be plotted through this landscape hostile to the concept of freedom of action. Covenant and counter-covenant stress the need for subjection. Diabolus' declaration to the inhabitants of Mansoul that,

> *they should never desert him, nor his Government, nor yet betray him, nor seek to alter his Laws: but that they should own, confess, stand by, and acknowledge him for their rightful King in defiance to any that do or hereafter shall, by any pretence, Law, or title what ever lay claim to the Town of* Mansoul.　　　　　　　　　　　　　　　　　(p. 31)

is echoed in its sinister, authoritarian tone by the language Shaddai uses when addressing his own followers: 'But if they shall notwithstanding thy Summons and the producing of thy Authority, resist, stand out against thee, and rebel: then do I command thee to make use of all thy cunning, power, might, and force to bring them under by strength of hand' (p. 38). The individual registers as little more than a pawn in this clash of wills. 'Authority', 'command', 'power', 'might', 'force', 'strength', this is the language of subjection and subjugation, calling for severe limitation of the individual will. We have here what amounts to an early version of that most Calvinist of political doctrines: the individual must be 'forced to be free'.[13]

To stress predestination and its inevitability of operation to this extent is to minimise the scope for individual development, a problem which calls forth one of the author's periodic 'doctrine softening' exercises. He chooses to emphasise the exciting and thrilling aspects of election, in an applied version of Haller's 'vision of adventure for courage to undertake':[14]

So *Diabolus* commanded that his *Drummer* should beat a Charge against the Town, and the Captains also that were in the Town sounded a Charge against them, but they had no Drum, they were Trumpets of Silver with which they sounded against them. Then they which were of the Camp of *Diabolus* came down to the Town to take it, and the Captains in the Castle, with the slingers at *Mouthgate* played upon them *amain*. And now there was nothing heard in the Camp of *Diabolus* but horrible rage and blasphemy; but in the Town good words, Prayer and singing of Psalms: the enemy replied with horrible objections, and the terribleness of their *Drum*; but the Town made answer with the slapping of their slings, and the melodious noise of their Trumpets. (pp. 197–8)

There is at least the illusion of free will at such junctures, with the individual heroically choosing to resist intense Diabolonian pressure. It might also be seen as an act of will to call on the fortifying power of Calvinist logocentricity ('good words') as a counter-determinism to Diabolonianism. Forcing the individual to be free in such cases means forcing him to take sides, which effectively masks the author's doctrinal severity by appearing to involve the individual in the struggle taking place. Doctrine is thus humanised to some degree, although the paradox remains unresolved.

Bunyan also makes extensive use of millenarian imagery to soften the impact of doctrine:

But when they set out for their march, Oh how the Trumpets sounded; their Armor glittered, and how the Colours waved in the wind. The Princes Armor was all of Gold, and it shone like the Sun in the Firmament. The Captains Armor was of proof and was in appearance like the glittering Stars. (p. 69)

Election can seem like a particularly vivid adventure when so pictured, especially when compared to the terrible landscape of reprobation:

And now did *Mansoul* seem to be nothing but a den of Dragons, an emblem of Hell, and a place of total darkness. Now did *Mansoul* lye (almost) like the barren wilderness; nothing but nettles, briers, thorns, weeds, and stinking things seemed now to cover the face of *Mansoul*. I told you before, how that these *Diabolonian* Doubters turned the men of *Mansoul* out of their Beds, and now I will add, they wounded them, they mauled them, yea, and almost brained many of them. Many, did I say, yea most, if not all of them. (pp. 204–5)

The stark contrasts of colour and tone play their part in forcing the individual to be free, thus drawing attention away from the works/faith paradox at the heart of the text. Indeed, engagement in the struggle begins to suggest works in a subtle way, since there is an active element involved which, strictly speaking, should be incidental to faith and the bestowal of grace.

The violence of the conflict also encourages the taking of sides. One party wounds, mauls and brains, the other inflicts 'a very great slaughter' on the enemy, 'killing many that were stout and sturdy, and wounding of many that for *Diabolus* were nimble and active'. The author loads the argument very noticeably here, insisting that 'all these were *Diabolonians*, there was not a man, a native of *Mansoul* hurt' (pp. 89–90). Mansoulians may suffer wounding, mauling and braining but not, significantly, killing, since they are of the elect and thus bound for everlasting life – the ultimate long-drawn-out condition. The effect is once again to divert attention away from the paradox by dwelling on the consequences of predestination rather than the logic (or illogic) of the theory. The nature of these consequence brings the author's severity and intolerance to the fore, but also holds out the possibility of comfort to the elect, whose despair at the prospect of wounding, mauling and braining can be balanced by the knowledge that if they really *are* of the elect, slaughter at least will not be their lot. It is a delicate balance, but then that is in the nature of Calvinism. Not all commentators would agree that Bunyan is demonstrating his intolerance at such junctures. Dugdale, for example, argues that 'religious errors' may be 'hunted down and slaughtered, but not one person of flesh and blood the slightest injury suffers', which is very much like special pleading; the suggestion being that where Bunyan is apparently intolerant it does not actually matter since the Diabolonians at the receiving end 'are no more than personified abstractions'. Exactly why it is more acceptable to shed the blood of a personified abstraction than that of any other fictional character it would be hard to say, unless of course, like Dugdale, you are committed to the view that Bunyan had 'a long-suffering, kindly, peaceful, and tolerant spirit' (the urge to liberalise Bunyan dies hard).[15] It would be more realistic to admit the presence of an intolerant streak in Bunyan's character which has to be seen in the context of a totally different cultural ethos. Diabolus, for example, is treated harshly in the manner of an age well versed in the art of legally-administered cruelty.[16] He is bound to the wheels of Emmanuel's chariot and the victor then proceeds to 'ride in triumph over him quite through the Town of Mansoul' (p. 92). The intolerance that is an integral part of an exclusivist doctrine such as Calvinism becomes very apparent at moments like these. Perhaps there is, too, a note of revenge, which speaks volumes for the frustration of the socially and politically repressed nonconformist. Whether Calvinism was more or less intolerant than the other theological factions of the time is a moot point; but it seems fruitless to deny that Bunyan could be as élitist as any of his fellow-believers when it came to the topic of reprobation and the art of forcing sinners to be free.

The point of working so hard to mask the paradoxes of Calvinist soteriology is to maintain the drive towards resolution, and a network of images of enclosure is to be noted in the text to reinforce this tendency. The initial Diabolonian revolt is quelled and the participants banished 'down into the horrible Pits' by Shaddai, there to be 'fast bound in Chains' (p. 10). Diabolus addresses those of his loyal subjects 'that lurked in Mansoul' from 'the dark and horrible Dungeon of Hell' (p. 176), where the forces of good have confined him. Defeated elements of the Diabolonian faction are 'buried in the Plains about *Mansoul*' (p. 226). Good seeks to hide evil; evil seeks to enclose itself against outside interference by turning Mansoul into a garrison, and becoming, in Hard-Heart's phrase, 'impenetrable' (p. 125). Each side strives to impose its own will on experience but can achieve only partial and temporary satisfaction in the midst of the cycle of recurring figures.

Theologically it all makes perfect sense. Evil is to be seen as a permanently dangerous principle lurking beneath the surface of each electee's life. The elect will always be subject to temptation, and that is why, paradoxical though it may seem in narrative terms, Diabolus can be left to roam free and to prosecute his anti-Mansoulian activities while his followers are being rounded up for trial. Narrative practice has to be put very firmly in theological perspective here, as elsewhere in Bunyan. It also explains why, in the book's closing pages, Diabolonian activists are to be found in the house of one Evil-Questioning, creating unrest amongst the still-existent disaffected. The work of fiction, like the evil it incorporates into its narrative frame as the enemy to be faced, does not close: it merely acknowledges a temporary lull in the proceedings. The end of the text signals the beginning of yet another cycle of struggle, and anxiety is to be fostered by God as a means of controlling Mansoul:

> *And dost thou know why I at first, and do still suffer* Diabolonians *to dwell in thy walls, O* Mansoul? *it is to keep thee wakening, to try thy love, to make thee watchful, and to cause thee yet to prize my noble* Captains, *their Souldiers, and my mercy . . . I therefore left them in thee, not to do thee hurt, (the which they yet will, if thou hearken to them, and serve them) but to do thee good, the which they must if thou watch and fight against them.* (p. 249)

The existential edge to Calvinist soteriology comes sharply into prominence at such points. The 'kingdom within' is clearly no easy option, and as is later to be the case with Sartre, it is anxiety that individuates and keeps the individual aware of the very delicate balance of the human condition.[17] Perpetually recurring anxiety becomes the individual correlative of the universally-operative, perpetually-recurring figure of good and evil.

If there is the illusion of freedom of action as regards the elect, there is no mistaking the author's anti-free will sentiments when it comes to the reprobate. One of the major targets of Shaddai and Emmanuel is Lord Willbewill, by whose agency Mansoul is 'brought under to purpose, and made to fulfil the lusts of the will and of the mind' (p. 22). Nothing could better illustrate the commitment to willlessness in Calvinist predestinarian theory than this attack on the mind. Freedom of thought is not to be countenanced lest it lead to freedom of action, the illusion of which is useful in smoothing over a paradox on occasion, but whose reality is inescapably identified with reprobation. Willbewill and his henchman Mr Mind are forcibly to be brought back within the ranks of the elect, on pain of 'a strict amendment of their lives' (p. 185). Will and thought need to be kept firmly in check, and we are back with the paradoxical idea of the will-to-resistone's-will. The free actions in *Holy War* continue to be those of the Diabolonians, whose persistence generates the recurring cycle and the text's dynamism. As is the case with *Badman*, it is only the villains of Bunyan's fiction who would seem to have the power, and the will, to decide the course of their own personality development; to be free agents in the 'quest for individuation' (the dynamic properties of the villains suggests a further parallel with *Paradise Lost* and that arch-quester for individuation, Satan). The power to decide for oneself is cunningly offered to Mansoul at one point by Diabolus: 'the ball is yet at thy foot, liberty you have, if you know how to use it' (p. 63); but the elect must decline such tempting possibilitics.

Reprobation, the condition of knowing how to use one's liberty, would appear to enhance this process of individuation. Indeed, this may well prove to be one of Bunyan's most enduring legacies to the development of fictional characterisation, albeit an unconscious one. It is interesting to note that Defoe is to concern himself almost without exception with protagonists whose actions, in Bunyan's terms of reference, would probably cause them to be classified as reprobates. The fact that they are in the main no less likely to receive dispensations from divine providence (Roxana being the notable exception), while it confuses the moral issue somewhat, also provides a more realistic index of the psychological complexity of human behaviour. All the ingredients for this pyschological realism are present in Bunyan nonetheless, and perhaps never more so than in *Holy War*'s long-drawn-out dialectical struggle between the individual will and the forces that seek to repress it. The major problem confronting the author of election-based fiction – the severely teleological effect on narrative of the underlying predestinarian scheme to which he is committed – has been mitigated in this instance, and Bunyan has shown one way that such fiction can be opened out into larger-scale forms. Perhaps Kaufmann's complaint about the static quality of conversion narrative fiction can be answered by Bunyan's practice in *Holy War*, where narrative line develops a sense of drama by posing the question, When will conversion occur? rather than, How will conversion occur? The shift to 'when' means that an individual's spiritual development can be traced with a sense of psychological exactitude, with the narrative still conforming to the ruthless linearity of purpose that Calvinist predestination demands. A more complex debate between free will and necessity can thus be set up. All that is required is to people the incidents of this fundamental conflict with individuals rather than types and we have the landscape of the modern psychological novel – in point of fact, Defoe territory.

What is being suggested, therefore, is that for all its traditional elements *Holy War* represents a significant extension of the author's range. It is not simply the epic scale on which he is working (by comparison both *Badman* and *Pilgrim's Progress* are more intimate dramas), but the greater sophistication which informs his handling of theological material. There is no less a desire than before for ultimate solutions on the author's part, and no less awareness of the need to counteract paradox's power to create a gap between desire and fulfilment. The apparatus of Calvinist closure technique – assertion, division, the Word – is very much in evidence, but here it is never quite allowed to resolve the debate. It is noticeable that the set-piece trial scene in *Holy War*, so often a means of resolving issues of conflict in Puritan prose fiction, is here merely a prelude to further struggle.[18] Emmanuel's remarks in the narrative's final stages that '*I came once and twice, and thrice to save thee from the poyson of those arrows that would have wrought thy death*' (pp. 249–50) perform a similar function in their ambiguity: salvation on several occasions (once, twice, thrice) creating grounds for presumption; its failure to be permanent, grounds for despair. The text's ultimate deferral of resolution ('hold fast') constitutes a refusal to take refuge in teleology as a way of excising anxiety from the electee's experience.[19] Indeed, it is the fact of the teleology which both creates and provides succour for (but, crucially for narrative purposes, only temporarily) the individual's sense of *angst*: '*it is to keep thee wakening, to try thy love, to make thee watchful*'. And on this manifestly open-ended note, paradox firmly to the fore, Bunyan's most ambitious and most formally experimental narrative concludes. The 'enigmas of experience' are to have the last word.

The ideology on view in *Holy War* can certainly be described as repressive and soteriologically élitist (practically a 'racial theory of inheritance of salvation' in Hill's view[20]), but in its anxiety-creating potential it can also be considered to have a radicalising and liberating effect on the individual electee. An extreme form of self-analysis is being encouraged, and proficiency in the semiotics of soteriology becomes a matter of the utmost importance in the struggle for self-determination – a phrase which in its ambiguity is well suited to describe the mixture of subversiveness and authoritarianism being postulated as an identifying characteristic of Calvinism. Bunyan's stress on predestination gives a particularly sharp edge to the self-analysis since it destroys the notion of self-recovery ('*The way of back-sliding was thine, but the way and means of thy recovery was* mine' (pp. 246) as Emmanuel admonishes Mansoul), thus removing the element of contingency from damnation, and forcing the individual to examine his psychology even more minutely than the outwardly-visible works that might be read as evidence for an inward fitness for grace. What Bunyan requires is a despair-ridden obsessional self-analysis that acknowledges a right to presumption as long as it is never claimed: a forcing to be free through intense engagement with paradox rather than a striving to be free through performance of works. The absence of certainty that this involves, the reliance on 'hints' as opposed to hard proof, is radically individuating against the grain of soteriology's predeterminism. Predestinarian sectarians reach subversive individualism by many different routes, but they do seem to reach there in the end – the authoritarian imperatives of their ideology notwithstanding.

The self, therefore, remains under siege, but in the act of resistance it asserts its discreteness of identity. Individual existence is transformed into a drama on the large scale, and the anxiety and fear that was only too real a part of the Restoration nonconformist's daily experience is turned into a favourable soteriological sign. The semiotics involved have both the precision and the sense of paradox that we have come to expect from the predestinarian outlook. Anxiety and fear are positive signs, doubt and incredulity are negative. The division between anxiety (which must take account of the 'he that never doubted never beleeved' principle) and doubt (of election, vocation, grace, and so on through the list of soteriology's various aspects) may seem all but indistinguishable to the non-predestinarian, but to the predestinarian it is a yawning (and of its essence unbridgeable) chasm. Mercy is seen to apply on one side of the chasm, justice on the other, and once again it is a case of being able to manipulate justice according to the rules of paradox: if free will works tactically to damn your target then stress free will, if predestination seems more appropriate to the situation then stress that. Justice can always be made to apply either way: paradox gives you that flexibility of manoeuvre. *Holy War* teaches how to develop the will-to-resist-one's-will and identifies this as a sign that will draw divine mercy. The discrimination between this kind of will and the will-to-resist-the-divine-will, which latter entity is no less God-given than the former, is of the subtlest: but it is in that critical space that Bunyan's narrative project goes to work and where his subversive potential proves to be greatest.

A self under siege is a self under paradox is a self under anxiety. Within that spectrum the conflict between free will and determinism is at its most spirited, and Bunyan's negotiations with his belief-system only succeed in sharpening that opposition. Strive though he may, Bunyan can never consistently prevent soteriological paradoxes from putting themselves forward, and in *Holy War* we are left well short of the resolution that is imposed on the author's other texts. It is as far as he will allow himself to go on this road, and he draws back in his last work of fiction, *Pilgrim's Progress* Part Two, which proves to be another neatly resolved narrative invoking death to usual effect. But the anxiety-creating potential of predestinarian soteriology is clear for all to see, as are free will's culturally subversive implications. Working from a similar ideological base, Defoe will contrive to exploit these subversive implications yet further in fictions which maintain an even more problematical relationship towards resolution than those of his predecessor.

Chapter Six

THE ISOLATED SELF
Robinson Crusoe and A Journal of the Plague Year

WITH Defoe we enter an even more complex set of
negotiations with paradox than obtains in Bunyan's
world, and in the next two chapters I shall be dealing with the
dialectic of free will and determinism in four of Defoe's
fictions: *Crusoe, Journal, Moll* and *Roxana*. The concern will be
to explore Defoe's dialogue with the closures (metaphysical
and ideological) of conversion narrative, dividing the texts
above into two groups in order to trace the strategies adopted
on behalf of the isolated self (*Crusoe, Journal*), and the social
self (*Moll, Roxana*). Necessity may present in a subtly different
form in each group – further divided, and crucially so as far as
the free will problem goes, by gender – but it is always the
narrative of predestination which marks out the terrain of
negotiation. Whether Defoe himself was committed to predestination is debatable,[1] but in the guise of providence he is in
a continuing dialogue with the notion throughout his fiction.
At the very least, as Bastian has argued, there is a residual
Calvinism to be noted in the author.

While clearly working within the structures of the narrative of predestination, Defoe seems concerned to exploit the
attendant paradoxes for their own sake to a significantly
greater degree than Bunyan does. The motivation involved
would seem to be strongly ideological. Defoe's characters are
notably *angst*-ridden, and it is an *angst* which unmistakably
derives from their collision with the contradictions and
paradoxes of their belief-system. Defoe's fictions are to be

read as sustained expositions of what happens when free-willed individuals are made to live through the paradoxes – ideological and ontological – of their existence. The author is particularly adept at bringing his characters into conflict with their ideology. Crusoe, for example, is consistently obliged to question the values of patriarchy as found in family life and religion. It becomes his creator's task to reconcile Crusoe's extreme individualism to society, patriarchy and Protestant values after his island sojourn, but this reconciliation takes place very much on Crusoe's own terms (I am inclined to agree with McKeon's verdict that there is an 'inescapable aura of irony' about much of Crusoe's 'long passage out of sinfulness',[2] but I would question the extent to which that remains the case in the narrative's later stages). To the end of his career the hero remains defiantly free willed. The siege mentality noted in *Holy War* is particularly evident in *Crusoe* (a network of imagery reinforcing it), and in this sense the assertion of self effectively undermines the dominant values not just of patriarchy but of Calvinism too. This subversive-ness is latent in Calvinist theory and its many paradoxes, as Calvinist soteriology is latent in dissent, and Defoe's engagement with these forces a continual process of negotiation to be carried out. In the act of negotiation, individual free will and determinism (divine, social and genetic varieties) clash. It is one of the major ironies of Calvinism that a strict application of its soteriological theory ultimately subverts that same theory, and it is this quality above all that renders it a dynamic source of narrative.[3]

We might say that Defoe is crucially concerned with the politics of autonomy in *Crusoe*, and a similar concern is to be expressed in *Journal*. Once again circumstances conspire to isolate the narrative's hero, H.F., who is left with no option but to fall back on an internally flawed belief-system in making life-or-death decisions. H.F. manages simultaneously to uphold and to undermine predestination in a neat enactment of paradox where he thinks one thing but does another. By remaining in plague-visited London on the grounds that God has the power to strike him dead whatever his location (impeccable providential reasoning), he displays a sense of fatalism quite consistent psychologically with predestinarian doctrine (that H.F. also presents several strongly-worded arguments *against* the cult of fatalism only adds to the paradox). By observing later in the text, however, that flight is the best remedy from plague, H.F. would appear to call into question the extent of God's power and the efficacy of predeterminism. The text's ultimate commitment seems to be to free will (although in an interestingly guarded, thought-only manner), and yet again isolation, as in *Crusoe*, encourages a sense of selfhood and individual autonomy rather than any ego-deflating recognition of God's power to dispose. Paradox is perhaps to be regarded not as an inhibiting factor to character development, but as possessing a very positive dimension for the individual; enabling him, for example, to create room for manoeuvre within personally threatening situations where necessity apparently has the upper hand. The dynamism of Defoe's fictions is crucially dependent on this particular property of paradox.

In all the works by Defoe under consideration in this book, dominant cultural values, including soteriological beliefs, are put under stress and shown to contain logical contradictions which problematise human decision making. Defoe's protagonists must learn to live with the anxiety and insecurity that exposure to such contradictions creates, and this almost inevitably reinforces their acute sense of self. In tracing the psychological effect of ideological contradiction on his characters Defoe reaches to the heart of one of the major Western cultural dilemmas – the conflict between freedom and necessity. The paradoxes of Calvinism give him the basis he needs to mount a penetrating and ideologically-loaded critique against authoritarianism in its many guises, but no easy closures or resolutions are permitted in what proves to be an intensely-fought dialectical struggle. It is to the specifics of that struggle in *Crusoe* and *Journal* that we now turn.

Recent scholars have gone to great pains to situate Defoe in historical context and to establish his credentials as heir to, and synthesiser of, a wide range of cultural traditions.[4]

Defoe's synthesis, however, is infinitely more sophisticated than that of his precursors in the field of Puritan and dissenting prose fiction, and marks a particularly significant advance on traditional practice in terms of characterisation and notions of being. In the process he demonstrates how the medium can be made to develop a high degree of sensitivity to ideology. Defoe pushes the conversion narrative tradition of prose characterisation to its limits, and his work constitutes a revolution in this respect. Stated briefly, this revolution consists in a reorientation of the ontological anxiety of his characters from the realm of the supernatural (Christian heaven) to that of everyday reality. Calvinist overtones certainly remain (the paradoxes particularly so, as we shall discover) but the spiritual aspect of 'pilgrimage' is ultimately more questionable in Defoe's world than in Bunyan's; as Zimmerman notes, 'Defoe presents characters who have been taught to assume souls but have difficulty finding them'.[5] In Bunyan the cause of spiritual crisis lies outside the human realm *per se*, with all the contradictions that this involves in terms of the validity of human action. Given divine predeterminism, what price free will? In Defoe, on the other hand, the causal factors increasingly come to be located in the social domain, thus allowing significantly greater scope for human action – and for social criticism. There is a pattern not just of spiritual evolution to be noted in a text like *Crusoe*, but also one of socio-economic evolution (although Macey rather considerably overstates the case in claiming that: 'Gold – or sterling its English equivalent – is clearly the goal that motivates all of Defoe's novels'[6]). It is a pattern that will tend to bring Crusoe into collision with the authoritarian mechanisms of his ideology. In countering these, in adopting an adversarial posture towards both man *and* God, he calls into question some of the most fundamental assumptions on which his ideological discourse is based. The virtue of literary texts then becomes that they highlight the false resolutions and real debates in the process of constructing ideology as an object. *Crusoe* is to be extremely revealing about the ideology of its time, its false resolutions and its real debates, by putting that ideology to what Macherey has called the 'test of the written word'.[7] Fiction writing becomes a form of guerrilla activity directed against the dominant power-structures of Defoe's society, and Crusoe one of the author's prime instruments of resistance.

Defoe makes extensive use of the conventions of spiritual autobiography in *Crusoe* (as Starr notes, 'the hero's vicissitudes, highly individual and complex as they appear to be, actually follow a conventional and regular pattern of spiritual evolution'[8]). We shall be tracing the effect of this practice upon his protagonist's ontological condition. In an ontological sense we are dealing with a supreme individualist in the person of Crusoe, whose 'quest for individuation' takes a radical form. He symbolises bourgeois individualism – the 'possessive', property-biased variety outlined by Macpherson it would seem[9] – taken to its limits, very much testing its interplay of the economic and the spiritual by the written word (double-entry spiritual book-keeping being one of the more obviously revealing illustrations of the interplay in action in the hero's life). From the start, Crusoe is seen to have an active, dynamic nature, which treats the environment as something to be engaged with and exploited by act of will, rather than merely a hostile landscape to be wandered through in the unassimilated fashion of a Christian (the physical is much more sharply demarcated from the metaphysical in Defoe than Bunyan, with time, place and circumstance being carefully, almost relentlessly, notated). Will sets itself against nature, that most insistent of givens, in what amounts to an act of defiance to all things that would inhibit the dynamism of individuality. The crucial difference to be noted between Defoe's and Bunyan's practice is that Crusoe's alienation is self-willed rather than forced on him by divine predeterminism, as is Christian's experience. Starr's contention that Crusoe is 'mastered by events rather than master of them' would seem questionable.[10] The relationship between hero and event in *Crusoe* is significantly more dialectical than Starr would allow. Crusoe expends much time in *trying* to become 'master of events', and to some extent he succeeds.[11]

Will plays a key role in the narrative, therefore, and proves to be a rich source of tensions for both author and character. It is a factor in Crusoe's adventures from the very beginning of his career, where it is made clear that he feels himself compelled to break with his background in a wilful act of individuation – 'I would be satisfied with nothing but going to Sea' – which involves a personal challenge to patriarchal authority:

> My Inclination to this led me so strongly against the Will, nay the Commands of my Father, and against all the Entreaties and Perswasions of my Mother and other Friends, that there seem'd to be something fatal in that Propension of Nature tending directly to the Life of Misery which was to befal me.   (p. 3)

With the introduction of this 'fatal propension' we find ourselves in the world of Calvinist soteriology. Crusoe stands as the wilful creator of the impulse to defy traditionally-sanctioned authority ('Commands' plus 'Entreaties' plus 'Perswasions' equalling 'ideology'), and, as the originator of his own sin, he can be held responsible for all the misfortune that will subsequently come his way. Fatal propension becomes, in effect, a weapon directed against authority in general and its hostile attitude towards the individual concerned to work out a pattern of socio-economic evolution. The trait will consistently bring Crusoe into confrontation with his culture and its false resolutions, and it will serve an interrogating function for its author. In fact, we could see the inner dialectic of the text as a case of fatal propension versus false resolution: the one postponing assimilation, the other actively willing it.

Misfortune arrives swiftly in the form of a storm at sea. The threat of absorption by alien forces that intrudes at this point is a recurrent one in the text, with society, nature and cannibals all seeking to enclose the hero's physical self at one time or another (hence what Zimmerman calls Crusoe's fear 'of being dematerialized'[12]), and the tone adopted by Crusoe is recognisably Calvinist:

I was most inexpressibly sick in Body, and terrify'd in my Mind: I began now seriously to reflect upon what I had done, and how justly I was overtaken by the Judgment of Heaven for my wicked leaving my Father's House, and abandoning my Duty; all the good Counsel of my Parents, my Father's Tears and my Mother's Entreaties came now fresh into my Mind, and my Conscience, which was not yet come to the Pitch of Hardness to which it has been since, reproach'd me with the Contempt of Advice, and the Breach of my Duty to God and my Father. (p. 8)

The idea of a deliberately-induced 'hardening of the heart' as a prelude to further personal misfortunes is squarely within the Calvinist tradition (*Grace Abounding*, for example, teems with such sentiments), as is the hero's resumption of his former carefree outlook when the storm abates: 'my Fears and Apprehensions of being swallow'd up by the Sea being forgotten, and the Current of my Former Desires return'd, I entirely forgot the Vows and Promises that I made in my Distress' (p. 9). Such escapes invariably curtail any move towards the suspension of wilful activity on Crusoe's part. He is only too willing to allow despair to be overcome by presumption, and not even the almost immediate repetition of this first storm-encounter can inhibit the fatal propension: 'my ill Fate push'd me on now with an Obstinacy that nothing could resist' (p. 14). Dynamism has now taken over. What is not clear yet is which of the two paths – election or reprobation – it is propelling Crusoe down, although the signs are not very propitious: *'depend upon it, if you do not go back, where-ever you go, you will meet with nothing but Disasters and Disappointments till your Father's Words are fulfilled upon you'* (p. 15). Turning back, of course, is the one option that neither Calvinist nor Ramist theory allows for, and in this sense Crusoe is being very traditional in carrying on.

If Crusoe's early conduct is soteriologically suspect (far too little in the way of despair, far too much in the way or presumption) it is also individuating, and, I would argue, subversive. Only his commitment to his fatal propension lifts Crusoe from the mass of his fellows, who presumably remain under the protection of their mediating 'Fathers' in a state of anxiety-free subjection ('following their affairs like other folk' in approved Anglican fashion one might say). I am arguing for fatal propension as an intrinsically more dynamic concept than 'hardening of the heart': as the concept that pushes a fictional character across the boundary that separates everyman-figures from discrete, self-motivated individuals. The Defoe protagonist acts, the Bunyan protagonist reacts, and therein lies a world of difference. Action forces false resolutions to disclose themselves; fatal propension becomes the interrogator of its culture.

The pattern established in this initial phase is to recur throughout the narrative until the hero is cast upon his island 'Despair' (where the early imbalance towards presumption is to be severely redressed). Crusoe consistently refuses to pay proper heed to providentially-inspired signs and fails to read them for what they really are: direct warnings from heaven. Not until he is marooned on the island will he devote himself wholeheartedly to the question of his own salvation. In Calvinist terms, Crusoe's failure to analyse the meaning of the signs he is given, to put the signifying events of his observation knowledge together with the signified doctrines of his discourse knowledge, is to be seen as deliberate policy on his part. The fatal propension derives from *him*, not God, and it is in his articulation of this phenomenon that Defoe suggests the way out of the closed structure of conversion narrative fiction. The fatal propension must be brought into the realm of human decision and into dynamic conflict with the various determinisms of the character's existence. Which is to say that the character, whether of elect or reprobate status, must participate in the dialectic. In Calvinist soteriological theory this is an option open to the reprobate only, since they alone can be held responsible for the content of their actions ('the cause and occasion of it are found in themselves'). In *Crusoe* the boundaries are becoming blurred, leaving at least the possibility of a real battle between man and God – and that possibility for the elect no less than the reprobate. Calvinist certainties too are coming under scrutiny.

Election demands that doctrinal belief and sense-experience, discourse and observation, be correlated in what is effectively a recasting of the individual's epistemological experience to conform to the required Calvinist model, and Despair creates the right conditions for this. Crusoe conceives of the process in ontological terms as a correlation of mind and body, but it is striking, and subversive, that the body, driven by fatal propension as it is, invariably seeks to evade such resolutions in *Crusoe*. Indeed, the body has to be disabled – by isolation and ill-health – before Crusoe will start to reflect in earnest on his spiritual condition, finally submitting his experience to semiotic analysis in an act of self-interrogation: 'Now I look'd back upon my past Life with such Horrour, and my Sins appear'd so dreadful, that my Soul sought nothing of God, but Deliverance from the Load of Guilt that bore down all my Comfort'. The heightened sense of self-consciousness involved at this point is very much that of the spiritual autobiographical tradition. What Crusoe is beginning to do is to organise his experience around the focal points of Calvinist soteriological theory, with salvation functioning as the major criterion against which all other experiences ought to be measured. Isolation, Crusoe's 'solitary Life', is now seen to have a meaning in the universal scheme. It is the state necessary to induce the realisation of conversion, therefore 'I did not so much as pray to be deliver'd from it, or think of it; It was all of no consideration in Comparison to this' (p. 97). 'This' being the process by which the hardened sinner is prepared for election. Temporarily, at least, discourse and observation, mind and body, are in a state of conjunction, and Crusoe is reconciled to his condition: 'I began to exercise my self with new Thoughts; I daily read the Word of God, and apply'd all the Comforts of it to my present State' (p. 113).

Yet ontological security is not quite so easily reached as might appear. Alienation from God may have been overcome, but not alienation from man; if anything, reconciliation with God has had the effect of reinforcing alienation from his fellow man in Crusoe's case. Crusoe's sense of security has been bought at the expense of total exclusion from all social intercourse; that is, by the most rigorous process of self-enclosure (note his tendency to fortify himself and to retreat from the outside world at the least hint of danger). The post-conversion phase of the narrative is mainly concerned with Crusoe's struggle to defend his solitude (for which we may read identity) from the encroachments of society, and then his gradual re-engagement with mankind on terms suitable to the possessive individual; this being the pattern of socio-economic evolution which continues its guerrilla activity against the pattern of spiritual evolution, persistently under-mining the latter by refusing to accept its concerns as dominant. Defoe's contemporaries were well aware of the presence of this inner tension. When Charles Gildon has his satirical Crusoe complain that 'when you bring me again to a Sense of the Want of Religion, you make me quit that upon every Whimsy', he is acknowledging the subversive dialectic within the text.[13]

Conversion does not eradicate anxiety from Defoe's world therefore, and those ontologically worrying gaps between discourse and observation open up again, indicating that the problem of identity is far from solved. The conversion-experience constitutes merely a brief interlude in a lifetime riddled with anxiety, the ontological complexity of which becomes greater as the pattern of socio-economic evolution unfolds in the post-conversion sequence. Pre-conversion anxiety is of a more predictable and immediate type, invariably assuming the form of anguished responses to natural disasters, as in the case of the storms during the first, monitory, voyage at sea: 'Then all Hands were called to the Pump. At the very Word my heart, as I thought, died within me' (p. 12). Crusoe's failure to heed providence at this point only succeeds in prompting an even more dramatic recurrence of the storm while on a journey to the Guinea coast. This time the insertion of providence into human affairs results in the ship being run aground, and Crusoe's thoughts again turn to death. It takes such an extreme set of circumstances, however, before he will readily acknowledge divine imperatives. It is characteristic of all the disasters that befall Crusoe in the pre-conversion phase that they deflect him from his path through life; that is, from the pilgrimage that fatal propension seeks to map out. It is a case of alternate sequences of activity and captivity. The flight from his family background, for example, is followed by a series of storm-torn voyages. Captivity by heathens occurs, to be succeeded by escape and life as a Brazilian colonist; which latter experience is conceived of by Crusoe as a form of captivity to one driven by a 'Desire of rising faster'. Fatal propension continues to be a critical factor in his adventures, Crusoe speaking of himself as being 'the wilful Agent of all my own Miseries' (p. 38) in accepting the offer of further voyages once settled.

The various states of captivity that take place before the island experience – captivity by family background, captivity by pirates, captivity by success in the middle station of life – are all states which deal with the relationship of individual and society. On Despair it is more a case of imprisonment within the self; the ultimate fate, it could well be argued, of all those who operate according to the tenets of possessive individualism. The relationship between self and society cannot be ignored indefinitely, however, and it returns to haunt Crusoe after his conversion in the form of that footprint on the sand and those hordes of barbaric savages who inhabit the fringes of his island consciousness. The Sallee episode of captivity is particularly revealing since much of what happens there prefigures Crusoe's later experience on Despair. He is 'colonised' by the Moors in a manner remarkably similar to his own later treatment of Friday (in Lockean terms, Crusoe becomes a servant and his labour the property of his master[14]). Reduced to performing 'the common Drudgery of Slaves' (p. 19), Crusoe contemplates escape: and so it comes to pass, but not until two years of captivity have elapsed. It is entirely typical of the spiritual autobiographical tradition that this period can be glossed over with so little comment. It is also only too typical of Crusoe's relations with society, which are usually felt to be personally restricting. Existence in society is, until a very advanced stage in the narrative, seen to have a neutralising effect on Crusoe, as if it represented a digression from the real business of life (the construction of an autonomous self) and consequently hardly worth recording. Seven years of settled existence in England on Crusoe's return from Despair are similarly glossed over in a few terse sentences, being treated merely as an interlude between two sets of adventures (with his marriage 'just a short experiment in curbing natural instinct' as Rogers has drily noted[15]).

Throughout the pre-conversion phase we note a complete distrust on Crusoe's part of the whole concept of society, each settled period merely serving to reveal his intense dissatisfaction with any kind of organised social existence. He appears to be fleeing from the community as much as from providence – in which case the work seems particularly subversive. There had always been an uneasy relationship between individual and community in Puritan thought, which carried over into much nonconformism. While religious radicalism had a distinct tendency to individualise human beings in a fairly radical manner, such individualisation usually found its expression in collective action of one kind or another: separatist churches, political groupings, colonial activity, and the like. Bunyan provides a model in this respect. The being who in *Grace Abounding* seems so totally isolated from his fellows as to appear almost other-worldly, is also the hugely successful lay preacher noted for his pastoral work amongst his parishioners ('Bishop Bunyan'). His career would seem to suggest that there is an ever-present set of tensions and discrepancies between the individualising and group-bonding tendencies within nonconformism. Contemporary Anglicanism, as we have noted, was considerably more successful in reconciling individual and group, with its conception of the Church as a mediator between man and God: that 'vertuous mediocrity' celebrated by Simon Patrick in *Parable*. Mediation there has the effect of playing down tensions between individual and society, whose power, as represented by the established Church, is designed to prevent the growth of any overt sense of individualism. The aim is to preserve an unequal relationship between pilgrim and ideology; that is, to subordinate the individual, most particularly the enthusiastic individual, to the collective will. Fatal propension, and anything that may induce it is carefully concealed in the name of 'vertuous mediocrity': that false, but highly effective, resolution to the real debate of individual versus society.

In contrast, by endowing his protagonist with a drive that throws him into constant collision with both providence and society, Defoe brings to the surface all the latent tensions in his ideology between radical individualism and authoritarian collectivism, free will and predeterminism. Crusoe's fatal propension uncovers gaps in his ideology: gaps between theory and practice which tend to be a breeding ground for ontological insecurity. The sense of anxiety felt by the hero in the pre-conversion phase stems from a fear of the de-individualising (and will-limiting) power of providence and society. Conversion appears to effect reconciliation with God, which leaves the matter of reconciliation with society to be dealt with in the narrative's post-conversion phase, where the pattern of socio-economic evolution has to be worked through.

We might now explore the nature that social reintegration assumes, beginning with some speculation as to why the process might be felt to be necessary. The text opens with a defence of the 'middle Station of Life' by the hero's father, which could be considered the equivalent of an argument from works, in that it implies that the performance of the duties of this state will lead to salvation. An individual who so performs will go 'silently and smoothly thro' the World, and comfortably out of it' (p. 5). Crusoe's rejection of this argument does indeed result in the '*Disasters and Disappointments*' (p. 15) that another recognisably patriarchal figure insists that it will: and what we might call the patriarchal conspiracy against the hero continues, with God providing appropriately argument-clinching catastrophes to order. Crusoe takes on patriarchy; patriarchy exacts its revenge. All of which sounds very much like an argument for the validity of middle-station life and against fatal propension: for a mediated rather than a self-created existence. Conversion proceeds to bestow meaning on what went before in Crusoe's life – the ever-branching experiences of the pre-Despair 'quest for individuation' – and holds out the promise of doing the same for the future. It gives the electee a grid to apply to his previously formless observation knowledge, thus making it conform to a system whose teleological bias represents a negation of the individual will: that will which manifested itself as fatal propension in Crusoe's case. In other words, it brings him back within the orbit of predeterminism, and by extension suggests that he should have submitted to social determinism and the middle state when first advised to do so. It is entirely possible to argue, however, that it is only through following his fatal propension that Crusoe had reached conversion; that it is a necessary part of the process in the sense that without despair there can be no conversion ('no fears, no Grace'), and the propension has very definitely led him to Despair.

This seems to open up an interesting gap between the text's two main patriarchal figures, Crusoe's father and God. The father has argued against fatal propension, God ultimately rewards it; yet these two figures are identified very closely in the work and Crusoe accords them the same respect (and, we might add, disrespect). From which it might be deduced that Crusoe is punished for not obeying his father, but was carrying out God's purposes in so doing; which amounts to saying that he both should and should not have gone through with his fatal propension. We are in classic Calvinist paradox territory here; but it has the appearance of reprobation rather than election since will is being allotted a major role, and in Calvinist theory only reprobates can choose to follow, or be made to follow, the dictates of their will. Nevertheless, evil consequences appear to be nil on this occasion, which can always be explained away if need be by reference to God's mysteriousness of purpose, or some such similar contradiction-masking device of Calvinist theory. Divine authority seems to have triumphed over fatal propension, and Crusoe's 'election' demands that he must display no more tendencies towards free will, or opposition to society's resolutions. Presumably he can also be returned to the middle station of life when opportunity admits, and take his place in the activities of the community. If Crusoe resists this process, or exhibits free-will-like characteristics after the event, then it suggests that his 'election' needs to be reassessed.

Crusoe certainly appears to have a strong, inbuilt resistance to the reintroduction of the other. It could be argued that this is hardly presented to him in an appealing form: cannibals representing the ultimate threat to the individual – total absorption into the body of the other. Yet as with Christian's lions, the appearance may be far worse than the reality; this too could be a 'trial of faith'. Self continues to intervene and to treat human contact as potentially contaminating. When contact presents itself it is noticeable how swiftly Crusoe withdraws behind the barricades of self:

> When I came to my Castle, for so I think I call'd it ever after this, I fled into it like one pursued; whether I went over by the Ladder as first contriv'd, or went in at the Hole at the Rock, which I call'd a Door, I cannot remember; no, nor could I remember the next Morning, for never frighted Hare fled to Cover, or Fox to Earth, with more Terror of Mind than I to this Retreat.   (p. 154)

The completeness of his self-absorption is signalled by the language Crusoe uses in this passage: 'castle', 'hole' and 'retreat' all conjuring up images of withdrawal and hiding. This is not much reminiscent of the landscape of election. Neither does post-conversion Crusoe display the consistent faith in providence that the grateful electee should, remaining instead the 'strange, whimsical, inconsistent Being' satirised by Gildon.[16] The desperate creature who calls upon providence to deliver and protect him during conversion ('*Jesus, thou exalted Prince and Saviour, give me Repentance!*' (p. 96)) disappears, to be replaced by a calculating possessive individualist equally divided by a fear that the savages will devour him and that his property will be invaded. Religion and spirituality certainly tend to recede as self-interest comes to the fore:

> Thus my Fear banish'd all my religious Hope; all that former

Confidence in God which was founded upon such wonderful
Experience as I had had of his Goodness, now vanished, as if he
that had fed me by Miracle hitherto, could not preserve by his
Power the Provision which he had made for me by his
Goodness: I reproach'd my self with my Easiness, that would
not sow any more Corn one Year than would just serve me till
the next Season. (p. 156)

Providence is eventually permitted to re-enter the argument,
however, and we soon find ourselves back in the spiritual
autobiographical tradition with events being subjected to
intense semiotic analysis. Yet it is illuminating to analyse the
passage above for evidence of paradox at work even when
self-interest is in the ascendancy.

The first point to note is the characteristically Calvinist
transition from predeterminism to free will. We move from
the sentiment: 'as if he that had fed me by Miracle hitherto,
could not preserve by his Power the Provision which he had
made for me by his Goodness', directly into: 'I reproach'd my
self with my Easiness, that would not sow any more Corn one
Year than would just serve me till the next Season'. That is, we
move from the omnipotent God who has it in his power to
predestinate every incident in the history of the universe
(including Crusoe's failure to 'sow any more Corn') to self-
criticism. God may predetermine, but the individual must
accept the blame for his own misfortunes. Why a storm can be
seen as a providentially-inspired event but a failure to store up
corn cannot, must remain a mystery to all but the subtlest of
Calvinist minds (once again we have the sense of there being a
step missing in the argument, of the type that makes 'a man
madde' if he is a reprobate). It would seem as if a certain
disjunction exists between Crusoe's practical behaviour and
his metaphysical beliefs at this point. If he is to be reproached
with his 'easiness' then presumably he must also be praised for
his ability to rectify the situation. Economic man begins to
take on a life of his own outside the confines of his theological
belief-system, opening up a gap between man and God which
creates a particularly fertile area for ontological tensions.

It would be tempting to see this dichotomy as the product of a clash between the author's own spiritual and secular concerns; that is, as representative of a collision between early capitalist ideology (of the expansionist kind) and an inward-looking Calvinism which was gradually losing its force as a determinant of social attitudes – and to some extent this is the case. Everything that happens in *Crusoe* can be made consistent with Calvinist theory, in the sense that the theory's internal contradictions allow for a situation in which God predestinates but the individual can be held responsible for his own actions. It is called reprobation. If Crusoe were indeed a reprobate we might say that Defoe was observing the paradoxes of Calvinist soteriology with great precision. Reprobating Crusoe would run counter to much of the text, however, and we might open out the debate to obtain a wider perspective on the author's problem. Defoe is grappling with something very fundamental: the conflict between free will and determinism that has become such a notable feature of Western culture. The Defoe protagonist confronts a range of authoritarian cultural formations – Calvinism, patriarchy and capitalism being the most prominent – which seek to hide their contradictions from him. He must plot his way through the dialectics of tension that this confusion of cultural formations creates, striving to maintain his individuality and to maximise his scope for the exercise of the free will that ensures that individuality. Where Defoe uses the Calvinistic Puritanism of the conversion narrative as his immediate point of reference, we would now most likely take some aspect of modern social or psychological theory, which so often seems to run counter to our perception of reality, substituting subcognitive imperatives of deterministic cast (economic, genetic, etc.) where the individual sees freedom of choice. The respective patterns of thought are not really so dissimilar, however, in that some point or other of the belief-system is seen to be creating tensions in the individual's life, and these are manifesting themselves in the form of anxiety-states concerning the extent of one's freedom of action.

Sartre's Roquentin, Beckett's Vladimir and Estragon, and

Defoe's Crusoe are all trapped in a no man's land between freedom and determinism.[17] It hardly seems to matter whether the source of the tension lies in physiology, psychology or soteriology, the effect on the character will be remarkably similar: ontological insecurity. Defoe's creations put up the braver fight perhaps, but they are dealing with the problem at a relatively early stage when a degree of optimism (enough to inspire a certain fierce energy) is still possible. Writers like Sartre and Beckett have come on to the scene at a time when such expenditure of personal energy has been discredited by several centuries of failure to resolve the basic problem.

Defoe's virtue lies in his attempt to encompass the contradictions of his own belief-system: to construct a character who is simultaneously a free agent (free to sin or to do good) and a pawn in a universal game (predetermined to be elected or reprobated as the case may be). It is hardly to be expected that he will resolve this dilemma – as formulated it may well be incapable of resolution – but Defoe must be given credit for his effort to tackle this seemingly intractable problem, which in his universe reveals itself as the conflict between the early capitalist possessive individualist and the patriarchal cultural formation (in both its divine and secular guises) confronting and obstructing him. Anxiety becomes the bridge between the two apparently irreconcilable states of freedom and determinism: the external realisation of a deep-seated insecurity which marks all Defoe's characters, and an index of their awareness of the many false resolutions attached to their condition. Anxiety discloses ideology's effacements of debate, in other words, in a manner which strikingly prefigures its role in Heideggerean phenomenology (where anxiety serves as a bridge between 'being' and an awareness of being's essential contingency[18]). It is Crusoe's fate to have to act out all the contradictions of Defoe's belief-system, and in so doing he highlights the presence of a gap between man and God – a gap which will have almost endless repercussions in modern Western thought, and which hints at a contingent quality to being-in-the-world. The minute that God's will fails to be a satisfactory source of explanation, the minute this will can be successfully challenged, then the possibility of contingency discloses itself, trailing anxiety in its wake. Latent in Defoe's fiction is the disturbing realisation that to escape determinism is not necessarily to escape anxiety (the anxiety which comes from doubt as to the precise nature of one's predestined fate) but to be confronted by yet another variety of it: the anxiety created by the *lack* of any omnipotent being, by the fact of life's sheer arbitrariness. Interrogation of an ideology in *Crusoe* opens up this disquieting prospect.

The basic binary opposition of individual and society is eventually to be resolved on terms favourable to Crusoe; a network of quasi-contractual obligations being set up in the gap between the free will of the one and the determinism of the other in an attempt to keep society at bay. Contract effectively becomes the individual's new means of fortification. It is worth noting that possessive individualism too, paradoxically enough, requires this reintegration into society, despite the many threats of compromise to the purity of one's identity that the process involves. We might say that possessive individualism requires the other, in that without the other there is effectively no self and no possession: possession being at the expense of someone else in both the Hobbesian and Lockean states of nature, where it is a case of exploit or be exploited (and as Birdsall has neatly put it, 'what point is there to strutting if there is no one present to applaud?'[19]). This means that there is a clear necessity for *some* human contact, no matter how minimal; but since contact always holds out the threat of assimilation it has to be done in a manner in which self can control other, thus continuing to assert identity in the act of exploitation: a case of 'no contact without contract'. More and more, contract rather than conversion comes to constitute the text's real debate, implying that conversion may be only a false resolution to the possessive individualist – and that really would qualify as subversion of an ideology. Under such a reading, conversion might simply be a local tactical man-oeuvre in a more protracted process of negotiation between Crusoe and the objects of his alienation; an admission that some complicity with history and tradition is unavoidable, without thereby counting as total acceptance of their objectives (at best, Crusoe on the island remains, in Novak's words, a 'suspicious despot'[20]).

Friday, a highly symbolic figure as far as the narrative's pattern of socio-economic evolution is concerned, is immediately transformed into a productive servant whose labour will henceforth accrue to Crusoe's account, this being the minimum contact possible in order to re-establish oneself as a social being. The relationship which accordingly is constructed – quasi-contractual, exploitative – is to form the basis for almost all of Crusoe's subsequent social relations. When other Europeans arrive on the island, for example, he promptly institutes a legalistically-inclined bond with them ('they should swear upon the Holy Sacraments and the Gospel, to be true to me'), and prudently extracts the promise from their erstwhile leader 'that he would bring a Contract from them under their Hands for that Purpose' (p. 245). Hegemony over others is now actively sought as a way of protecting one's personal autonomy. Marx made the point that 'Robinson Crusoe's products were exclusively individual, and were therefore useful objects for himself alone'.[21] We can now see that this applies to people no less than to things in the possessive individualist's world.

The opportunity to direct others bound by contract means that re-entry into society is rendered relatively painless to Crusoe, since its constraints are considerably minimised. This would hardly qualify as surrender to the collective, however, or even tacit acceptance of his father's 'middle Station of Life' argument. Crusoe's strategies still seem designed to defer absorption into the body politic, for all that social being appears to have the providential seal of approval (it being a way of 'sliding gently thro' the World' (p. 5)). What few examples of collective action we find in Crusoe's post-reconciliation career tend to indicate just how reluctant a *zoon politikon* and believer in providence he remains. Providence certainly provides no solace during an attack by Pyrrenhean wolves, who are beaten off by the combined efforts of the group:

Upon which I order'd our last Pistol to be fir'd off in one Volley, and after that we gave a Shout; upon this, the Wolves turn'd Tail, and we sally'd immediately upon near twenty lame Ones, who we found struggling on the Ground, and fell a cutting them with our Swords. (p. 301)

The contrast with Christian's passage through the Valley of the Shadow of Death, sustained by nothing more than his faith in God, is very telling. Crusoe's faith is placed in a fowling-piece and strategic collective action, which collectivity remains acceptable only so long as it prevents some greater evil from occurring (and no greater evil can be said to exist for the discrete individual than total absorption into the body of the other).

Belief in providence remains similarly strategic and selective. A journey from Portugal to England by ship is rejected because 'I had been very unfortunate by Sea' (p. 288), and when the vessel in question miscarries, Crusoe's decision appears to have been providentially-vindicated. Yet the same character is daring providence again as the narrative draws to its close, by undertaking a new sea voyage in accordance with the dictates of his fatal propension. In fact, providence serves a largely retrospective function in Crusoe's case. It enables him to structure his past rather than his future, which latter always remains a *possible* field of operations for free will. It is a guide to action only when he chooses to permit it to be so. Again, this could be seen as good Calvinist theory. Only the individual can sin, and he alone is to be held responsible for his sins. By shadowing the theory this faithfully, Defoe is opening up a gap between Crusoe's theory and practice. Indeed, as the work ends, a very perceptible gulf exists between man and God, and Crusoe is paying attention to the warnings of providence only when it suits his purpose: fatal propension consistently winning out over divine imperatives.

The narrative, revealingly enough, ends as it began, with the hero poised to resume his travels on the high seas, unrepentant and individualistic to the last: 'my Wife dying, and my Nephew coming Home with good Success from a

Voyage to *Spain*, my Inclination to go Abroad, and his Importunity prevailed and engag'd me to go in his Ship, as a private Trader to the *East Indies*' (p. 305). So in his sixties, in a typical act of presumption ('my Inclination' well to the fore again, as it was in his early career) Crusoe resumes his wanderings. Sill's otherwise quite persuasive reading of the book as one in which 'Defoe sought to develop in Crusoe a model of moral restraint',[22] rather breaks down at this point in the face of Crusoe's undimmed impetuosity. It is hard to interpret Crusoe's action as anything other than a challenge to God's authority; an assertion of individual free will against an authoritarian and deterministic ideology; a refusal to accept false resolutions to intractable problems. Free will ('my Inclination') is being exalted by the author, who allows his narrative to have the most open-ended of conclusions, Crusoe happily contemplating the continuation of the real debate in other far-flung arenas. In typically iconoclastic fashion, Bell regards the ending as merely 'a kind of advertisement for the *Farther Adventures*',[23] but this is a little too reductive (if true in its limited way). Rather that, given Defoe's concerns, 'to conclude a life is to falsify it';[24] to set up a sequel is to reveal something about the character's continued pretensions.

The narrative closes, therefore, on a subversive rather than an authoritarian note, signalling a victory for personal auton-omy and against social being; for self and its defence-mechanisms as against the insistent pressures of ideology. In spiritual terms we would seem to be stranded between election and reprobation, since Crusoe is being very selective about which events he regards as providential in origin. In living through the paradoxes of Calvinist soteriology (which in effect provide the materials and conditions for the system's own interrogation) Crusoe gravitates increasingly towards the active side of his personality, becoming more dynamic and physically-oriented as the narrative progresses, more the author of his self and his conceptual mechanisms (holding out the same possibility to the reader too, of course, as John Preston has noted of such fictions[25]). He moves steadily away from a Bunyanesque interiorisation of experience to an ideological position which depends on action and presumption; although in common with the Bunyan hero he retains an intensely egocentric outlook on life, in which other beings are to be treated with caution. As viewed from behind the barricades of self, others represent a threat to the continued existence of that self. Crusoe seems to be calling into question not just the dominant assumptions of mainstream post-Restoration culture, but also the dominant assumptions of its Calvinist-influenced dissenting counter-culture. Interrogation can hardly be carried much further. In modern terms of reference, what the character is refusing to accept is necessity – in both its historical and metaphysical guises – and to a greater degree than any of his literary contemporaries, Defoe reaches to the heart of that major Western cultural dilemma: the conflict between freedom and necessity. Refusing to resolve this particular narrative represents a continuing commitment to the debate on this issue. The best that can be said at the end of part one of Crusoe's adventures is that an uneasy truce has been negotiated on behalf of the isolated self. When Curtis complains that *Crusoe* eventually declines into a mere 'adventure story',[26] she underestimates quite seriously the complexity of Defoe's narrative project and the negotiations it demands between hero and belief-system.

Although it is set in the firmly social context of the City of London, there are striking parallels to be noted between *Crusoe* and *Journal*, particularly as regards isolation of the self and fear of the other. In both texts the individual comes to regard social contact as potentially contaminating. This effect is created in *Journal* by the extremely powerful and suggestive metaphor of a plague within the context of a large city, giving the author the opportunity to examine once again the effects of isolation on the individual; few things being more isolating than the circumstance of a city-wide epidemic. Isolation within plague-stricken London is seen to have much the same character as isolation on Despair. It is similarly conceived of as being providentially-inspired. In H.F.'s words:

It came very warmly into my Mind, one Morning, as I was

musing on this particular thing, that as nothing attended us
without the Direction or Permission of Divine Power, so these
Disappointments must have something in them extraordinary;
and I ought to consider whether it did not evidently point out, or
intimate to me, that it was the Will of Heaven I should not go. It
immediately follow'd in my Thoughts, that if it really was from
God, that I should stay, he was able effectually to preserve me in
the midst of all the Death and Danger that would surround me;
and that if I attempted to secure my self by fleeing from my
Habitation, and acted contrary to these Intimations, which I
believed to be Divine, it was a kind of flying from God, and that
he could cause his Justice to overtake me when and where he
thought fit.[27]   (pp. 10–11)

'Flying from God' is, of course, precisely the sin that Crusoe
commits; this is what his fatal propension amounts to. H.F.'s
refusal to fly, on the other hand, represents a submission to an
impersonal and determinist metaphysical scheme, raising
afresh the free will problem in dissenting prose fiction.

There is the most careful balance observed in *Journal*
between despairing and presuming over the outcome of
the free will/determinism conflict, as the treatment of the
subject of fatalism in the work demonstrates. To the non-
predestinarian, fatalism may seem an entirely valid response to
such an inhuman doctrine, with Antilegon's observation, 'if
God hath decreed mens destruction, what can he do withall?
who can resist his will?' cogently expressing the psychology
involved. H.F., however, committed as he is to the despair/
presume balancing act as a strategy to cope with providential
disposition, is at pains to exclude fatalism from the election
process of survival. He relates how his brother,

proceeded to tell me of the mischievous Consequences which
attended the Presumption of the *Turks* and *Mahometans* in *Asia*
. . . and how presuming upon their profess'd predestinating
Notions, and of every Man's End being predetermin'd and
unalterably before-hand decreed, they would go unconcern'd
into infected Places, and converse with infected Persons, by

which Means they died at the Rate of Ten or Fifteen Thousand a Week, whereas the *Europeans*, or Christian Merchants, who kept themselves retired and reserv'd, generally escap'd the Contagion. (pp. 11–12)

Fatalistic presumption is, it would seem, just as bad as optimistic presumption, and although H.F. has his own form of predestinating notion – 'nothing attended us without the Direction or Permission of Divine Power' – this does not extend to a fatalism that would exclude anxiety: 'I went Home that Evening greatly oppress'd in my Mind' (p. 12). Those who fail to be as scrupulous in observing the despair/presume balance attract divine justice rather than mercy:

> Then, with a kind of *Turkish* Predestinarianism, they would say, if it pleas'd God to strike them, it was all one whether they went Abroad or staid at Home, they cou'd not escape it, and therefore they went boldly about even into infected Houses, and infected Company . . . and what was the Consequence? But the same that is the Consequence in *Turkey*, and in those Countries where they do those Things; namely, that they Were infected too, and died by Hundreds and Thousands? (p. 193)

Fatalism begins to equal reprobation and the paradox of reprobation intrudes itself into the argument. Reprobate fatalists bring about their own destruction ('they went boldly about'), even though it is acknowledged to be the case that nothing attends us 'without the Direction or Permission of Divine Power', and that, if it so chooses, that same power can preserve us 'in the midst of all the Death and Danger' connected with plague. Curtis comments on a sense of tension between H.F. and his fellow-Londoners, which she attributes to Defoe's 'habitual unconscious desire to have things two ways at once'.[28] These two things she takes to be a desire to impose, and a desire to escape, order; but while this captures the sense of paradox in Defoe's outlook, it misses its very real, Calvinist-derived judgemental side. We can now see what is wrong with these fatalists' conduct, of course: they display no anxiety, that critical sign of the elect temperament. Yet why anxiety should be any more efficacious in the face of predestinarian omnipotence than fatalism remains, as usual, paradoxical.

H.F. manoeuvres between despair and presumption with all the skill and confidence of one who feels himself to have gone through the conversion experience, ('It came very warmly into my Mind, one Morning'), and consequently to be under divine direction ('it was the Will of Heaven I should not go'). His strategies are subtle, his negotiations at times devious, often depending on an ability to separate thought from action in the struggle against necessity. He takes on the appearance of one of those chosen to 'walke thinly in the streets' while the reprobate around him – who in the narrative run through the gamut of types marked out by Theologus in *Pathway*: heretickes, swearers, drunkards and all – are systematically cut down in the name of divine justice. The essentially solitary character of electee pilgrimage that promotes such an intense sense of self is revealed to H.F. in a chance reading of the 91st psalm: '*A thousand shall fall at thy side, and ten thousand at thy right hand: but it shall not come nigh thee. Only with thine Eyes shalt thou behold and see the reward of the wicked*' (p. 13). H.F. proceeds to drift 'solitarily' through a nightmare landscape in which individuals are reduced to mere statistics (namely, those chilling mortality lists with which the text is punctuated) and all human contact is, if possible, to be shunned: 'I went up *Holbourn*, and there the Street was full of People; but they walk'd in the middle of the great Street, neither on one Side or other, because as I suppose, they would not mingle with any Body that came out of the Houses' (p. 17). To disregard such precautions and connect with the other is to prejudice the integrity of the self and, in effect, to be sucked into a determinist scheme which admits of no remission. H.F. resists, and maintains a scrupulous detachment from his fellow men: a solitary observer of a catastrophe which assumes millenarian proportions, who wanders around London commenting on the follies of a doomed race in the throes of 'a National Infection' (p. 33). The image he presents is much like that of a nonconformist suffering through the Restoration settlement, and indeed the plague is a gift to the metaphor-seeking dissenting author.[29] As Starr notes, 'Defoe is just as much concerned with persuasively interpreting the plague as with graphically recreating it',[30] and that motivation may well be accredited with ideological overtones in terms of the history of dissent.

H.F.'s personal solution to the spread of the epidemic is to cut himself off as much as possible from the rest of humanity, retiring into his own dwelling for several days at a time in an act of self-enclosure which recalls Crusoe's retreat to his 'fortification'. This withdrawal into self is broken only by occasional sorties into the streets where H.F. unfailingly notes 'the many dismal Scenes before my Eyes' (p. 80), such as the forcibly shut up infected houses which form such a potent image of ideological closure by the collective will against individuals: 'here were just so many Prisons in the Town, as there were Houses shut up; and as the People shut up or imprison'd so, were guilty of no Crime, only shut up because miserable, it was really the more intollerable to them' (p. 52). Such practices effectively isolate H.F. as much as those enclosed, and enhance his sense of special status in relation to his fellow men. Elect and reprobate are seen to be locked into their separate spheres of development at the whim of impersonal outside forces, permanently alienated from each other by their respective ontological conditions.

The lone forays into the stricken city, suggestive of nothing so much as the archetypal Defoe image, a ship journeying into a storm, merely reinforce the impression of solipsism in the text and in many ways this is Defoe's bleakest statement in this regard. All human contact is, if possible, to be avoided; if indulged in, it is to be followed by a swift retreat to one's 'fortification'. We are back with a vengeance in Tawney's 'hostile landscape'; a landscape in which disease lurks around every corner (like those persistent Diabolonians in *Badman*), and death can strike at any moment; where every human being must be classed as a potential enemy, and individuals scuttle furtively through the streets afraid of the

contaminating touch of their fellows. It constitutes one of the
most effective metaphors for a solipsistic universe that could
possibly be imagined; a universe where self and other confront
one another, can *only* confront one another, in an atmosphere
of mutual suspicion and hostility. The social contract here is at
its most minimal. Yet in the sense that it represents an antidote
to ideological closure, such solipsism can be considered to
have a subversive quality. H.F. defers absorption into the
body politic for the soundest and most pragmatic of reasons;
in his case it is quite literally a matter of life and death to
emphasise one's discreteness.

Journal features many of the conventions of the spiritual
autobiography in its narrative structure; such as a basic sense
of conflict between man and providentially-generated natural
disasters; a conversion scene (it is possible to make a case for
H.F. as Defoe's least problematical electee); a clear-cut division between saved and damned; and the total belief in God's
omnipotence and omnipresence in human affairs. Belief in
providence is very strong indeed in the text, as H.F. reveals
when noting that, in a case of conscience regarding his duty,
an individual,

> should keep his Eye upon the particular Providences which
> occur at that Time, and look upon them complexly, as they
> regard one another, and as altogether regard the Question before
> him, and then I think, he may safely take them for Intimations
> from Heaven of what is his unquestion'd Duty to do in such a
> Case. (p. 10)

Those who mock providence, such as the raucous tavern
crowd encountered by H.F. at one point, will be made to pay
for it: and in exemplary Calvinist fashion, with their lives. Yet
as in *Crusoe* Defoe, through the agency of his leading
character, is to suggest doubts about providence which can
only appear as subversive in the context of his work; as witness
the following sentiments delivered by H.F. in the immediate
aftermath of the plague:

> Upon the foot of all these Observations, I must say, that tho'
> Providence seem'd to direct my Conduct to be otherwise; yet it
> is my opinion, and I must leave it as a Prescription, *(viz.) that the*
> *best Physick against the Plague is to run away from it.* I know People
> encourage themselves, by saying, God is able to keep us in the
> midst of Danger, and able to overtake us when we think our
> selves out of Danger; and this kept Thousands in the Town,
> whose Carcasses went into the great Pits by Cart Loads; and
> who, if they had fled from the Danger, had, I believe, been safe
> from the Disaster. (pp. 197–8)

This is a curious passage in many ways and it certainly merits
comment. The italicised section would appear to run directly
counter to one of the narrative's major themes, God's
omnipotence ('he was able effectually to preserve me in the
midst of all the Death and Danger that would surround me').
Even the narrator himself admits as much ('I know People
encourage themselves, by saying, God is able to keep us in the
midst of Danger'), and in so doing sets up a considerable
tension within the ideological subtext of *Journal*.

If providence can be called into question, as it patently is
being here, where does one stop? What would be the point of
running away from the plague if God 'could cause his Justice
to overtake' any individual 'when and where he thought fit'?
What is the point of observing 'particular providences' and
'looking upon them complexly' if a rational argument, *'the best*
Physick against the Plague is to run away from it', can be produced
as contrary evidence? Determinism too is being called into
question at this point, and human reason is being presented as
an alternative source of insight: an insight which can set itself
up against providence's directives. Starr refers to H.F.'s
desire, as both character and interpreter, 'to maintain an
outlook that is at once reasonable and religious';[31] but that
synthesis is clearly beginning to fracture. The passage becomes more subversive the more one analyses it; an island of
human rationality in a sea of Calvinist determinism; a plea for
free will from within the confines of a belief-system which
hardly allows for it – except in the negative and paradoxical

sense of the 'alwaies free unto evill' will to reprobate oneself. Such tensions can only increase the feeling of ontological insecurity to which the Calvinist temperament is notoriously prone. The logic of H.F.'s argument pushes us towards reprobation as the model for the human condition, since only the reprobate have the character traits he sees as necessary to the proper defence of the self. Even the elect can see the desirability of personal responsibility. H.F. approves of free will, even if he does not have the courage to carry through its promptings. The most cautious of guerrillas, H.F. will commit himself no further than acknowledging the real debate on the occasion of this particular false resolution's disclosure. The character stands poised on the brink of free will: a somewhat reluctant advocate of its virtues, whose observation knowledge runs subversively counter to his discourse knowledge. Wilfulness and will-lessness are made to confront each other in a typically searching Defoean manoeuvre. At times like these, with theory and practice in complete opposition, there is more than the suggestion of someone interrogating an ideology.

This is the only point in *Journal* when free will and determinism are allowed to confront each other quite so starkly. Despite H.F.'s acknowledgement of the benefits of flight and his criticism of those who take God's protection for granted, the narrator himself has followed the dictates of providence, remaining in the plague-ridden city until the bitter end. Discourse knowledge wins out, but observation knowledge is increasingly making its presence felt, opening up interesting possibilities concerning the estrangement of human beings from their God which will not be fully addressed in Defoe's work until *Roxana*. The contradiction in question is very much a consequence of Calvinism's inherently paradoxical character, stemming from the doctrine that although God is the sole determinant of human action, man is still to be held responsible for his sinning nature and consequent decline into reprobation. In this respect Defoe is simply reproducing the paradoxical metaphysics of his belief-system.

Flight from the plague sounds like flight from divine

justice, a decidely reprobate characteristic, and there is a fascinating dialectic of justice and mercy to be observed in the text. Ostensibly, as the 91st psalm reference would indicate, this is a justice-conscious text:

> I look'd upon this dismal Time to be a particular Season of Divine Vengeance, and that God would, on this Occasion, single out the proper Objects, of his Displeasure, in a more especial and remarkable Manner, than at another Time . . . it could not but seem reasonable to believe, that God would not think fit to spare by his Mercy such open declared Enemies, that should insult his Name and Being, defy his Vengeance, and mock at his Worship and Worshipers, at such a Time.

Couched in between these framing arguments from divine justice, however, is a note of doubt that recalls the discussion of Badman's death: 'it was no certain Rule to judge of the eternal State of any one, by their being distinguish'd in such a Time of general Destruction, neither one Way or other' (p. 66). There is, therefore, no room for complacency on the individual's part. One should not despair; one may *not* be an object of God's displeasure. One should not presume; there being 'no certain Rule' for man to make soteriological judgements by. The acknowledgement of lack of certainty from man's perspective captures the sense of ontological insecurity basic to Calvinism, and all H.F.'s decisions during the plague have to be plotted against this background of uncertainty. The overall paradox of the narrative is that while the individual is powerless against the plague – especially a plague with divine sanction – his decisions as to his conduct are nevertheless to be regarded as significant. To stay or go, to tempt God or submit to his will, all can have a bearing on one's ultimate fate; but as the drama is unfolding, with the peculiar urgency that plague imparts to Ramist disjunction, the individual can never know with certainty what that ultimate fate is going to be; and it is in that space created by doubt that free will can subversively go to work. H.F. responds to a catastrophe outside his control, knowing that the plague is no respecter of persons and believing it to be of providential origin, while nevertheless harbouring in his mind a subversive suspicion that freely arrived at personal decisions can materially affect the outcome of the catastrophe (*'the best Physick against the Plague is to run away from it'*). The character may be caught within paradox, and he may even acquiesce to it, but he maintains an inner sense of resistance to its manoeuvres. He even enacts paradox's operation within himself by doing one thing (staying in London) but believing another (the virtue of flight). Like the judges of *Badman* he can emphasise whichever side of the paradox best suits his needs at any time.

It is all too easy to see paradox as an inhibiting factor; it creates considerable, and continuing, anxiety in the individual, and it leaves a permanent residue of unpredictability in his life. Looked at from a non-predestinarian perspective paradox can appear alienating and radically destabilising. Yet it also has its positive side where the politics of autonomy are concerned. As H.F.'s career would indicate, it can provide the soteriologically-conscious individual with room for negotiation within what is, after all, an impossible situation. Between absolute despair and absolute presumption there is space for free will to operate productively, especially when thought and action are allowed to be at variance. When that happens, paradox permits the individual to think the unthinkable about his belief-system. H.F. shows his predetermined nature by staying, but his freedom by thinking of going – and eventually by thinking the *preferability* of going. While not perhaps as reluctant a pilgrim as Hunter finds Crusoe to be, he has some of that potential within him. The effect of the thought/action dichotomy is appropriately paradoxical, in that in its intriguing juxtaposition of submission and resistance it both validates and casts doubt on the theological scheme being used by the character. The issue of autonomy may keep on insinuating itself, but the scheme still sets the agenda and provides the ground-rules for negotiation. A graphic example of this latter point can be found in H.F.'s post-epidemic reflections on providence and causality. The plague is 'a distemper arising from natural causes . . . really propagated by natural means', but no less divinely ordained since 'the Divine Power . . . thinks fit to let His own actings with men, whether of mercy or judgement, to go on in the ordinary course of natural causes'. It is the paradox of reprobation cunningly applied. In the realm of 'human causes and effects' some measure of blame and responsibility can be attached to individuals, but as the agenda for the causal process is set elsewhere ('the Divine Power has formed the whole scheme of nature and maintains nature in its course') a degree of judgement is always inscribed in that blame and responsibility.

Neither are we necessarily justified as readers in seeing a satisfactory resolution to H.F.'s pilgrimage through the plague. Infections come and go, and H.F.'s position at the end of the narrative might be summed up as being simultaneously post-plague and pre-plague, with all the considerable scope for anxiety that such a situation of limbo allows; there being no effective guarantee against the return of 'the secret Conveyance of Infection imperceptible, and unavoidable' (p. 194). H.F. remains poised, like Mansoul, 'between the two worlds', trusting, in the despair/presume manner, that providence will continue to intervene on his behalf – once, twice and thrice. In consequence we leave him just as much trapped in his isolation as ever, and just as much in fear of the contaminating power of the other: a character located at the very fracture-point of his belief-system. Social existence provides little in the way of succour against theological or metaphysical determinism, and H.F. is still acutely aware of his isolated, and soteriologically vulnerable, selfhood as he concludes his journal:

> A dreadful Plague in London was
>   In the year Sixty Five,
> Which swept an Hundred Thousand Souls
>   Away; yet I alive!

(p. 248)

'Yet I alive': the phrase perfectly captures the essence of the electee temperament in its blend of triumph, solipsism and wariness. It confronts soteriology in the name of identity, and in so doing places free will at the forefront of the negotiations.

Journal is in many ways the author's most metaphysical text, and indeed its social critique is more oblique than the other Defoe works considered here: more a case of the narrator being made to comment on individual human follies – 'the foolish Humour of the People, in running after Quacks, and Mountebanks, Wizards, and Fortune-tellers, which they did . . . even to Madness' (p. 35) – than on the contradictions of the social system in question (with the qualification previously registered of the plague being a gift for dissenting seekers after metaphor). That said, it does highlight the contradictions of soteriology in a particularly stark form that we can now see contains the essence of the modern free will problematic. The strategy of outward submission but inward resistance (a guerrilla 'kingdom within' serving free will) is one way of coping with the dictates of necessity, Crusoe's more overt, possessive individualist resistance is another (Crusoe being the character who *does* take flight). In each case, however, what the author derives from Calvinist conversion narrative is what might be called the ultimate problem of modern Western metaphysics: What happens when a free human being meets a determinist metaphysical system? The answer given by these texts is personal anguish and feelings of ontological insecurity, but also a more refined and intensely-experienced sense of self and personal identity. In *Moll* and *Roxana* yet other strategies for negotiation will be examined, as Defoe turns from the isolated to the social self.

Chapter Seven

WOMEN AND PARADOX
Moll Flanders and *Roxana*

I N *Crusoe* and *Journal* Defoe is not so much breaking with
Calvinism, as demonstrating its dialectical strength by the
act of foregrounding its internal contradictions and subjecting
them to the 'test of the written word'. For all its apparently
repressive and authoritarian nature, Calvinism can be a
peculiarly dynamic ideology to the extent of supplying the
materials and conditions for its own interrogation. Any writer
who cares to take the paradox of reprobation literally enough
will soon find himself engaged in doing precisely that. The
interrogation continues in *Moll* and *Roxana*, where it takes on
a more sharply social–critical aspect. By constructing narratives around women, Defoe is able to explore the conflict
between freedom and necessity in individual existence at one
of its most problematical points: gender. Autonomy becomes
an altogether tougher proposition when gender enters the
debate. Given the specifics of their social position, women are
simply more subject to necessity. Defoe's women are to be
confronted by a formidable array of determinisms – physical,
social and divine – and then expected to survive as best they
can. The underlying paradox is that they have no control over
those determinisms but will nevertheless be held responsible
for all decisions and actions taken to protect themselves
against deterministic pressures. It will be the free will problem
at its most intense in Defoe's fiction, with necessity presenting
much in the manner of predestination (it certainly has that
same sense of inexorability).

Moll is forced to negotiate her survival in a money-obsessed world in which women are particularly at risk, and poor women almost insufferably so. If, as Zimmerman has suggested, money is the 'metaphor that she uses to articulate her private needs',[1] then it is a metaphor that Moll is poorly placed to articulate. This state of affairs continually entangles her in the workings of paradox; social morality demanding that she respect the rights of property, the imperatives of personal survival that those rights must be transgressed. Her progress to what we assume to be a state of grace in her old age, consists of a series of collisions between the will to survive and necessity in its many forms: collisions which repeatedly call into question the prevailing values of her culture. These collisions provoke a sense of ontological insecurity which is clearly conducive to self-realisation, further problematising patriarchal ideology. Paradox is therefore having a marked effect on Defoe's characterisation practice. Moll maintains a sense of humanity throughout her experiences and Defoe would seem to side with her in her many dubious transactions with the paradoxes of her existence, but the same cannot be said of Roxana. With a few significant exceptions of late, critics have tended to be either baffled or offended by this text, effectively the 'Badwoman' of Defoe's *oeuvre*, particularly by the bleakness of its ending (none more so on the latter score than Bram Dijkstra, whose severely economic reading of the work leads him to conjecture that Defoe may not have written the final paragraph[2]). If we approach it, however, as a sustained act of engagement with the paradox of reprobation (the individual at once predestined to damnation, yet responsible for her own sins) then the text reveals itself as a savage piece of anti-patriarchal social criticism, as well as a very significant contribution to the debate on personal identity. Roxana is presented as a woman caught between a survival-seeking free will and an implacable necessity which seems particularly directed against women. She is, in other words, both free *and* determined. Acute ontological insecurity would seem to be the almost inevitable concomitant of this irresolvable dialectic, and Defoe is ahead of his time in articulating this. There is in fact a recognisably existentialist quality to much of Defoe's writing, and never more so than in *Roxana* where the ever-insistent closures of ideology mean that a character is constantly obliged, in the manner of the Sartrean individual, to make critical moral choices with bad faith seemingly always lurking in the background. Passivity is all but impossible under these circumstances, and resistance becomes a way of life.

Moll and *Roxana* illustrate the progressive concern shown by the author with the pattern of socio-economic evolution and its ethics. This has the effect of raising the level of tension in the lead characters' lives since it involves exposing them to a wider, and less easily definable, range of necessities and determinisms, thus setting ever more complex problems of correlation between discourse knowledge and observation knowledge. Tension is also heightened by making the two protagonists women, thereby rendering them that much more vulnerable to socio-economic pressures than Crusoe.

The roots of ontological crisis come to be located, therefore, increasingly obviously within the social sphere, until by *Roxana* we are dealing with an analysis of society on the author's part which, in its insistence on the determining influence of economic factors on social being, strikingly prefigures Marxism. Lukács has argued that such clear-sightedness as regards the personal and psychological impact of bourgeois economic practice is a characteristic of capitalism's early period, and might almost be referring to Defoe when he observes that:

> This development of the commodity to the point where it becomes the dominant form in society did not take place until the advent of modern capitalism. Hence it is not to be wondered at that the personal nature of economic relations was still understood clearly on occasion at the start of capitalist development, but that as the process advanced and forms became more complex and less direct, it became increasingly difficult and rare to find anyone penetrating the veil of reification.[3]

Defoe certainly seems to qualify as one of those able to penetrate the 'veil of reification', and as an analyst of bourgeois economic practices and their implications for human relations he has few peers. His grasp of the new economic order as it applies to women is particularly acute and ahead of its time, and Roxana might almost be a Brechtian figure in her dispassionate use of sex as a commodity. The more acute his socio-economic analysis, the more complex the negotiations that Defoe's characters must conduct with false resolution, and the more complex the negotiations the more acute those characters' sense of ontological insecurity.

Moll is never quite as dispassionate a character as Roxana, and for all that the pattern of socio-economic evolution is beginning to dominate, her narrative retains a spiritual dimension (although of a fairly residual sort some would argue). Starr, possibly too unproblematically, sees the narrative as being 'in comformity to the classic pattern of spiritual rebirth',[4] and argues a current of sympathy between author and character: 'we are invited to abhor Moll's crimes, but urged not to despise the criminal herself . . . the narrative seeks to deflect our severity from the doer to the deed, and to retain sympathy for the erring heroine'.[5] Others have been less persuaded by the 'rebirth' argument.[6] We might also query the exact extent of the sympathy of an author who remarks of a post-conversion character that she 'was not so extraordinary a Penitent as she was at first' (p. 5) (although of course we might always wonder about the exact narrative status of the editor). Irony, in the guise of a veiled attack on a character capable of bad faith in relation to her soteriological system, becomes a possibility here. Feminist critics have tended to stress the sociological critique implicit in Defoe's handling of Moll's 'crimes', and I would agree with Mason's sentiments on this: 'It is probable that Defoe uses the characterisation of Moll to expose the faulty laws of the time and the resulting social conditions, Moll is involved in evil deeds not only because of the flaws in her own character but also because society does not offer her adequate alternatives'.[7] In exposing these faulty laws and social conditions Defoe probes deeply into the problem of gender, an area where ideology is particularly riven by contradictions and where false resolution abounds.

As is usually the case with Defoe protagonists, Moll has to be isolated in some way in order to focus attention on the development of her identity. This time the strategy is orphanhood – or as good as, her mother having been transported for theft. Moll is left 'a poor desolate Girl without Friends, without Cloaths, without Help or Helper in the World'; a situation very much akin to Crusoe's on his island Despair, for all that she inhabits a social, essentially urban-centred world. We might say that Moll is in society but not of it. Moll's basic plight, therefore, is that from the very beginning she lacks *context*. Her life is to be a constant struggle to integrate herself into a social group, a battle to attain a sense of security which has been denied her from birth. In fact, her birth has only been achieved by the expedient of her mother having 'pleaded her Belly' (p. 8) while under sentence of death for theft. Insecurity seems to have been built into Moll's world-picture from her days in the womb, and has a correspondingly sharper edge than that of Crusoe's, whose own insecurity develops at a much later point in life. Moll is forced into a confrontation with the harsh realities of her world at a very early stage in her career, when, at the age of eight, she finds herself ordered into domestic service by the local magistrates. Describing herself as having 'a thorough Aversion' to such an outcome, Moll is reduced to a state of chronic insecurity, able to do nothing 'but Work and Cry all Day' (p. 10), a clear indication that her insecurity will have an economic basis. It is this economic deficiency which is to dog her for the remainder of the narrative.

Yet another factor has to be taken into account in this context: Moll's sex. As a woman she is automatically a member of an extremely vulnerable social grouping. Penniless, friendless and female is not a good combination of qualities in this world, and all Moll's troubles are to stem from this particularly adverse conjunction. Being a woman means that she is even more at the mercy of contemporary socio-economic pressures than any male orphan would be in similar circumstances. Compare the fate of Colonel Jack and his companions when they are orphaned, for example:

> I WAS almost 10 Year old, the Captain 11, and the Major about 8, when the good Woman my Nurse died . . . the good Woman being dead, we the three *Jacks*, were turn'd loose to the World, as to the Parish providing for us, we did not trouble our selves much about that; we rambl'd about all three together, and the People in *Rosemary-Lane*, and *Ratcliff*, and that Way knowing us pretty well, we got Victuals easily enough, and without much Begging.   (p. 8)

Far from being able to act independently, Moll is placed in a world which appears to demand of her that she find the protection of a male if she is to ensure survival. To fail to do so is to be forced into a life of subterfuge, since few other options are open to a single woman. She can, of course, survive at the level of domestic servant – a role she instinctively rejects, but which circumstances inexorably propel her towards. When eventually she lands in that position she is soon made to realise just how difficult it is for a friendless, penniless woman to remain out of trouble. Like Tess Durbeyfield after her, Moll is to discover that 'in inhabiting the fleshly tabernacle with which Nature had endowed her she was somehow doing wrong'.[8] Ontology conspires against her and she is to become the target of attention of the household's elder son.

While there is undoubtedly a vein of proto-feminist social criticism running through *Moll*, it is probably true to say that Defoe's strategy in making his protagonist a woman is mainly designed to increase the sense of isolation and vulnerability felt by a character in society. Moll's basic plight is rendered more critical thereby, her range of options being drastically fore-shortened by gender as well as by class. Her social position is made that much more tenuous, her fight for independence and her quest for identity that much more difficult. This distinction needs to be kept firmly in mind when assessing Moll's role in the narrative, and I would suggest that her status as a

woman, crucial though it obviously is to developments, is of
secondary importance to the author. It acts as a device for
heightening the irony, since women, by definition, are more
prone to ontological insecurity than are men.

Economics and class (another area rich in false resolutions)
conspire particularly strongly against single women, and it is
to Defoe's credit that he keeps the real debate well to the fore.
Moll's position in the Colchester household is very clearly
false. Although technically a servant, she shares many of the
privileges of the daughters, being educated alongside them:

> the Lady had Masters home to the House to teach her Daughters
> to Dance, and to speak *French*, and to Write, and others to teach
> them Musick; and as I was always with them, I learn'd as fast as
> they; and tho' the Masters were not appointed to teach me, yet I
> learn'd by Imitation and enquiry, all that they learn'd by
> Instruction and Direction. So that in short, I learn'd to Dance,
> and speak *French* as well as any of them, and to Sing much better,
> for I had a better Voice than any of them.

This latter point about having superior abilities is stressed by
Moll, who notes that she has 'Gifts of Nature' which 'their
Fortunes could not furnish' (p. 18). The irony is that fortune
has the greater efficacy in this world, and that all Moll's natural
gifts cannot guarantee her an untroubled existence. As one of
the daughters puts it, in a particularly devastating analysis of
Moll's status which certainly penetrates the 'veil of reification':

> *Betty* wants but one Thing, but she had as good want every
> Thing, for the Market is against our Sex just now; and if a young
> Woman have Beauty, Birth, Breeding, Wit, Sense, Manners,
> Modesty, and all these to an Extream; yet if she have not Money,
> she's no Body, she had as good want them all, for nothing but
> Money now recommends a Woman; the Men play the Game all
> into their own Hands.   (p. 20)

Moll's isolation is once again highlighted. Being a woman is
liability enough; being a woman without money is a double

liability, highly unlikely to be overcome. Moll's creation of a discrete identity starts from the critical disadvantage that 'she's no Body' in social terms, effectively lacking everything in the contemporary marriage market. Borsay has noted of this market that, 'to simplify matters considerably, the woman brought wealth and the man status; a woman was as beautiful as she was wealthy, a man as handsome as he was superior'.[9] When Moll observes of a new husband, poor but gentlemanly, that 'a Fortune would not have been ill bestow'd on him, for he was a lovely Person indeed: of generous Principles, good Sense, and of abundance of good Humour' (p. 151), she neatly confirms Borsay's point about the respective contributions expected of the sexes.

Observation would suggest that salvation is primarily an economic matter in this world, where the individual will strive to correct any discrepancies between natural gifts and personal possessions (the discourse knowledge and observation knowledge respectively of a capitalist society). Moll's route to this salvation must be plotted through a hostile landscape of predatory males, who, as representatives of a socio-economic system anxious to maintain the differentials between its elect and the rest of mankind it exploits (no rich without poor; no elect without reprobate), generally seek to exert control over her and to inhibit her quest for individuation. Conversion in Moll's case becomes a question of transforming oneself from exploited to exploiter: a 'best physick' calling for considerable application of the will, given the position of massive disadvantage from which she starts. Predatory males and their socio-economic system – with all the many closure-mechanisms they can command – represent the givens against which Moll's will must assert itself in the bid to establish independent identity. There is to be no submission to one's social destiny but, as with Crusoe, active participation in the dialectic. Moll is, however, more at risk from social pressures than Crusoe, and we might say that 'fatal propension' is thrust upon her by males only too ready to exploit that discrepancy between gifts and possessions that marks her early career. The elder brother of the Colchester household provides the first instructive example:

> THEN he walk'd about the Room, and taking me by the Hand, I walk'd with him; and by and by, taking his Advantage, he threw me down upon the Bed, and Kiss'd me there most violently; but to give him his Due, offer'd no manner of Rudeness to me, only Kiss'd me a great while; after this he thought he had heard some Body come up Stairs, so he got off from the Bed, lifted me up, professing a great deal of Love for me, but told me it was all an honest Affection, and that he meant no ill to me; and with that he put five Guineas into my Hand, and went away down Stairs.
>
> (p. 23)

Moll's reaction to this incident is as confused as we might expect such a cunningly-conceived blend of sex and money to be to a 'no Body' of a servant: 'I WAS more confounded with the Money than I was before with the Love; and began to be so elevated, that I scarse knew the Ground I stood on' (pp. 23–4). At this first assault on her personal integrity Moll is found unprepared. There seems to be little in the way of discourse knowledge to fall back upon (an absence usually associated with reprobate tendencies), and it is revealing that her temptation is conceived of not in spiritual but in economic terms. Spiritual consciousness will develop only slowly, and almost exclusively in response to economic dilemmas, to which it appears to stand in an epiphenomenalistic relationship.

Salvation-as-economic is effectively salvation-by-works, since the process of acquisition demands active participation from the individual, who must seek through works to maximise her economic power. Defoe's language brings this out in a graphic manner when Moll, five guineas in hand, describes how her seducer 'falls to Work with me again as before, only with a little less Introduction' (p. 24). The road to conversion begins with a fall from spiritual grace in pursuit of economic grace, suggesting just how close the relationship between the two has become. That such a fall is involved is

only really acknowledged after seduction and its accompanying economic transaction:

> My Colour came, and went, at the Sight of the Purse, and with
> the fire of his Proposal together; so that I could not say a Word,
> and he easily perceiv'd it; so putting the Purse into my Bosom, I
> made no more Resistance to him, but let him do just what he
> pleas'd; and as often as he pleas'd; and thus I finish'd my own
> Destruction at once, for from this Day, being forsaken of my
> Vertue, and my Modesty, I had nothing of Value left to
> recommend me, either to God's Blessing, or Man's Assistance.
>
> (pp. 28–9)

Money may alienate her from both God and humanity, but at
the same time Moll is only too aware of its necessity. At least
part of her regret may be put down to a consciousness of
having sold her only marketable product, her virtue, too
cheaply. Spiritual consciousness tends to remain a secondary
consequence of economic calculation in Moll's world. Despair
is first economic and *then* spiritual.

Moll is, of course, still prey to the attentions of any other
male who cares to try her virtue. Given that she is prudent
enough to conceal her liaison, her status in others' eyes is still
that of an unattached, unprotected female, in which guise she
attracts an offer of marriage from the family's younger
brother. It is characteristic of her position that the discrepancy
between gifts and possessions noted earlier is still there to be
exploited, as it is once more by the elder brother:

> he Reason'd me out of my Reason; he conquer'd all my
> Arguments, and I began to see a Danger that I was in, which
> I had not consider'd of before, and that was of being drop'd
> by both of them, and left alone in the World to shift for myself.
>
> (p. 57)

Her range of options yet again seems to be very limited. Moll
is treated much like a possession; passed on from one brother
to another as from owner to owner, with little real opportunity

to follow her own inclinations being granted her. The price of her 'honour' is £500 offered by the penitent elder brother for her consent to marry the younger. Moll's status is that of any commercial object; subject to transaction with little regard being paid to such amorphous, and manifestly non-commercial, considerations as personal feelings. She has, in effect, been reified: turned into a commodity pure and simple. To the males in her world she is essentially property, a Xury or Friday for disposal purposes. If she benefits from her reification more than these latter figures do, she is nevertheless as little the author of her own destiny at this point. Social pressures work on her much as the hand of God does on a Calvinist; they enclose her by necessities, which induce despair, call presumption into question, and enhance awareness of personal identity. The conversion from exploited to exploiter can only take place through the direct experience of these necessities and their paradoxes. In true empiricist fashion the observation knowledge must be gathered before a discourse can be compiled to explain it.

Reification is the ultimate form of ideological closure since it denies selfhood, even of the rudimentary 'vertuous mediocrity' variety. Dependence on the male gives none of the security, false though it may be, of dependence on the mediating theologian figure of the Anglican tradition. There is always the fear of 'being drop'd'. Yet in 'no fears, no Grace' manner, reification also creates the conditions for selfhood in the midst of denial. Paradoxes abound here. Self soon works out that the only way to escape from reification is to reify others, but to do so is to intensify the other's conception of selfhood, thus putting one's own self more at risk in the exploitation stakes. Since everyone is using the same metaphor of articulation, and since this metaphor demands that the other be reified and exploited, collisions seem bound to occur. The ultimate paradox of capitalism presents itself: all cannot be exploiters, but the only way to avoid exploitation is to become an exploiter oneself. The tension-inducing possibilities of existence in a world where exploiters constantly lurk around every corner, and grace is almost inevitably a short-term phenomenon, are considerable, and Defoe is subjecting the paradox responsible for the tension to a much more thorough-going examination than in *Crusoe*. Self and other cannot so easily escape each other's orbit in this instance, and will is given much more difficult terrain on which to assert its freedom.

The other who puts Moll most at risk is the predatory male, whose appearance on the scene usually heralds some new check on her quest for individuation; pregnancy being one of the most obvious, as well as one of the most difficult to reconcile with the imperatives of the pilgrimage to economic grace. Pregnancy in Defoe functions in much the same way as a lapse from grace does in Bunyan's world. As the consequence of sin it arrests the individual's progress. It becomes the female equivalent of Crusoe's periodic captivities, and it is significant that both Moll and Roxana regard children in the nature of an inconvenience deflecting them from the journey through life ('pregnancy is weakness' in eighteenth-century fiction, as Spacks has noted[10]). Roxana presents the more extreme example in this respect, but even Moll evinces a fairly pragmatic, even cavalier, attitude towards reproduction and parenthood. At one point she admits that she 'would have been glad to miscarry' (p. 161), and on the death of her first husband she quite willingly parts with her offspring to alleviate her economic problems, effectively 'orphaning' them off to their fate as her mother earlier had done to her. Mason is not totally convinced by Defoe's handling of the children issue, arguing that 'Moll and Roxana seem like men with scattered progeny of whom they are vaguely aware, but about whom they have little or no interest'.[11] Given Roxana's contention that the best way to ensure survival is to adopt masculine traits ('seeing Liberty seem'd to be the Men's Property, I wou'd be a *Man-Woman*' (p. 171)), Defoe may well be making a subtle, and pro-feminist, point which Mason is missing. She is suggesting a failure of understanding on Defoe's part whereas it would in fact seem that he is displaying all too real an understanding of the impossible position of the single-parent family in his age, and that this particular penetration of the ideological veil actually provides more ammunition for Mason's essentially positive view of Defoe in feminist terms.

Neither children nor conventional bourgeois family life would appear to have much place in Defoe's fictional world, for all that he can wax the moralist on such topics in his non-fictional guidebooks.[12] What is important for Moll is independence, ontological and financial, and not ties, familial or otherwise. Her primary objective is to exploit her immediate environment as best she can. Children do not provide suitable material for exploitation and can thus be disposed of with minimal concern for the ethics of the situation. Moll can articulate the odd conventional sentiment regarding children – 'to neglect them is to Murther them' (p. 174) – but the real debate is economic, and self-interest invariably wins out. The negotiations are particularly clinical at such points and all the more a reflection on the hypocrisies of Moll's society. Discarding children indicates the lengths to which the possessive individualist will go to protect her identity in the pursuit of transformation from exploited to exploiter. Will must be exerted in the most uncompromising way against the pressures which patriarchy can bring to bear on the individual woman, since dominance over men can only be maintained by act of will, women having no real legal status. In the eyes of the law Moll remains the property of her husband (servant status applying to her both inside and outside marriage), and it is force of personality that must substitute for contract in her case. Economic election brings wealth to Moll and her last husband, but the security it provides is essentially his. When he remarks that, 'I have married a Fortune, and a very good Fortune too' (p. 341), he might well add, 'and legally it is now mine'. Moll has revealed herself to be a considerable asset, but an asset belonging to another's estate.

Moll's identity is formed in a series of conflicts with men (an implicit binarism is to be noted here which encourages Ramist-like assertiveness on the personal level), and she cannot help but be aware of her dependent status after her experience with her first lover. Her life takes on a predominantly economic character from that point onwards. Moll's pilgrimage has to be conducted through a world full of predators, while fighting to maintain her independence against the closures and captivities they would force upon her. Such independence as she creates can only be partial, since it is subject to restriction the minute it comes into contact with a male – even one as undemanding and pliable as her last husband. Defoe charts his way through the material in the manner of a division-conscious Puritan preacher; division in this case meaning the ever-branching sequences of conflict and choice which Moll's life breaks down into. Disjunction does seem to be very much a law of God here, and in its relentless generation of new states it enacts the doctrine of deferral; closure is constantly being sidestepped by the creation of yet another disjunction, and, soteriologically speaking, where there is disjunction there is hope. Only death could effect closure in such cases, and first-person narrative, of course, works against this: 'no Body can write their own Life to the full End of it, unless they can write it after they are dead' (p. 5).

All of which would suggest a basic sympathy on the author's part for a character beset by the necessities of the new socio-economic order. Moll will apparently be forgiven the moral compromises dictated by forces outside her control, and rewarded by a conversion scene which will provide the means to interpret her past experience: a discourse to organise her fund of observations. This will be her escape-route from the ideology which is allowing her so little room for man-oeuvre, and it enables Moll and her husband to end their days together 'in sincere Penitence for the wicked Lives we have lived' (p. 343). Yet despite the spiritual turn, Defoe is begin-ning to say some uncomfortable things about social being under early capitalism. The individual is left exposed by such a system, which provokes a desperate kind of free will in defence against its pressures. The necessity to transform oneself into an exploiter is masked somewhat by the fact of conversion, which puts a dubious spiritual gloss over the heroine's actions, but to an even greater extent than in *Crusoe* there is a suggestion of false resolution about this which the author's exposure tactics do nothing to ameliorate. It is not a self-produced fatal propension which underscores Moll's behaviour but the insistent promptings of socio-economic necessity: 'Give me not Poverty least I Steal' (p. 191). Such poverty poses particularly severe problems for women, whose only effective anti-poverty strategy is sex (whether disguised as marriage or not), and Defoe certainly highlights this real debate in the narrative by pointing out just how limited an option this actually is: 'it was past the flourishing time with me when I might expect to be courted for a Mistress; that agreeable part had declin'd some time, and the Ruins only appear'd of what had been' (p. 189). 'Agreeable parts' gone (and these must surely qualify for the false resolution category), Moll is left with little alternative but to act out the contradictions of her exploit-or-be-exploited ideology in the most direct manner: by stealing.

The economic dilemma involved is extreme enough to trigger a secondary spiritual reaction, and it is noticeable how skilfully Defoe interweaves spiritual and economic considerations to indicate the complex nature of his character's plight:

> it was then particularly heavy upon my Mind, that I had been reform'd, and had, as I hop'd, repented of all my pass'd wickednesses; that I had liv'd a sober, grave, retir'd Life for several Years, but now I should be driven by the dreadful Necessity of my Circumstances to the Gates of Destruction, Soul and Body; and two or three times I fell upon my Knees, praying to God, as well as I could, for Deliverance; but I cannot but say my Prayers had no hope in them; I knew not what to do, it was all Fear without, and Dark within; and I reflected on my pass'd Life as not sincerely repented of, that Heaven was now beginning to punish me on this side the Grave, and would make me as miserable as I had been wicked. (p. 193)

Moll mentions both soul and body, but the main fear seems to be of a physical nature – fear of Newgate and its consequences: 'Lord, said I, what am I now? a Thief! why I shall be taken next time and carry'd to Newgate and be Try'd for my Life! and

with that I cry'd again a long time' (pp. 192–3). Moll is caught
between 'dreadful Necessity' and the ethics, both human and
divine, of the situation. Such gaps conventionally call forth
angst in the Defoe protagonist, thus enhancing the process of
individuation. A Crusoe-like fatal propension now enters
Moll's personality and it is during this criminal phase that she
displays her greatest ingenuity – and we could say develops
most in terms of identity. Defoe brings Moll into conformity
with the spiritual–autobiographical tradition by putting her
into Newgate, and having her undergo what can reasonably
be described as a conversion experience:

> I now began to look back upon my past Life with abhorrence,
> and having a kind of view into the other Side of time, the things
> of Life, as I believe they do with every Body at such a time,
> began to look with a different Aspect, and quite another Shape,
> than they did before. (p. 287)

The repentance is genuine enough to generate a reprieve from
the death sentence, and in the style of spiritual autobiography
Moll can begin anew: in this case in the rather forbidding
context of the new world of the American colonies, where she
achieves a more lasting brand of economic success too (subject
to the qualifications previously noted about male preroga-
tives).

Conversion might be read as submission to the will of the
collective, or alternatively as a strategic act on the character's
behalf. It is only when 'I had nothing before me but present
Death' (p. 286) that Moll will become really serious about her
spiritual condition – as usual it is in the nature of an
afterthought to economic failure. In the context of the whole
narrative, conversion seems cursory; a strategic response to
yet another potentially de-individualising act by the collective.
The real Moll is not the being who looks on her past life with
abhorrence from the confines of a prison cell, but the energetic, possessive individualist busily stockpiling goods in the
Americas. The former defers closure on behalf of the latter.
Even the Newgate experience is undercut with economic

calculations which cast doubt on the spirituality of the proceedings. Consider the governess's cynical aside to Moll: 'did you ever know one in your Life that was Transported, and had a Hundred Pounds in his Pocket' (p. 294). This particular argument proves to be invalid in Moll's case, but in its insistence on the primacy of economic factors it keeps the real debate well to the fore (and money certainly eases Moll's entry into the colonies). It is in the highlighting of the paradoxes of the contemporary socio-economic system that the narrative's subversiveness essentially lies.

We are back with the idea of election as a local tactical move in a protracted set of negotiations, and the long-term sincerity of Moll's spiritual turn can certainly be questioned: indeed the author/editor invites us to do just that in the preface. What he also invites us to do, in a significant gesture of mercy towards his put-upon character, is to reflect on the degree of injustice involved in her case. Gender is seen dramatically to reduce what limited freedom is available in the face of the many necessities of human existence, and to create further problems in the already murky area of individual moral responsibility. In many ways morality is on trial in *Moll*, for all that some critics have found the text to be a study in amorality.[13] Perhaps we have yet another uneasy truce at the end of the narrative, but it is clear that when it comes to disclosing ideological contradiction, gender is one of the most effective weapons to hand for the interrogator of an ideology.

The paradoxes of the contemporary socio-economic system are exposed with even greater vigour in *Roxana*, which remains Defoe's most trenchant piece of ideological critique. *Roxana* is the most problematical of Defoe's narratives, and critics do seem to have difficulty in assessing its moral and literary value. As with *Badman* and *Holy War*, there is something of a critical barrier to be surmounted with this work. In recent years some critics have begun to surmount this barrier – Richetti, Birdsall, Bell and Backscheider come most readily to mind[14] – but with a few such significant exceptions the general tone of the critical heritage on the work is one of perplexity, as the following selection of views suggests. For Brown, *Roxana* 'is either the most resolved of all the dialectical struggles between self and other in Defoe's fiction or the most unresolvable'. Dobrée is considerably harsher in his verdict:

> It was Defoe's last attempt at novelistic fiction, and had he been able to carry it through, it might have constituted another forward step in the art; but he abandoned it, feeling perhaps that he was faced with a technical problem, as well as a moral one, that he could not solve, or had not the leisure to attempt.

Starr feels the book lacks organic unity (which quality he found in *Moll* with its spiritual rebirth theme): 'Instead of sustaining a double vision that would make her appear at once sympathetic and reprehensible, much of the book oscillates between extremes of identification and repudiation, with the latter ultimately dominant'. Even more damagingly, he refers to *Roxana* as a work whose 'shape is distended by the inclusion of much spiritually unassimilated narrative', which suggests structural as well as spiritual and ideological flaws to be taken into account. Zimmerman sees Defoe as having exhausted a line of development in the text, and remarks that 'there are no solutions in *Roxana*, only fewer evasions'. Sutherland complains that 'there is no conclusion at all' to the narrative. For Shinagel the ending is to be regarded as 'a potential second thought rather than evolving out of the action', and McKillop is similarly disappointed, remarking on 'an abrupt and perfunctory biographical conclusion'.[15]

Such criticism underestimates the work's value quite drastically. Rather than Brown's 'either/or' reading of the text I would substitute a reformulated inclusive one: *Roxana* is both the most resolved of all the dialectical struggles in Defoe's fiction *and* the most irresolvable. Furthermore, this is entirely consistent with Calvinist soteriological theory as well as a logical development of the conversion narrative tradition. The 'gravitational pull' of Calvinism on Defoe is probably at its strongest in *Roxana*. (Backscheider has argued that 'in spite of her faults, Roxana may be the most Calvinistic of all of

Defoe's protagonists',[16] but I would want to put it much more forcefully than that and proceed from a *'because* of her faults' position.)

Roxana confusingly features many of the conventions traditionally associated with election, such as anxiety, sense of sin and sense of repentance, but the heroine's ultimate fate argues against soteriological success:

> I can say no more now, but that, *as above,* being arriv'd in *Holland,* with my Spouse and his Son, *formerly mentioned,* I appear'd there with all the Splendor and Equipage suitable to our new Prospect, *as I have already observ'd.* Here, after some few Years of flourishing, and outwardly happy Circumstances, I fell into a dreadful Course of Calamities, and *Amy* also; the very Reverse of our former Good Days; the Blast of Heaven seem'd to follow the Injury done the poor Girl, by us both; and I was brought so low again, that my Repentance seem'd to be only the Consequence of my Misery, as my Misery was of my Crime.
>
> (pp. 329–30)

The paradox of reprobation will surely enable us to square the anomaly between election–suggestive signs and reprobate fate. Defoe's achievement in *Roxana* is to incorporate this paradox into the narrative such that its full implications for the art of characterisation are revealed. Aporias will not be disguised, and the heroine must learn to live with the consequences. This forward step in the art, by which literary enquiry is opened up to the philosophically fertile field of identity, is achieved by taking the paradox quite literally. Defoe attempts to give equal weight to both sides of the equation: to present us with a character who is both free *and* determined. In doing so, Defoe is operating at the very limits of his belief-system (where unopposable morality meets opposing data) since his literal interpretation of its doctrines involves the articulation of its internal contradictions.

It is when we come to deal with the reprobate that paradox really comes to the fore. God has predetermined the characters of the reprobate, those 'vessels made for dishonor' in Calvin's

telling phrase, but *they* are responsible for the judgements that
he passes on them since 'they do not cease by their continual
crimes to arouse God's wrath amongst themselves' (*Institutes*,
II, 961). In which latter case God is absolved of all blame. A
reprobate is both severely predetermined and the possessor of
a free will, a contradictory as well as an unfortunate combination since free will is always a God-defying characteristic in the
Calvinist scheme of things. This leads to the interesting
conclusion that the reprobate are more free than their elect
counterparts because they are the only ones allowed to put
their 'alwaies free unto evill' will into operation: even if this
can only be done in the self-defeating sense of opposing the
unopposable. Free action is at least a possibility in their case,
and there are certain subversive implications to be noted in
asserting one's will against an ultimately determining authority. This is what is at issue in *Roxana*; at which point the free-
willed individual and the necessities of her existence are locked
in conflict: the opposition of the unopposable. Roxana is a
character at the mercy of forces outside her control, whose
exercise of free will in response to those forces merely succeeds
in intensifying her plight. There is no question that Roxana is
operating under the kind of necessities which make a mockery
out of the notion of individual moral responsibility:

> The House, that was before handsomely furnish'd with Pictures
> and Ornaments, Cabinets, Pier-Glasses, and every thing suit-
> able, was now stripp'd, and naked, most of the Goods having
> been seiz'd by the Landlord for Rent, or sold to buy Necessaries;
> in a word, all was Misery and Distress, the Face of Ruin was every
> where to be seen; we had eaten up almost every thing, and little
> remained, unless, like one of the pitiful Women of *Jerusalem*, I
> should eat up my very Children themselves.   (pp. 17–18)

Trapped in the 'Misery and Distress' caused by her husband's
imprudence, as well as by the limitations imposed on her by
gender, Roxana might seem to have vanishingly small pros-
pects of retaining her moral integrity. Nevertheless, opposition to necessity by the free and determined being will entail

moral responsibility. Roxana is made to live out this paradox, and, unlike Badman, to be aware that she is living through it and so to experience the very considerable sense of ontological insecurity such a realisation induces. The result is the most complex dialogue with closure in Defoe's fiction, given that his theory demands that he pass judgement on such a wilful character. Yet paradoxically, Roxana's strength of will is the only means she has of resisting the pressures of a social system of which the author himself is openly, and often scathingly, critical.

Patently, something is wrong with a society which can so consistently push individuals into compromising situations, and Defoe is beginning to be very critical indeed of the dominant ideology of his time in *Moll*. He can only go so far in attacking it, however, through the conversion narrative, since this eventually precludes the detailed analysis of precisely those issues that the pattern of socio-economic evolution so insistently raises – issues like moral responsibility. Conversion represents an evasion of such an issue because the electee, the recipient rather than the instigator of grace in Calvinist soteriology, is effectively absolved from personal responsibility for her actions. Ultimately, election blunts Defoe's social critique by offering false resolutions to a complex dialectic: resolutions that the author himself seems less and less convinced by. It will only be when he moves outside the conventional spiritual autobiographical form, which the pattern of socio-economic evolution increasingly seems to be impelling him to do, that Defoe can properly confront the issue of moral responsibility – and Calvinist soteriology provides him with the means to do so in the guise of reprobation. Only the reprobate have the free will that ensures that they can respond subversively to necessities and determinisms, and also be held responsible for the actions they take; thus enabling the author to condemn both the system that provokes the will into operation and the will that freely chooses to seek success within that system. Reprobation becomes the channel by which Defoe can make his most significant contribution to the debate on identity, since if the doctrine is taken literally enough then the massive logical paradox that lies at the heart of Calvinist soteriology stands revealed – and it is this same paradox that lies inscribed within social being. In his uncompromising articulation of the contradictions of this most paradoxical of Calvinist doctrines, Defoe is subjecting his own ideology to intense scrutiny: negotiation with paradox leads to interrogation of an ideology. Given the inherently dynamic properties of paradox, however, it can withstand such scrutiny, disclosing in the process its very considerable value as an instrument of social criticism and metaphysical speculation. Reprobation overcomes teleology by setting up a perpetual dialectic between closure and deferral in the individual's life, which in Roxana's case promotes the most extreme levels of personal anxiety to be found anywhere in Defoe's already highly anxiety-conscious fiction. Starting with very similar materials to *Moll*, Defoe proceeds by way of reprobation to present the problem of identity in its starkest form in *Roxana*, minus the false (that is, aporia-disguising) resolutions of conversion and election. It will be the over-despairing personality in a situation which excludes presumption.

Roxana is, like Moll, up against some fairly inflexible givens of existence in the early stages of the narrative: being friendless, penniless and female leaving little room for manoeuvre:

> It must be a little surprizing to the Reader to tell him at once, that after this, I never saw my Husband more . . . But you will easily allow, that as Time run on a Week, two Weeks, a Month, two Months, and so on, I was dreadfully frighted at last, and the more when I look'd into my own Circumstances, and consider'd the Condition in which I was left, with five Children, and not one Farthing Subsistance for them . . . What to do I knew not, nor to whom to have recourse. (pp. 12–13)

Distributing children (essentially unwanted possessions in Defoe's world) amongst relatives proves a harder task for Roxana than Moll, and it is significant that the opposition comes mainly from the women of the family, including her particularly intransigent sister-in-law:

> What *says she*, do you want to have four Children to keep? Have we not Children of our own? Would you have these Bratts come and eat up my Children's Bread? No, no, let 'em go to the Parish, and let them take Care of them, I'll take Care of my own. (p. 22)

This could be construed as the new, strident voice of bourgeois capitalist self-interest, but it is also worth noting that it comes from a woman; that is, from someone who is more likely to have to suffer from the consequences of her husband's charity than he is. With the example of Roxana before her eyes it is only too easy to see how a rejection of increased commitments could come about. Taking gender into account, we might be inclined to gloss the sister-in-law's action as the prudent response of a woman afraid of the future and her own economic vulnerability. Perhaps women, being that much more at risk, have just cause to be more realistic about these things than men do.

Socio-economic necessities of a desperate kind, therefore, lie behind the action that stands as an original sin in Roxana's life, the liaison with her landlord in the aftermath of her husband's desertion. The dialogue with Amy on the subject of being the target of the landlord's attentions is quite explicit on this point:

> What, consent to lye with him for Bread? *Amy, said I*, How can you talk so?
> Nay, Madam, *says Amy*, I don't think you wou'd for any thing else; it would not be Lawful for any thing else, but for Bread, Madam; why nobody can starve, there's no bearing that, I'm sure.   (p. 28)

If we analyse Roxana's original impulse towards sinful behaviour in terms of a dialectic between freedom and necessity, it has to be admitted that she does not have a great deal of choice at this point. Starvation is staring her full in the face:

Poverty was my Snare; dreadful Poverty! the Misery I had been in, was great, such as wou'd make the Heart tremble at the Apprehensions of its Return; and I might appeal to any that has had any Experience of the World, whether one so entirely destitute as I was, of all manner of all Helps, or Friends, either to support me, or to assist me to support myself, could withstand the Proposal.

This is quite clearly an argument from necessity and it seems designed to elicit some degree of reader sympathy: 'that it may move the Pity, even of those who abhor the Crime ' (p. 39). Free will can seem a rather artificial concept when confronted by such economic necessities as the 'Argument of wanting Bread' (p. 43). At such points the 'veil of reification' is comprehensively penetrated, and Roxana is persuaded to take the uncompromising, but mercilessly logical, decision to reify herself with a view to manipulating the exploiters of her world as much as possible. In paradoxical fashion, this leads straight back to free will. Self-reification, like self-enclosure, argues free will in the sense that the individual consciously attempts to turn necessity to her personal advantage. Will-lessness in this case would only result in a reification to one's disadvantage, thus hindering the transition from exploited to exploiter that the ambitious, possessive individualist seeks. Paradox is clearly underpinning the construction of character.

The logic of self-reification may be admirable, but it raises some uncomfortable ethical questions concerning the degree to which feeling and emotion should be subordinated to economic considerations. Roxana's society would seem to demand the most rigorous subordination, and her economic success appears to provide spectacular justification for her reading of the situation. Yet Defoe is ultimately critical of a system which so completely disregards all but the material side of life. The fact that Moll never carries subordination to these extreme lengths is an argument in her favour as regards election (Defoe allows her to strike a genuine note of emotional sincerity on several occasions, as when her impoverished husband Jem deserts her: 'NOTHING that ever befel me in my Life, sunk so deep into my Heart as this Farewel: I reproach'd him a Thousand times in my Thoughts for leaving me, for I would have gone with him thro' the World, if I had beg'd my Bread' (p. 153).) The correlation between economic and spiritual success that we can note in *Crusoe* and *Moll*, contingent though it is perhaps, is conspicuous by its absence in *Roxana*. Economic success and spiritual success are mutually exclusive phenomena in the latter work. One can only be achieved, it would seem, at the expense of the other. Roxana is to be outstandingly successful in the former sense but not in the latter, and her ultimate fate, as expressed in the text's chilling final paragraph, signals reprobation and authorial disapproval: 'Here, after some few years of flourishing, and outwardly happy Circumstances, I fell into a dreadful Course of Calamities'. There is a marked contrast between these anguished sentiments and *Moll*'s peaceful conclusion, with the heroine and her husband reunited in England, 'where we resolve to spend the Remainder of our Years in sincere Penitence for the wicked Lives we have lived'. Crusoe's reference to his further adventures, while perhaps not definable as peaceful, is nevertheless similarly optimistic. *Roxana*'s despairing conclusion compares unfavourably to either of these, and it could be assumed that she is being punished for her spiritual sins.

In strictly economic terms there is no doubt as to her success, and we find her dwelling on wealth and the power it brings at various points in the text:

> now I was so far from Poor, or the Danger of it, that I had fifty Thousand Pounds in my Pocket at least; nay, I had the Income of fifty Thousand Pounds; for I had 2500 *l*. a Year coming in, upon very good Land-Security, besides 3 or 4000 *l*. in Money, which I kept by me for ordinary Occasions, and besides Jewels and Plate, and Goods, which were worth over 5000 *l*. more, these put together, when I ruminated on it all in my Thoughts, as you may be sure I did often, added Weight still to the Question, as above, and it sounded continually in my Head, what's next? *What am I a Whore for now?* (pp. 202–3)

It is all too significant that Roxana can only contemplate giving up the 'works' that have brought her success when she has acquired enormous wealth. She continues to be driven by an inner urge to amass wealth by any means, that has all the force of the classic Calvinist sinner's surge to reprobation. The manner is that of the reprobate wilfully embracing her own fate ('she could not but know' as Bunyan might have put it), and Defoe comes across as a particularly trenchant critic of what has since come to be called the 'cash nexus' society.

One problem we have in *Roxana* is that Defoe can on occasion give the impression of approving of the heroine's ill-gotten gains, as in the episode in which she places her financial affairs in the hands of the famous Sir Robert Clayton. Yet while apparently commending his character's financial prudence ('Sir Robert . . . applauded my Way of managing my Money, and told me, I shou'd soon be monstrous rich' (p. 171)), Defoe nevertheless condemns his heroine to ultimate disaster with that 'Blast of Heaven' pursuing her, presumably, to the grave. Defoe the moralist cannot quite condone the prostitution that generates Roxana's material for investment: a prostitution which on the face of it is a perfectly logical extension of the possessive individualist creed as far as the friendless, penniless woman is concerned (what Novak has called her 'occasionally bitter feminism'[17] has been learned the hard way). Roxana seems permanently poised between determinisms which seek to overcome her will to survive and determinism-defying remedies whose cure invariably proves to be worse than the disease. Passivity will lead to immediate physical ruin, activity to eventual spiritual ruin. Either way, moral responsibility will be attached to the individual.

Fear of 'dreadful Poverty', then, is to form the primary motivation for Roxana's behaviour. While we might sympathise with it as a motive in the initial stages of her career when economic necessity presses, we must surely come to question its validity later on, especially when Roxana herself comes to ponder her conduct: '*What am I a Whore for now?*' The argument that is advanced is a revealing one: 'but as Necessity first debauch'd me, and Poverty made me a Whore at the beginning; so excess of Avarice for getting Money, and excess of Vanity, continued me in the Crime, not being able to resist the Flatteries of Great Persons' (p. 202). Necessity may prompt, but Roxana's character does the rest. Indeed, necessity might be seen as merely providing her with a ready excuse for actions that she finds desirable. She certainly seems to enjoy the acquisition of wealth, even though she recognises that its procedures are incompatible with spiritual salvation:

> I had a Terror upon me for my wicked Life past, and firmly believ'd I was going to the Bottom, launching into Death, where I was to give an Account of all my past Actions; and in this State, and on that Account, I look'd back upon my Wickedness with Abhorrence.   (p. 129)

The moral dilemma under consideration is whether necessity can condone a sequence of actions such as Roxana embarks upon after it 'first debauch'd' her. One of the best places to explore such a question is in the episode concerning Roxana's daughter Susan. Economic necessity is the determining factor of Roxana's behaviour in disposing of her children after her first husband's death, but circumventing this particular necessity only defers the problem. Susan returns to plague her mother, demanding a recognition that Roxana's career cannot tolerate: 'the Business was, how to get clear of the Girl's Suspicions, and of the Girl too, for it look'd more threatening every Day, than other' (p. 281). Amy, acting here, as so often is the case, as Roxana's *alter ego*, does away with the paradox that is Susan. 'Fortunate mistresses' cannot be seen to have pasts which include daughters. Susan becomes a fact which cannot be faced in the discourse of mistresshood, and Amy's solution constitutes the strongest possible response to such opposing data. Defoe is at pains to describe the daughter's pitiful condition and dwells upon it much to Roxana's disadvantage, suggesting a marked shift of authorial sympathy compared to the Clayton episodes:

> she was resolv'd she would take so much *Knight-Errantry* upon her, that she wou'd visit all the Airing-Places in the Nation, and

even all the Kingdom over, ay, and *Holland* too, but she wou'd
find me; for she was satisfy'd she cou'd so convince me that she
was my own Child, that I wou'd not deny it; and she was sure I
was so tender and compassionate, I wou'd not let her perish after
I was convinc'd that she was my own Flesh and Blood.   (p. 308)

Susan is clearly searching for an identity, but it is in the nature
of self in the possessive individualist scheme of things to want
to deny such a state of awareness to the other. The other is
there to be reified and exploited and can only be considered an
enemy in the identity stakes, where its claims on the self will
be treated as a bid for hegemony. The Roxanas of this world
can only reject such a state of affairs.

Susan's murder (as we are invited to conjecture it) is
presented as a direct, inescapable consequence of Roxana's
mode of life, and in this sense she has to be held ultimately
responsible (note her plea of '*Lord be merciful to me*' (p. 323)
which suggests complicity of some kind in the deed). Defoe
gives her economic success – an all-but-unbroken run of it
after the initial brush with poverty – and social prestige ('my
Spouse saluted me one Morning with the Title of *Countess*'
(p. 261)), but he does not shrink from leaving her in dire straits
at the close of the narrative. Which means that he is holding the
character responsible for her actions in line with the paradox of
reprobation. Necessity, conceived of by Roxana as an absolute
force like God, provides a determining condition, but she condemns herself by moving wilfully from poverty to avarice to
vanity. In the final analysis, even extenuating circumstances,
such as being a woman and hence particularly vulnerable to
socio-economic necessities, do not constitute grounds for
excusal of Roxana's behaviour. The entailment of moral responsibility on free will holds, despite the presence of determining givens such as gender and economics. To oppose the
unopposable is to draw blame on oneself. Both doer and deed
are to be held culpable in Roxana's world.

Opposing the unopposble in Roxana's case involves a fairly
radical attitude to the givens of existence which consistently ex-
poses the internal contradictions of her ideology. Necessity all

too often presents a male face in her world, and all too often the male exploiter tries to disguise his intentions and the nature of the real debate taking place. Sexual designs can come masked as altruism:

> He said, That was all he desir'd of me, that his Reward would be, the Satisfaction of having rescued me from Misery; that he found he was obliging one that knew what Gratitude meant; that he would make it his Business to make me compleatly Easie, first or last, if it lay in his Power; and in the mean time, he bade me consider of any thing that I thought he might do for me, for my Advantage, and in order to make me perfectly easie.   (pp. 30–1)

The heroine's resistance by means of deferral soon brings the real issues to the surface:

> he shew'd me a Contract in Writing, wherein he engag'd himself to me; to cohabit constantly with me; to provide for me in all Respects as a Wife; and repeating in the Preamble, a long Account of the Nature and Reason of our living together, and an Obligation in the Penalty of 700 *l.* never to abandon me; and at last, shew'd me a Bond for 500 *l.* to be paid to me, or to my Assigns, within three Months after his Death.   (p. 42)

Roxana's tactics have succeeded in exposing the real nature of relations between the sexes in her world. Offers of help to penniless, friendless women will invariably have a hidden agenda – money for sex – that has to be recognised and turned to account, if the identity-preserving transition from exploited to exploiter is successfully to be negotiated (as it is here in another case of 'no contact without contract'). The choice that presents itself to Roxana in this instance is stark, as Amy points out: 'Your Choice is fair and plain; here you may have a handsome, charming Gentleman, be rich, live pleasantly, and in Plenty; or refuse him, and want a Dinner, go in Rags, live in Tears; in sort, beg and starve; you know this is the Case, Madam' (p. 40). Such false resolutions as sentiment and affection (the stock-in-trade of the exploiting class, as Roxana and Amy are becoming aware) can be ignored; actions must be tailored strictly to the 'Argument of wanting Bread'.

If relations between the sexes really are a money-for-sex affair (and the young Roxana is given little incentive to believe otherwise), then it would seem to one's disadvantage not to acknowledge this fact at all times, whether or not the 'Argument of wanting Bread' still applies. Roxana carries such thinking to its logical conclusion, operating according to this economic criterion in every encounter with males in such a way as to disclose the basic hypocrisy of patriarchy:

> at last I was very handsomely attack'd by a Person of Honour, and (which recommended him particularly to me) a Person of very great Estate; he made a long Introduction to me upon the Subject of my Wealth: Ignorant Creature! *said I to myself*, considering him as a LORD; was there ever Woman in the World that cou'd stoop to the Baseness of being a Whore, and was above taking the Reward of her Vice! *No, no, depend upon it, if your Lordship obtains any-thing of me, you must pay for it.* (p. 183)

Necessity is playing no part in episodes like this, and Roxana stands condemned by her own words; but it is characteristic of her progress to damnation that it represents as much of a condemnation of the society that made her as of the heroine herself. Social being has very much determined Roxana's personal consciousness, and that being has demanded desperate measures of the individual will in its opposition of the unopposable. Doer and deed are both products of an inexorable social process.

Social being, as Roxana can clearly perceive, distinctly favours the male sex – that most unattainable of elects as far as any woman is concerned. If opposing the unopposable were to be taken to its logical conclusion then even gender, surely the least alterable of givens, would be challenged. The heroine's declared wish to be a 'Man-Woman' might be read as just such a challenge, perhaps as a desire to distance herself from the compromising condition of womanhood:

my Heart was bent upon an Independency of Fortune; and I told
him, I knew no State of Matrimony, but what was, at best, a
State of Inferiority, if not of Bondage; that I had no Notion of
it . . . that I knew no Reason the Men had to engross the whole
Liberty of the Race, and make the Women, notwithstanding any
desparity of Fortune, be subject to the Laws of Marriage, of their
own making; that it was my Misfortune to be a Woman, but I
was resolv'd it shou'd not be made worse by the Sex; and seeing
Liberty seem'd to be the Men's Property, I wou'd be a *Man-
Woman*; for as I was born free, I wou'd die so.   (pp. 170–1)

These are brave words, but they merely succeed in highlighting the paradox that informs Roxana's whole career. To be
such a creature as a '*Man-Woman*' is to embody all the
contradictions of the heroine's existence, and graphically to
illustrate the incompatibility of necessity and free will. Roxana
may freely assume the male role in economic matters, 'seeing
Liberty seem'd to be the Men's Property', but the facts of
gender will defeat her in the end – as the case of Susan so
tragically bears out. If one is a woman then one's actions are
necessarily circumscribed; the patriarchal conspiracy of God
and male-dominated society is utterly unopposable at this
point. No 'best physick' exists. In this instance to wish for
man-womanhood might be construed as an ultimate act of
vanity on Roxana's part, since she is calling into question not
just an entire social system but God-given ontological categories too. The irony of the episode is underlined by Roxana's
remark that, 'as I was born free, I wou'd die so'. In neither the
social nor the spiritual sense can this be said to be true, and the
exposure of the character's pretensions serves to cast further
doubt on her code of ethics: doubt which will be amply
confirmed by the death of Susan.

We have now established the existence of a restricted
mode of being in both the public and private spheres of
Roxana's life, with faulty laws and social conditions much in
evidence; which is to say that necessity places her at a
disadvantage in both spheres. This raises anew the question of
moral responsibility. If Roxana has so little freedom of action

how can she be held accountable, let alone the author of her
own destiny? I have already argued that Defoe holds Roxana
responsible for Susan's death (hence that 'Blast of Heaven' as
the narrative concludes), presenting the event as a consequence of Roxana's freely-chosen, if also necessity-generated,
course of actions, and we might generalise from this concerning the relationship between responsibility and necessity in the
work as a whole. In ethical terms, the problem is that Roxana
allows an early encounter with economic necessity to blind her
to the moral implications of all her subsequent actions.
'Circumstances were my Temptation' may move pity once,
but not an indefinite number of times; certainly not when a
character reaches the level of economic sophistication that her
dealings with Sir Robert Clayton declare. Clayton onwards,
little heed is paid to the dictates of necessities other than
economic ones, as a wilfully self-reified (and by implication,
self-reprobated) Roxana embarks on a career whose actions
become increasingly contingent in terms of any moral scheme
other than the most personalised form of possessive individualism. She chooses to act in such a way as to realise only
one aspect of her character – economic greed – and she is to be
regarded as a victim of a powerful conjunction of social and
spiritual pressures; keenly aware of the former ('the Misery I
had been in, was great, such as wou'd make the Heart tremble
at the Apprehensions of its Return'), and aware enough of the
latter to indulge in a series of deceptions and strategies of
deferral until the 'Blast of Heaven' finally catches up with her.
The ritual storm at sea may provoke fear – 'I had a Terror upon
me for my wicked Life past' – but it can be deflected in an
authority-defying way that speaks volumes for the character's
refusal to accept responsibility for her own actions: 'I had no
Sence of Repentance . . . only such a Repentance as a Criminal
has at the Place of Execution, who is sorry, not that he has
committed the Crime, as it is a Crime, but sorry *that he is to be
Hang'd for it*' (p. 129). At such times Roxana's inability to
correlate discourse knowledge and observation knowledge is
made very clear indeed, but as a reprobate she has to suffer the
fact that the line of communication between them has been

cut, and she must rely instead on that good old Ramist type of argument-form, assertion. It is a poor kind of proof-technique but it is all that she has, and at the very least it is applied consistently; assertion of the will providing Roxana with her main method of countering necessity in all its many forms. Her freedom of action actually does remain very limited (she can defer necessity but not banish it completely from her experience), but she is apparently given the opportunity to develop in her own individual way; the catch being that Amy's 'fair and plain' choice amounts to a case of 'damned if you do, and starved if you don't'. Roxana is at once victim of socio-economic pressures and active element in their development; a perfect exemplar of the paradox of reprobation.

What has just been suggested is that any apparent authorial identification with Roxana's plight is mainly designed to lull us into a false sense of security. Jane Jack has argued that although 'Defoe has been prepared to play some of her cards for her . . . at the end he is not willing to cheat on her behalf' (*Roxana*, p. xii). The reason he is not willing to do so may be because towards the end of his career Defoe retains a Calvinist bias to his moral outlook. The 'gravitational pull' maintains its hold on him and he thinks naturally within the framework of the narrative of predestination. Far from being 'a brilliant compromise' on the part of an author trying to strike a balance 'between sympathy and reprobation', as Jane Jack has it (ibid., p. xi), the ending of *Roxana* is a calculated exercise in shock tactics, which both establishes a moral position consistent with a body of thought (that stretching back through the Puritan tradition to Calvin) and discloses the paradox within that same body. 'Compromise' has the sound of something altogether less dynamic than what is taking place at this point. Defoe does *not* cheat concerning the paradox of reprobation. Roxana is made to be simultaneously a victim of circum-stances and the author of her own destiny; precisely the kind of paradox that theorists of identity have to wrestle with. We are to consider, therefore, that Roxana plots her own downfall, and that her particular pilgrimage through life takes the shape it does largely because of character failings on her part. But we must also assume the presence of an opposing power – 'Necessity', the 'Blast of Heaven' – which is constantly and inexorably placing the heroine in an intolerable position and forcing unequal negotiations on her. Roxana can freely choose her course of action when so positioned, but any choice she makes will inevitably be for the worse. Her reprobate character will see to that.

The work can be considered to remain essentially true to the ideals of Calvinism, therefore, while pointing the way to the psychological concerns of the modern novel. In the exposure of the paradox of reprobation and the refusal to disguise its effects on the individual, Defoe has broken through the limitations of the spiritual autobiography form, while retaining its sense of urgency and intensity. The benefits conferred on the practice of novel-writing by this reorientation are clear. The shift towards reprobation as a focal point not only increases the size of the domain of characterisation, thus opening up an enclosed discourse, but also deepens the complexity of the art, since reprobates by their very nature are infinitely more complex beings in motivational terms than their elect counterparts. For people like Roxana, from whom definite promptings of progress towards grace have been withheld, the construction of self is an intensely personal affair, since God, having anticipated their transgressions, has effectively left them to their own devices. There can hardly help but be an even sharper awareness than usual of one's identity in such circumstances. One is truly alone, with little option but to be self-reliant, with all the anxiety-generating potential inherent in such a state. Hence a sense of ontological insecurity comparable to *Grace Abounding* in its intensity; hence also general critical perplexity about this apparent confusion of soteriological signs.

The critical comments cited earlier seemed to point towards the breakdown of a signifying system in *Roxana*; the argument being that signs, such as anxiety and economic success, are no longer functioning as an infallible guide to action or soteriological status; but I would argue instead that it is a case of a signifying system being broadened in scope to have a wider field of operations: *ex*tension, not *dis*tension. Once this is done it seems inevitable that the paradoxes of the system will have to be confronted eventually. If you do this honestly enough, then the contraries involved will lead to progression; in this instance to a far richer and more responsive form within which to explore the mysteries of identity and the relationship between the individual free will and the necessities, physical and spiritual, of social existence. The author has created a site in *Roxana* for the study of the effects of the collision between the two phenomena: that which has no wish to be resolved and that whose entire function is to resolve. Defoe has not so much boxed himself into a corner as disclosed the rich seam of psychological and metaphysical complexity latent in Calvinist thought and fiction. By his doctrinaire insistence on the letter of the paradox he has brought its underlying contradictions to the surface. It is not the 'either/or' of Brown's reading that we have in *Roxana*, far less Dobrée or Zimmerman's 'dead end', but the much more confusing, as well as exciting, realistic and ideologically subversive, 'both/and': both free *and* determined. Paradox is now calling an entire value system into question.

A 'both/and' reading demands that we have both resolution and non-resolution at the end of the text, and in a very striking way we find this simultaneity inscribed in the last paragraph of *Roxana*. The author, through his character, passes judgement on that same character: 'I fell into a dreadful Course of Calamities, and *Amy* also; the very Reverse of our former Good Days'. The last sentence announces a particularly neat resolution: 'Repentance seem'd to be only the Consequence of my Misery, as my Misery was of my Crime'. The finality of the tone encourages us to see soteriological closure being applied to Roxana – at the last gasp as it were. It is a moral pronouncement any Calvinist theorist would readily accept. Yet within this resolution, non-resolution is insidiously asserting itself. The leading character is still alive, still deferring judgement in that last paragraph; refusing to disclose just *what* 'dreadful Course of Calamities' provided clinching evidence of reprobation in her case. The freedom to oppose

the unopposable is being exercised even as the narrative runs out, while the author concurrently insists on the necessity of ultimate damnation: free *and* determined. Even the resistance to judgement carries with it a Calvinist message. Calvin had spoken of there being 'no end to . . . the punishment of the wicked' (*Institutes*, II, 995): an apt moral to draw from *Roxana*'s
final sentences, with mental torment being projected beyond the narrative itself in the manner of some kind of living hell. The inscription of the paradox in the text seems complete as we observe *Roxana* moving to an appropriately arbitrary conclusion. Defoe has not only exposed the paradox, he has rendered it dynamic.

The combination of the free will of the reprobate and the anxiety of the elect proves to be a particularly volatile one, and no final conclusions about the nature of identity are to be drawn from *Roxana* – except that ontological insecurity seems to be a difficult state to avoid for the bulk of mankind. Perhaps final conclusions are not really in order in this area. The relative degree of freedom we possess is still very much a matter of debate in philosophical and scientific circles, yet most of us go on believing, or at least pretending, that freedom of action exists and that individuals have the ability to make moral choices. Free will and determinism (whether of a metaphysical, physiological or socio-economic kind) still represent the poles of the debate, and too much speculation on the reasons for, and causes of, our actions is still very likely to result in anxiety-states when we realise the lack of available solutions; the chronic, nagging, frequently over-despairing anxiety that underlines Roxana's life remains very much part of the twentieth-century cultural experience. To that extent *Roxana* is a very modern and very metaphysical work, and a particularly penetrating contribution to the debate on the problems of identity.

Chapter Eight

CONCLUSION

THE foregoing textual studies enable us to situate Bunyan and Defoe in a general sense within the free will/ determinism debate as it continues to tax us to the present day. Their fictions can be regarded as mapping the terrain of operations *vis-à-vis* authority, and paradox is a major weapon in their armoury. Paradox is an essentially anti-authoritarian device in Bunyan and Defoe's narrative practice, and gives the authors considerable scope for social critique and metaphysical speculation. Pushed far enough, however, paradox also reveals the limitations of human endeavour, and both authors have to work out how to accommodate this less than comforting knowledge within their narrative codes. The narrative of predestination provides a framework that encompasses some of the most fundamental and pressing problems of individualism and personal identity, and has considerable resonance still in the late twentieth century. The inscription of paradox within these texts imparts to them a particularly dynamic quality, as the relentlessly unfolding process of negotiation obliges the self in question to assert its claims to survival in a continuous dialectical struggle. In the hands of Bunyan and Defoe the narrative of predestination, through concentration on its paradoxes, becomes a site for social criticism as well as for the exploration of the effects of the free will debate on the nonconforming (in an ideological as well as theological sense) individual. The consequence for the individual is feelings of anguish and ontological insecurity, and it is largely through their brilliant articulation of these psychological states that these dialectical texts retain their power to shock and trouble. Our own culture has been no more lastingly successful in resolving the paradoxes inherent in the free will debate.

I have tended throughout to treat free will and determinism as mutually exclusive contraries. Present-day philosophers are more likely to see them as matters of degree, arguing that in given areas we have a greater or lesser degree of freedom, are more or less determined in our actions. Each context must then be subjected to careful scrutiny. Reformulating and recontextualising the problem is a traditional philosophical pastime, and there have been several sideways shifts in this particular debate: shifts into physics, psychology, physiology and politics, for example. Jennifer Trusted has argued that determinism, of whatever kind, is a metaphysical thesis, and that metaphysical theses lie beyond logical proof; they 'cannot be established as true or false by appeal to observation or by appeal to deductive reasoning; they are statements of metaphysical belief and must be assessed along with other beliefs in the system'[1] (not a move calculated to endear itself to the predestinarian, whose starting point is that his soteriological thesis simply *is* true[2]). The particular context must be scrutinised, in other words. Trusted also comes out strongly in favour of moral responsibility for the most pragmatic of reasons:

> We cannot help holding ourselves and others responsible for actions save in very special circumstances. In addition we make moral judgements, and this also reflects our concept of a person. It is not a contingent fact that there is no human society in which there are not moral values for, if a society of human-looking creatures who did not have moral values were found, we should not judge them to be truly human.[3]

One could chip away at such a conclusion. It veers perilously close to being an argument from tradition ('we make moral judgements' implies that we always have, it is conventional to do so). Then too, arguments from human nature ('we cannot help') can be notoriously transitory; Bunyan could have argued in his day that, 'we cannot help holding ourselves as being bound by the principles of soteriology', since the contents of the Bible were not then regarded as 'contingent facts'. The argument is, however, very typical of the commonsensical, late Wittgensteinian approach to intractable metaphysical problems, where the questions we would ask take the form: 'What do people actually do, and how do they actually behave?' Contexts are to be analysed, behaviour analysed, and free will to some extent marginalised as an issue. Ways around the free will problem certainly exist, therefore, and in everyday life, as Trusted justifiably notes, we have such a strong commitment to the notions of free will and moral responsibility that we continue to act as if there were, to all intents and purposes, *no* free will problem. Pragmatism generally rules in this area: although we might still be interested in discovering the exact extent of that domain of 'very special circumstances'.

When we come to reflect on the nature of the pressures facing us as individuals, however, the possibility of free action begins seriously to diminish. This need not necessarily cause any problems to the individual – lack of free will does not *entail* anxiety (fatalism, resignation, even euphoria, are no less defensible responses) – but it *might*, and to that extent the problem is never really solved. It depends on the nature of the individual psychology, and on the prestige and power of the determinist scheme the individual is operating under. (The 'degree' argument only works for non-absolutists, and, as O'Connor points out, between absolutism and non-absolutism no accommodation is really possible: 'the very first premises of the arguments of one side will be unacceptable to the other'.)[4] If one does pursue the determinist line (which, as O'Connor has noted, is in many respects the more sustainable intellectually), then several disquieting consequences result. One is forced to recognise a disjunction between one's system of belief, plus its accompanying metaphysics, and the institutions and dominant ideology of one's society, largely grounded as they are in the notions of individual free will and personal moral responsibility. In such gaps, anxiety can still flourish. Pragmatism may generally rule, but it cannot completely legislate for the vagaries (and fears) of the individual psychology. What Bunyan and Defoe do is to disclose those gaps as experienced by sensitive individuals in the beginnings of modern culture, where a strongly defined predeterminism was still holding sway.

A further parallel with twentieth-century existentialist theory suggests itself here. To a significant extent our subjects' value lies in their articulation of the extreme case; for a Bunyan or Defoe character, as for a Sartrean one, Trusted's 'very special circumstances' are simply the norm.[5] There is no matter of 'degree' countenanced in Bunyan, and although there arguably is in Defoe, it is a matter of degree that has to coexist – albeit uneasily – with the perpetually menacing background presence of a providential determinism, that can assert itself with devastating effect when it so chooses. In the final analysis, as *Roxana*'s conclusion would seem to declare, it is not *really* a matter of degree; although there is considerable scope for negotiation until we reach that final analysis, and as long as the protagonist is constructing her narrative, the negotiations can continue.

Defoe's negotiations rely heavily on deferring that final analysis, whereas Bunyan, with the signal exception of *Holy War*, actively seeks to embrace it; but both authors' deployment of conversion narrative reveals the subversive potential of the Calvinist soteriological paradoxes inscribed within the form. Those paradoxes can be adapted to one's social–critical purposes (emphasise mercy or justice, free will or predeterminism as required), but they also fold back on themselves to disclose the contradictions of one's own position. They interrogate both the position that one wishes to attack and the position one wishes to protect. The written word systematically undermines the certainties apparently inscribed within one's soteriology, thus throwing culture and counter-culture wide open to interrogation, in a manner that is sensed somewhere in the minds of both these authors and their fictional creations. Badman's 'double death' can no more guarantee the desired divine judgement than can Roxana's final gesture of defiance deter the undesired one. The anxiety that permeates Bunyan and Defoe's fiction bears witness to both human limitations and intractable metaphysics. Anxiety, too, folds back on the soteriology that generates it, to demonstrate how that authoritarian-aspiring soteriology cannot effect complete closure on the individual will. To live through the anxieties of the Calvinist position is to defy its authoritarianism, and another paradox is enacted, more negotiations set in motion. As a recipe for an intensely experienced sense of self, paradox plus negotiation is hard to beat.

The major strategy of negotiation in Bunyan is to manipulate paradox against the reprobate, and so to insist on the inexorability of the judgement formed against them. Ignorance and Badman are seen to invite justice and the non-extension of mercy by a paradoxical conjunction of divine fiat and wilful behaviour: 'man falls according as God's providence ordains, but he falls by his own fault' (*Institutes*, II, 957). Christian and Mansoul have the paradoxes manipulated in their favour, which ought to suggest the absence of wilful behaviour in their case; but it is to be found in their character nevertheless, in the form of the will to resist diabolical temptation, the will-to-anxiety, and that particularly radicalising phenomenon, self-censorship of the will. Indeed election, given its necessary encounters with paradox, can only encourage the development of the individual will. So arbitrary is the disposition of divine providence in the matter of distribution of justice and mercy, that the individual is left unable to assume the certainty that predestination appears to offer. He is to remain, instead, prey to the competing attentions of despair and presumption, a cycle of conflict which, as *Holy War* bleakly announces, can describe a perpetually recurring figure through the individual's life (and universal history too). This may provide little comfort, but it does considerably enhance one's sense of self and personal identity in that characteristically subversive way of Calvinist paradox. Any fiction patterned on Calvinist spiritual autobiography will have to articulate the paradoxes encoded within its soteriology, and these will be at once repressive and individuating, productive of anxiety yet ultimately anti-authoritarian in their effect on individual action. The resultant negotiations will lead Bunyan further into the free will problem, and for all that he will refuse to acknowledge the reality of paradox (as Wiseman consistently refuses to in *Badman*, following on from Theologus' conduct in *Pathway*) it is in fact an integral part of his narrative structure. Bunyan becomes progressively more implicated in paradox's subversive action in his strategic deployment of it against the reprobate. Paradox, and particularly the paradox of reprobation, is the very basis of Bunyan's social critique, but it is also, eventually, the basis of a radical individualism at odds with the imperatives of predestination. In this sense, *Holy War* becomes his most subversive text, leaving as it does that radical individualism intact at the narrative's close.

Opposition to 'vertuous mediocrity' serves to foster radical individualism and wilful behaviour in the nonconformist, and Bunyan is very much concerned to demolish the claims of that politically-inspired theology throughout his fiction. Christian opts for the life of the 'soldier in hostile territory' rather than the temptations offered by such apologists for the 'vertuous mediocrity' school as Worldly-Wiseman: *'Why in yonder Village, (the Village is named* Morality) *there dwells a Gentleman, whose name is* Legality, *a very judicious man (and a man of a very good name) that has skill to help men off with such burdens as thine are, from their shoulders'* (p. 19). The offer of mediation will always be rejected by the electee like Christian in favour of the straight and narrow path, with not only its *'Wearisomeness, Painfulness, Hunger, Perils, Nakedness, Sword, Lions, Dragons, Darkness; and in a word, death'* (p. 18), but also its aura of personal adventure and opportunity for self-fulfilment. Part Two's pilgrimage gives us a sense of the gathered sectarian community resisting by its collective will the blandishments of 'vertuous mediocrity's' multitude of representatives. Mansoul, too, opts for a life of continual resistance. Those who, like Ignorance and Badman, take refuge in 'vertuous mediocrity', will be punished for their refusal to risk the tougher course of the 'Fanatick conventicle' (and what could be more productive of an intense sense of self than risk?). The overall picture to emerge from Bunyan's fiction is of a concerted counter-cultural opposition to a seemingly attractive, but in reality repressive, ideology based on the middle way. It is the mark of the electee to seek out the extreme situation: '*A good Man must suffer Trouble*' (p. 275) – with the accent falling very firmly on the 'must'.

Defoe's creations do not so much seek out the extreme situation as have it thrust upon them by circumstances: shipwreck, plague, orphanhood, gender. Behind the circumstances lie an omnipotent providence and a tradition of predestinarian belief (as encoded in spiritual autobiography, for example), and Defoe's characters restlessly search for signs, economic as much as anything, that providence has led them to a position where they can assume an elect pilgrimage in retrospect. The assumption is at best tentative for a character still in the throes of his or her career, at no matter how advanced a stage, and this sense of incompleteness actively promotes ontological insecurity (and perhaps also in Roxana's case a desperate hope that the completion will not turn out to be what both her observation and discourse knowledge are telling her it must inevitably be). 'No Body can write their own Life to the full End of it' can cut both ways; it can signal the very real grounds for ontological insecurity in the individual's life, as well as the still-existent scope for strategies of evasion. All Defoe's characters seek to evade providence's drive to completion in some way – Crusoe by further flight, H.F. by subversive thought, Moll by pragmatic remorse, Roxana by defiant gestures of self-assertion – but it is not just providence that they have to contend with, but a formidable array of necessities that come bearing the seal of ideological approval: necessities that present with all the force of predestinarian doctrine in a Bunyan narrative. Patriarchy, hierarchy and tradition are all to be challenged in Defoe's fiction, and in their various ways Crusoe, H.F., Moll and Roxana are opponents of 'vertuous mediocrity' (the 'middle Station' lauded by such as Crusoe's father). As rebellious spirits inspired by a 'fatal propension' (even if it is only the fatal propension to think the unthinkable, as in H.F.'s case), they will prolong the process of negotiation for as long as they can – even pushing it beyond the confines of the actual narrative, as both Crusoe and Roxana strive to do. In prolonging negotiation, they will assert the subversive claims of the individual will from within the heart of a literary genre originally designed to celebrate the irresistible workings of a predestinarian providence. In Defoe's handling of the narrative of predestination, both divine and ideological authoritarianism are to be confronted in what is a particularly far-reaching act of interrogation.

Defoe's characters are left free and determined as Bunyan's reprobates are left predestined to damnation but personally responsible for that damnation. The dilemma can be artfully disguised in Bunyan by skilful manipulation of soteriological paradox and a talent for logical sleight of hand. In Defoe the dilemma increasingly insistently intrudes itself into the proceedings, and its stark exposure in *Roxana* reveals the problem in all its very considerable depth. The politics of autonomy are now unmistakably on the cultural agenda. If free will is a matter of degree, then *Roxana* shows just how limited that degree can be (essentially a matter of deferring infinitely-applicable divine judgements from within a finite lifespan), as well as how unproductive of peace of mind. What Defoe reveals in his reworking of the conversion narrative, particularly in *Roxana*, is that there is ultimately much more scope for despair than presumption. When it comes to the extreme situation of a Roxana – and it is worth remembering that although it is an extreme it is based on that most banal of facts, gender – then despair will out. That potential for despair is always there in the background of the lives of Crusoe, H.F. and Moll too: ships can founder, plague return, wealth dissipate; life is always on a knife-edge in Defoe's universe.

I spoke earlier of there being a shift in concern from the realm of the supernatural in Bunyan to everyday reality in Defoe (although the supernatural still informs that reality). In that shift, paradox becomes less a means of demolishing your ideological enemies and more a method of disclosing human limitations in the face of necessity. Anxiety becomes progressively sharper as we move into the open-ended narrative (again, this tends to suggest *Holy War* as Bunyan's most radical text), the negotiations more complex, the sense of selfhood all the keener. In the process, the metaphysics of Calvinist soteriology is firmly inscribed into the discourse of the English novel, and it is in the articulation of those metaphysics, and the anxiety that they promote in individual consciousness, that I would locate the continuing fascination and relevance of Bunyan and Defoe's fictions.

NOTES

Chapter One Introduction

1. For Defoe, see particularly G. A. Starr, *Defoe and Spiritual Autobiography* (1965), and J. P. Hunter, *The Reluctant Pilgrim* (1966). For Bunyan, see particularly W. Y. Tindall, *John Bunyan, Mechanick Preacher* (1934), and R. Sharrock, 'Spiritual autobiography in *The Pilgrim's Progress*', *RES*, 24 (1948), 102–20. Spiritual autobiography in general is covered in P. Delany, *British Autobiography in the Seventeenth Century* (1969), D. Ebner, *Autobiography in Seventeenth-century England* (1971), O. Watkins, *The Puritan Experience* (1972) and P. Caldwell, *The Puritan Conversion Narrative* (1983). For an illuminating discussion of Bunyan's relationship to Calvinism, see R. L. Greaves, *John Bunyan* (1969). On Calvinism in England, see R. T. Kendall, *Calvin and English Calvinism to 1649* (1979).

2. In one of the more iconoclastic readings of Defoe in recent years, Ian Bell, in *Defoe's Fictions* (1985), has strenuously opposed theologically-based interpretations of Defoe's work. For Bell, 'Crusoe's God is . . . a narrative assumption', and the narrative 'cannot, then, be wholly assimilated to the world of spiritual autobiography' (pp. 98, 108). Refreshing though Bell can be on occasion, his overall reading of Defoe is somewhat reductive.

3. Daniel Defoe, *The Life and Strange Surprizing Adventures of Robinson Crusoe*, ed. J. D. Crowley (1972). All subsequent page references given in the text.

4. P. Macherey, *A Theory of Literary Production*, trans. G. Wall (1978), p. 132.

5. See paras 15 and 16, John Bunyan, *Grace Abounding to the Chief of Sinners*, ed. R. Sharrock (1962), p. 8. All subsequent page references given in the text.

6. See N. H. Keeble, *The Literary Culture of Nonconformity in Later Seventeenth-century England* (1987).

7. The line argued by C. Hill in *A Turbulent, Seditious, and Factious People* (1988). Also see A. West, '*The Holy War* and *The Pilgrim's Progress*', *MQ*, 8 (1953), 169–82.

8. See F. Bastian, *Defoe's Early Life* (1981).

9. W. J. Ong, *Ramus, Method, and the Decay of Dialogue* (1958).

10. John Bunyan, *The Pilgrim's Progress*, Parts One and Two, ed. J. B. Wharey, rev. R. Sharrock (1928, 1960), p. 38. All subsequent page references given in the text.

11. John Bunyan, *The Holy War*, eds R. Sharrock and J. F. Forrest (1980), p. 250. All subsequent page references given in the text.

12. John Bunyan, *The Life and Death of Mr Badman*, eds J. F. Forrest and R. Sharrock (1988), p. 17. All subsequent page references given in the text.

13. See *Grace Abounding*, paras 292–3, 320, for example.

14. Quoted by Alan Schneider in *Beckett at 60: A Festschrift*, ed. J. Calder (1967), p. 34. Beckett himself attributes the saying to St Augustine, but its precise source in his *œuvre* remains unclear.

15. N. H. Keeble, 'The way and the ways of Puritan story', *English*, 33 (1984), 209–32 (222).

16. See L. A. Curtis, *The Elusive Daniel Defoe* (1984).

17. Daniel Defoe, *Moll Flanders*, ed. G. A. Starr (1971), p. 287. All subsequent page references given in the text.

18. Daniel Defoe, *A Journal of the Plague Year*, ed. L. A. Landa (1969), p. 12. All subsequent page references given in the text.

19. Arthur Dent, *The Plaine Man's Path-way to Heaven*, facsimile of 1601 London edition (1974), p. 287. All subsequent page references given in the text.

20. Daniel Defoe, *Roxana*, ed. J. Jack (1964), p. 129. All subsequent page references given in the text.

21. Daniel Defoe, *Colonel Jack*, ed. S. Holt Monk (1965), pp. 307–8. All subsequent page references given in the text.

22. V. Ogden Birdsall begins to move towards such a reading of *Crusoe*, when she asks, 'is the form of the spiritual autobiography merely a kind of wishful thinking – a construction within which Crusoe attempts to hide in order to avoid too much exposure?' (*Defoe's Perpetual Seekers* (1985), p. 49).

CHAPTER TWO CALVINISM, PARADOX AND NARRATIVE

1. John Calvin, *Commentaries*, eds Joseph Haroutunian and Louise Pettibone Smith (1958), Introduction, pp. 42–3.
2. Francis M. Higman, *The Style of John Calvin in his French Polemical Treatises* (1967), p. 37.
3. F. Wendel, *Calvin*, trans. P. Mairet (1963), p. 263.
4. Quoted in ibid., p. 265.
5. E. A. Dowey, Jr, *The Knowledge of God in Calvin's Theology* (1952).
6. *Autobiography in Seventeenth-century England*, p. 31. See also A. Simpson, *Puritanism in Old and New England* (1955).
7. John Calvin, *Institutes of the Christian Religion*, I and II, trans. F. L. Battles (1961), II, 926. All subsequent page references given in the text.
8. *Calvin*, pp. 357, 358, 359.
9. *Style of John Calvin*, p. 34.
10. W. J. Bouwsma, *John Calvin: A Sixteenth-century Portrait* (1988), pp. 5, 161.
11. *Calvin*, p. 358.
12. W. Fraser Mitchell, *English Pulpit Oratory from Andrewes to Tillotson* (1932), p. 199. The sermon is by John White (1615).
13. For another example of Calvinism's impact on the sensitive individual see Delany on Norwood (*British Autobiography*, pp. 58–62). Watkins suggests that Norwood's 'life-pattern' strikingly prefigures that of Christian and Crusoe (*Puritan Experience*, p. 71).
14. On Calvin's anxiety see Bouwsma, *John Calvin*, and 'Anxiety and the formation of early modern culture', in *After the Reformation*, ed. B. C. Malament (1980), pp. 215–46.
15. Bunyan's description in *Grace Abounding* of an encounter with a group of these mid-century millenarians brings out their *carte blanche* tendencies quite graphically: 'my Calling lying in the Countrey, I happened to light into several peoples company; who though strict in Religion formerly, yet were also swept away by these Ranters. These would also talk with me of their ways, and condemn me as legal and dark, pretending that they only had attained to perfection that could do what they would and not sin. O these temptations were suitable to my flesh, I being but a young man and my nature in its prime' (p. 17).
16. J. McVeagh, *Tradefull Merchants* (1981), p. 49. Sharrock has observed of *Badman* that, 'though his parable explores some of

the new problems of the market, his heart remains in the simple village economy where the consumer's needs come first' (*John Bunyan* (1968), p. 112). M. McKeon, on the other hand, argues for a sense of economic modernity in Bunyan, whom he sees as a representative of the 'new Christian' capitalism of the period (*The Origins of the English Novel* (1987), pp. 311–12).

17. The most detailed study of Ramus is in Ong, *Ramus, Method*. Useful material on Ramus can also be found in P. Miller, *The New England Mind: From Colony to Province* (1953), and *The New England Mind: The Seventeenth Century* (1954); P. Miller and T. Johnson, eds, *The Puritans* (1938); and E. J. Ashworth, *Language and Logic in the Post-medieval Period* (1974). For editions of Ramus see *The Logike*, facsimile of 1574 Rolland M'Killwein translation (1970), and *Dialectica*, trans. R. F(age), Gent. (1632).

18. Puritanism is being defined as anti-humanist in relation to Renaissance humanism in much the same way that Althusser defines Marxism as anti-humanist in relation to modern bourgeois humanism. See ch. 5 of Althusser's paper 'From *Capital* to Marx's philosophy', in L. Althusser and E. Balibar, *Reading Capital*, trans. B. Brewster (1972).

19. Miller and Johnson have remarked that, for Ramus, 'thinking was not conceived as a method by which we compose our knowledge discovery by discovery, but as the unveiling of an ideal form' (*The Puritans*, p. 32).

20. Ibid., p. 30.

21. *Ramus, Method*, p. 7.

22. *Language and Logic*, p. 16.

23. *Ramus, Method*, pp. 63, 166.

24. Ong differentiates carefully between 'arts' scholasticism and 'theological' scholasticism: 'Although scholastic theology enjoyed a theoretical priority of dignity over other forms of scholasticism, as soon as one descends from the realm of theoretical relations into the real university theater where Ramism and other movements and countermovements took form, theology pales into insignificance behind the scholasticism of the arts course' (*Ramus, Method*, p. 132).

25. Quoted in ibid., p. 245.

26. Ibid., p. 225.

27. *New England Mind: The Seventeenth Century*, p. 125.

28. Quoted in *Ramus, Method*, p. 249 (Ong's translation).

29. 'Argument' is not the most precise of terms in the Ramist lexicon; as Miller notes, 'by the term "argument" Ramus

intended any word by which things are understood or represented in speech, any concept, any counter employed in
thinking' (*New England Mind: The Seventeenth Century*, p. 124).

30. *New England Mind: From Colony to Province*, p. 72.
31. *New England Mind: The Seventeenth Century*, p. 132.
32. *Ramus, Method*, p. 192.
33. *Language and Logic*, p. 16.
34. Quoted in *New England Mind: The Seventeenth Century*, p. 120.
35. Ibid., p. 136.
36. For more detailed treatment see J. B. Wharey, *A Study of the
Sources of Bunyan's Allegories* (1904), and M. Hussey, 'Arthur
Dent's *Plaine Man's Path-way to Heaven*', *MLR*, 44 (1949), 26–34.
37. J. B. Wharey, 'Bunyan's *Mr Badman*', *MLN*, 36 (1921), 65–79
(p. 65); L. B. Wright, *Middle Class Culture in Elizabethan England*
(1935), p. 253; Sacvan Bercovitch, *The Puritan Origins of the
American Self* (1975), p. 13.
38. H. Davies, *Worship and Theology in England*, I–V (1961–75), p. 56.
39. Arthur Dent, *The Opening of Heaven Gates* (1617), p. 43.
40. See W. Haller, *The Rise of Puritanism* (1938) on Puritan modes of
behaviour. For a sceptical view about standard conceptions of
Puritanism, see M. G. Finlayson, *Historians, Puritanism, and the
English Revolution* (1983).
41. M. Hussey, 'Christian conduct in Bunyan and Baxter', *BQ*, 14
(1951), 75–83 (p. 75).
42. Dent, *Heaven Gates*, p. 35.

CHAPTER THREE   PARADOX AND PROGRESS I:
The Pilgrim's Progress

1. See particularly *Literary Culture* and *Turbulent, Seditious*.
McKeon too finds subversive import in a text which 'recapitu-
lates the rise of the new gentility of early modern England'
(*Origins of the English Novel*, p. 311).
2. Wharey argues for Patrick as an influence on Bunyan in *Bunyan's
Allegories*; more recently P. Salzman, in *English Prose Fiction
1558–1700: A Critical History* (1985) has argued the opposite
view: '*Parable . . .* has never been a strong contender as a source
of Bunyan's allegory' (p. 241).
3. Quoted in J. Sutherland, *English Literature of the Late Seventeenth
Century* (1969), p. 301.
4. *Origins of the English Novel*, pp. 311–12.

5. S. Patrick, *The Parable of the Pilgrim* (1668), p. 2. All subsequent page references given in the text.
6. R. H. Tawney, *Religion and the Rise of Capitalism* (1926), p. 229.
7. The growth of individualism in the seventeenth century is covered in M. Bottrall, *Every Man a Phoenix: Studies in Seventeenth-century Autobiography* (1958), and J. Webber, *The Eloquent 'I': Style and Self in Seventeenth-century Prose* (1968).
8. *English Literature of the Late Seventeenth Century*, p. 332.
9. Brian Nellist makes a similar point, though without the Ramist reference, when he notes that in *Pilgrim's Progress*, 'Knowledge means submission to a succession of antitheses, always formulated in a fresh series, so that nothing can ever be predicted' ('*The Pilgrim's Progress* and allegory', in *The Pilgrim's Progress: Critical and Historical Views*, ed. V. Newey (1980), pp. 132–53 (p. 147)).
10. *English Literature of the Late Seventeenth Century*, p. 208.
11. When Salzman complains of a narrative 'overwhelmed by Patrick's didactic impulse' (*English Prose Fiction*, p. 242) he misses the point that this is precisely how Patrick, and Bunyan too for that matter, conceived of narrative form. This is yet another case of the ideology of form not being properly attended to by commentators.
12. J. A. Froude, *John Bunyan* (1880), p. 25.
13. H. Talon, *John Bunyan: The Man and his Works*, trans. B. Wall (1951), p. 57.
14. G. Rupp, *Six Makers of English Religion, 1500–1700* (1957), p. 90.
15. S. Fish would disagree over goal-directedness, and in *Self-consuming Artifacts* (1972) dubs the text 'antiprogressive' (p. 229). Fish's reading of *Pilgrim's Progress* is interesting in that he identifies the presence of paradox in the work, but disappointing in that he fails to see paradox's dynamic and self-realising possibilities. When he complains that the narrative works 'to subvert the confidence of pilgrim and reader alike' (p. 229), he is not taking into account that this is a requirement laid on the author by Calvinist soteriology. For an anti-Fish reading see J. R. Knott, Jr, 'Bunyan's gospel day: a reading of *The Pilgrim's Progress*, *ELR*, 3 (1973), 443–61.
16. V. Newey, 'Bunyan and the confines of the mind', in *Critical and Historical Views*, pp. 21–48 (p. 44). Keeble is one of the few critics to stress the doctrinal side of the work, and argues that we are unjustified in detaching this from its aesthetic side (see '*The Pilgrim's Progress*: a Puritan fiction', *BQ*, 27 (1980), 321–36).
17. Nussbaum notes a similar pattern in Bunyan's spiritual

autobiography, arguing that 'a subversive element creeps into *Grace Abounding* as the personal text replaces the scriptural one'. For Nussbaum, 'the very idea of salvation seems to hold within it both the promise and the threat of the loss of identity' ('"By these words I was sustained": Bunyan's *Grace Abounding*', *ELH*, 49 (1982), 18–34 (p. 22)). Newey too sees a dramatic conflict between 'self-affirmation and self-abnegation' lying at the heart of spiritual autobiography ('"With the eyes of my understanding": Bunyan, experience, and acts of interpretation', in *John Bunyan: Conventicle and Parnassus*, ed. N. H. Keeble (1988), pp. 189–216 (p. 207)).

18. M. E. Harding, *Journey into Self* (1956), p. 85.
19. U. M. Kaufmann, *The Pilgrim's Progress and Traditions in Puritan Meditation* (1966), p. 107. Wolfgang Iser too finds a sense of tension in a narrative in which 'the theological withholding of certitude stimulates human self-assertion' (*The Implied Reader: Patterns of Communication in Prose Fiction from Bunyan to Beckett* (1974), p. 24).
20. *Literary Culture*, p. 239.
21. R. Baxter, *The Saints Everlasting Rest*, 4th ed (1653), p. 217.
22. If 'Good Will' is acceptable, 'Free Will' never is: 'I am not a free-willer, I do abhor it', as Bunyan exclaims elsewhere ('Mr Bunyan's Last Sermon', in *The Works of John Bunyan*, I–III, ed. G. Offor (1860–2), II, p. 756).
23. For a recent interesting treatment of the subversive potential of marginal glosses in Bunyan, see V. Cunningham, 'Glossing and glozing: Bunyan's allegory', in *Conventicle and Parnassus*, pp. 217–40.
24. D. Seed, 'Dialogue and debate in *The Pilgrim's Progress*', in *Critical and Historical Views*, pp. 69–90 (p. 81).
25. J. Royce, 'The case of John Bunyan', *PR*, 1 (1894), 22–33, 134–51, 230–40 (p. 143).
26. *Bunyan's Allegories*, p. 97.
27. *John Bunyan*, p. 72.
28. M. Weber, *The Protestant Ethic and the Spirit of Capitalism*, trans. T. Parsons (1930), pp. 110–11.
29. *John Bunyan*, p. 141.
30. N. H. Keeble, 'The unity of *The Pilgrim's Progress*', in *Critical and Historical Views*, pp. 1–20.
31. For a feminist reading of Bunyan's treatment of women, see M. Olofson Thickstun, 'From Christiana to Steadfast: subsuming the feminine in *The Pilgrim's Progress*', *SEL*, 26 (1986), 439–53.

32. *The Man and his Works*, p. 111.
33. John Bunyan, *The Miscellaneous Works of John Bunyan*, IX, ed. R. L. Greaves (1981), p. 74.
34. *Origins of the English Novel*, p. 194. As Nussbaum notes of *Grace Abounding*, 'Bunyan disobeys God within the autobiography, but he disobeys within the limits of authority' ('Bunyan's *Grace Abounding*', p. 21). On the outside/inside distinction in *Pilgrim's Progress*, and its soteriological significance, see J. Turner, 'Bunyan's sense of place', in *Critical and Historical Views*, pp. 91–110.

CHAPTER FOUR PARADOX AND PROGRESS II:
The Life and Death of Mr Badman

1. E. Venables, *Life of John Bunyan* (1888), p. 190; *John Bunyan*, p. 110; *English Literature of the Late Seventeenth Century*, p. 335.
2. Sharrock has recently returned to the text in '*The Life and Death of Mr Badman*: facts and problems', *MLR*, 82 (1987), 15–29; but despite an interesting comparison between it and Conrad's *Heart of Darkness*, he still finds *Badman* very problematical.
3. See Keeble, *Literary Culture*.
4. *The Man and his Works*, p. 235.
5. As D. J. O'Connor has pointed out in *Free Will* (1971), 'the determinist seems to be in a slightly stronger position. What he needs to prove his case is more evidence of the same kind that he has already . . . What his opponent needs is a radically new insight into the difficulties of the problem' (p. 121). While conceding the claims of the determinist position, O'Connor opts for freedom as a matter of degree. So too does Jennifer Trusted in *Free Will and Responsibility* (1984), although her overall argument is more strongly pro-libertarian.
6. Quoting O'Connor again: 'it is extraordinarily difficult to put forward an argument for or against free will without covertly begging the question against the other side. This is because the libertarian and the determinist have world views that are utterly opposed to each other and offer little in the way of common ground that can serve as mutually acceptable premises for the controversy . . . Neither can afford to make the smallest concession without rendering his own position covertly inconsistent' (*Free Will*, pp. 122–3). The argument can become sharply political. It is a standard critique of Marxism, for example, that

it is determinist and therefore involves a denial of individual freedom.

7. *John Bunyan*, pp. 106–7.
8. 'Bunyan's *Mr Badman*', p. 79.
9. *Traditions in Puritan Meditation*, p. 28.
10. The diagrammatic schemas that Puritan theologians were so fond of devising are meant to function in just this way, with particular events being read off against an overall pattern. Notable examples can be found in Perkins, *The Golden Chain*, and Bunyan, *A Mapp Shewing the Order and Causes of Salvation and Damnation*.
11. For an early example of this practice in Bunyan, see *A Few Sighs from Hell*, particularly 'The Exposition' (*Miscellaneous Works*, I, eds. T. L. Underwood and R. Sharrock (1980)).
12. Bunyan has been variously described as supra- and infralapsarian. On the former, see Campbell, 'Fishing in other men's waters: Bunyan and the theologians', in *Conventicle and Parnassus*, pp. 137–51 (p. 147); on the latter, see Greaves, *John Bunyan*, p. 52. In psychological terms there seems little to choose between the positions.
13. U. M. Kaufmann, 'Spiritual discerning: Bunyan and the mysteries of the divine will', in *Conventicle and Parnassus*, pp. 171–87 (p. 184).
14. See also *A Treatise of the Fear of God*: 'when thou art dying, thou shalt not know whither thou art going, to wit, whether to Heaven or Hell' (*Miscellaneous Works*, IX, 455).

CHAPTER FIVE   SELF UNDER SIEGE: *The Holy War*

1. *John Bunyan*, p. 95. More recently Keeble, who is particularly attuned to the conflict element in the nonconformist literature of this period, has referred approvingly to the 'Miltonic balance' of *Holy War* (*Literary Culture*, p. 173). E. M. W. Tillyard too has admired the work's epic sweep, in *The English Epic and its Background* (1954). For a dissenting view, see J. B. Wharey, 'Bunyan's *Holy War* and the conflict-type of morality play', *MLN*, 34 (1919), 65–73, where the argument is that *Holy War*'s theme is that 'of a typical morality play rather than that of Milton's two great epics in one' (pp. 65–6).
2. *The Man and his Works*, p. 254. Echoes of Talon's view can be found in what is probably the most sympathetic reading of *Holy*

War in recent years, where it is described as a 'long, and possibly overloaded allegory' (E. B. Batson, *John Bunyan, Allegory and Imagination* (1984)). Even the editors of the new OUP edition cannot help complaining that, for all its 'human variety', *Holy War* lacks *Pilgrim's Progress*'s 'mythic power' (p. xxxv).

3. '*The Holy War* and *The Pilgrim's Progress*', p. 175. Tindall stresses the ideological significance of *Holy War* in ch. 7 of *Mechanick Preacher*, arguing for the work as a subtly-wrought political allegory in which Diabolus equals Charles II, and Mr Filth Sir Roger L'Estrange. In a more recent article M. Mullett has dubbed *Holy War* 'a Puritan Absalom and Achitophel' ('The internal politics of Bedford, 1660–1688', *PBHRS*, 59 (1980), 1–42, p. 35). Greaves too stresses the work's political dimension in 'John Bunyan's *Holy War* and London Nonconformity', *BQ*, 26 (1975), 158–68.

4. *Mechanick Preacher*, p. 148; *John Bunyan*, p. 136.

5. *Turbulent, Seditious*, p. 249.

6. *Literary Culture*, p. 143.

7. Hill argues that what looks like knowledge of Milton in Bunyan's work may have been derived from Benjamin Keach's *War with the Devil* (*Turbulent, Seditious*, p. 142).

8. See Wharey, 'Bunyan's *Holy War*', p. 66.

9. Friedrich Nietzsche, *Thus Spake Zarathustra*, trans. R. J. Hollingdale (1961), pp. 178–9.

10. Eugene Ionesco, *Plays*, I, trans. D. Watson (1958), p. 119.

11. *Literary Culture*, p. 206.

12. *John Bunyan*, pp. 143–4, 149, 150.

13. Jean-Jacques Rousseau, *The Social Contract and Discourses*, trans. G. D. H. Cole (1913), rev. J. H. Brumfitt and J. C. Hall (1973). With his Genevan background, Rousseau would no doubt be well versed in the paradoxes of Calvinism.

14. *Rise of Puritanism*, p. 37.

15. C. E. Dugdale, 'Bunyan's court scenes', *TSE*, 21 (1941), 64–78 (pp. 64, 74, 77).

16. Seen in such cases as the Star Chamber's punishment of Prynne, Bastwick and Burton in the 1630s.

17. See Jean-Paul Sartre, *Being and Nothingness*, trans. H. E. Barnes (1958), pp. 32, 35, 39–40 especially.

18. See R. Sharrock, 'The trial of vices in Puritan fiction', *BQ*, 14 (1951), 3–12.

19. Greaves sees the ending as articulating a non-militant 'spiritual millenarianism' that 'symbolised the increasing accommodation

of Nonconformity to the post-Restoration world' ('*Holy War and London Nonconformity*', p. 166).
20. *Turbulent, Seditious*, p. 241.

CHAPTER SIX   THE ISOLATED SELF:
Robinson Crusoe and *A Journal of the Plague Year*

1. Defoe 'refused to commit himself to a rigid doctrine of predestination' (M. E. Novak, *Defoe and the Nature of Man* (1963), p. 13); R. G. Landon has defined Defoe's outlook as 'Calvinstic theology tempered with the rationalism of Locke and the use of "natural law"' (Introduction to Daniel Defoe, *The History of the Devil* (1972), pp. viii–ix).
2. *Origins of the English Novel*, p. 332.
3. McKeon makes some broadly similar points when he refers to the presence of 'dialectical reversals' in *Crusoe*: 'the dominant, progressive ideology of the narrative, whose account of virtue delivered from early sin and then amply confirmed by the trials and rewards of providence is threatened repeatedly by the never articulated insight that virtue is nothing but the ability to invoke providence with conviction' (*Origins of the English Novel*, p. 337).
4. See particularly Starr, *Defoe and Spiritual Autobiography*, and *Defoe and Casuistry* (1971); Novak, *Defoe and the Nature of Man* and *Economics and the Fiction of Daniel Defoe* (1962); Hunter, *Reluctant Pilgrim*; for Defoe and popular literature, see Bell, *Defoe's Fictions*; Lennard J. Davis *Factual Fictions: The Origins of the English Novel*, places Defoe within a tradition of 'news discourse'; Pat Rogers, *Robinson Crusoe*, offers a useful survey of the major literary and cultural traditions on which Defoe was drawing.
5. E. Zimmerman, *Defoe and the Novel* (1975), p. 17.
6. Maccy, *Money and the Novel* (1983), p. 45. For Green (*Dreams of Adventure, Deeds of Empire* (1979)) Crusoe's socio-economic development illustrates the growth of imperialism. On Defoe and the imperialist ethic, also see Rogers, *Robinson Crusoe*, and McVeagh, *Tradefull Merchants*.
7. *Literary Production*, p. 132.
8. *Defoe and Spiritual Autobiography*, p. 15.
9. C. B. Macpherson, *The Political Theory of Possessive Individualism* (1962). Watt's view of Crusoe in *The Rise of the Novel* (1957) is similarly biased towards his economic individualism.

10. *Defoe and Spiritual Autobiography*, p. 18.
11. As J. J. Richetti argues in *Defoe's Narratives: Situations and Structures* (1975), p. 53.
12. *Defoe and the Novel*, p. 32.
13. C. Gildon, *The Life and Strange Surprizing Adventures of Mr D . . . De F . . ., of London, Hosier* (1719), p. viii.
14. 'Thus the Grass my Horse has bit: the Turfs my Servant has cut; and the Ore I have digg'd in any place where I have a right to them in common with others, become my *Property*, without the assignation or consent of any body' (J. Locke, *Two Treatises of Government*, ed. P. Laslett (1963), p. 330). For an anti-Lockean reading of *Crusoe* see M. Schonhorn, 'Defoe: the literature of politics and the politics of literature', in *English Literature in the Age of Disguise*, ed. M. E. Novak (1977), pp. 15–56.
15. Rogers, *Robinson Crusoe*, p. 76.
16. C. Gildon, *The Life and Strange Surprizing Adventures*, p. viii. In a more modern formulation, Crusoe becomes a perpetually 'restless seeker' (Birdsall, *Perpetual Seekers*, p. 47).
17. H. O. Brown sees Roquentin as one of Crusoe's 'heirs' ('The displaced self in the novels of Daniel Defoe', *ELH*, 38 (1971), 562–90 (p. 585)).
18. See M. Heidegger, *Being and Time*, trans. J. Macquarrie and E. Robinson, (1962), pp. 226–7.
19. *Perpetual Seekers*, p. 173.
20. M. E. Novak, 'Crusoe the king and the political evolution of his island', *SEL*, 2 (1962), 337–50 (p. 340).
21. Karl Marx, *Capital*, trans. E. and C. Paul (1930, rev. 1972), p. 252.
22. G. M. Sill, *Defoe and the Idea of Fiction* (1983), p. 169.
23. *Defoe's Fictions*, p. 109.
24. P. R. Backscheider, *A Being More Intense: A Study of the Prose Works of Bunyan, Swift, and Defoe* (1984), p. 177.
25. J. Preston, *The Created Self* (1970). Iser makes a similar point in *The Implied Reader* (1974).
26. *Elusive Daniel Defoe*, p. 72.
27. The issue of the morality of flight was a traditional one in plague literature. See L. A. Landa, Introduction to *Journal of the Plague Year*, pp. xxix–xxxiii, for a brief discussion of this literature.
28. *Elusive Daniel Defoe*, p. 72.
29. In an interesting reading, Rogers updates the metaphor of 'National Infection' to 1720 and the South Sea Bubble episode (*Eighteenth-century Encounters* (1985), pp. 164–6).

30. *Defoe and Casuistry*, p. 56.
31. Ibid., p. 54.

CHAPTER SEVEN WOMEN AND PARADOX: *Moll Flanders* and *Roxana*

1. *Defoe and the Novel*, p. 99.
2. B. Dijkstra, *Defoe and Economics* (1987).
3. G. Lukács, *The History of Class Consciousness*,, trans. R. Livingstone (1971), p. 86. For a Marxist reading of Defoe see A. West, *The Mountain in the Sunlight* (1958), pp. 59–109.
4. *Defoe and Spiritual Autobiography*, p. 157.
5. *Defoe and Casuistry*, p. 112. Richetti makes a similar point: 'As her experiences proceed, we are asked to admire her skill at disguise and escape rather than at crime itself' (*Defoe's Narratives*, p. 130). Perhaps it is a case, as it was with that earlier Puritan prose fiction writer Richard Bernard, of '*I tax the Vice, and not, any mans person*' (*The Isle of Man*, 4th edn (1627), author's preface). Taxing the vice and not the person was something that Bunyan, the more thoroughgoing Calvinist, would certainly not have countenanced.
6. Neither Bell, *Defoe's Fictions*, nor Curtis, *Elusive Daniel Defoe*, are particularly convinced by Moll's conversion. Elliott contends that 'Moll's repentances . . . are skin deep' (*Twentieth Century Interpretations of Moll Flanders*, ed. R. C. Elliott (1970) p. 5). For McKillop, *The Early Masters of English Fiction* (1956), Moll is an essentially crafty character with little religious sense. Van Ghent describes Moll's world as one 'astonishingly without spiritual dimension' (*The English Novel: Form and Function* (1953), p. 34), but leaves it open as to whether Defoe intends this as an ironical comment against the character.
7. S. Mason, *Daniel Defoe and the Status of Women* (1978), p. 18.
8. T. Hardy, *Tess of the D'Urbervilles*, ed. P. N. Furbank (1974), p. 57.
9. P. Borsay, 'The English urban renaissance: the development of provincial urban culture. c. 1680–1780', *SH*, 5 (1977), 581–603 (p. 595).
10. Patricia Meyer Spacks, *Imagining a Self: Autobiography and Novel in Eighteenth-century England* (1976), p. 60.
11. *Status of Women*, p. 53.
12. Mason points out that such discrepancies are not unusual in

Defoe's work: If Defoe really did not mean for women to be free and self-sufficient but dependent upon men, as he advocates in "An Academy for Women", his fiction contradicts his theory' (ibid., p. 118).

13. See R. A. Donovan, *The Shaping Vision: Imagination in the English Novel from Defoe to Dickens* (1966), for example. Koonce also refers to Moll's 'conveniently underdeveloped, sense of morality' ('Moll's muddle: Defoe's use of irony in *Moll Flanders*', *ELH*, 30 (1963), 377–94 (p. 380)). Edwards ponders the possibility that 'an explosion of Christian values might be among Defoe's purposes in writing *Moll Flanders*' ('Between the real and the moral: problems in the structure of *Moll Flanders*', in *Twentieth Century Interpretations*, pp. 95–107 (p. 96)).

14. The most positive reading of *Roxana* is probably Richetti's in *Defoe's Narratives*, in which the text is seen to reveal the power that self feels the need to exert over other in a bourgeois society. More recently Birdsall, *Perpetual Seekers*, Bell, *Defoe's Fictions*, and Backscheider, *Being More Intense* and *Daniel Defoe: Ambition and Innovation* (1986), have all shown themselves sympathetic to the text and the power of its ending.

15. 'The displaced self', p. 582; Dobrée, *English Literature in the Early Eighteenth Century* (1959), p. 425; *Defoe and Casuistry*, p. 166; *Defoe and Spiritual Autobiography*, p. 182; *Defoe and the Novel*, p. 181; Sutherland, *Daniel Defoe: A Critical Study* (1971), p. 206; Shinagel, *Daniel Defoe and Middle-Class Gentility* (1968), p. 193; *Early Masters*, p. 38.

16. *Being More Intense*, p. 129. Backscheider elsewhere makes the interesting suggestion that Defoe projects male fears about women on to Roxana – which may help to explain the unease displayed by so many male critics about her character (*Daniel Defoe*, pp. 208–11).

17. M. E. Novak, *Eighteenth–century English Literature* (1983), p. 63.

CHAPTER EIGHT   CONCLUSION

1. *Free Will and Responsibility*, p. 78.
2. His position being, as Richard Rorty has complained is a tendency of the absolutist outlook, that his particular discourse 'gives us a species of true sentence which is not *just* a true sentence, but rather a piece of Truth itself' (*Consequences of Pragmatism* (1982), p. xix). Calvinist logocentricity certainly

functions on just such a principle, hence that inclination noted by Higman to feel that logical contradiction is dissolved by mere exposure to appropriate scriptural texts.

3. *Free Will and Responsibility*, p. 166.
4. *Free Will*, p. 123.
5. 'We have undertaken to create a literature of extreme situations', as Sartre declared in *What is Literature?*, trans. Bernard Frechtman (1967), p. 164.

BIBLIOGRAPHY

PRIMARY SOURCES

Baxter, Richard, *The Saints Everlasting Rest*, 4th edn (London, 1653).

Bernard, Richard, *The Isle of Man*, 4th edn (London, 1627).

Bunyan, John, *Grace Abounding to the Chief of Sinners*, ed. Roger Sharrock (Oxford: Clarendon Press, 1962).

Bunyan, John, *The Holy War*, ed. Roger Sharrock and James F. Forrest (Oxford: Clarendon Press, 1980).

Bunyan, John, *The Life and Death of Mr Badman*, ed. James F. Forrest and Roger Sharrock (Oxford: Clarendon Press, 1988).

Bunyan, John, *The Miscellaneous Works of John Bunyan*, I, ed. T. L. Underwood and Roger Sharrock (Oxford: Clarendon Press, 1980).

Bunyan, John, *The Miscellaneous Works of John Bunyan*, IX, ed. Richard L. Greaves (Oxford: Clarendon Press, 1981).

Bunyan, John, *The Pilgrim's Progress*, Parts One and Two, ed. J. B. Wharey, rev. Roger Sharrock (Oxford: Clarendon Press, 1928, 1960).

Bunyan, John, *The Works of John Bunyan*, I–III, ed. George Offor (London, 1860–2).

Calvin, John, *Commentaries*, ed. Joseph Haroutunian and Louise Pettibone Smith (London: SCM Press; Philadelphia: Westminster Press, 1958).

Calvin, John, *Institutes of the Christian Religion*, I–II, trans. Ford Lewis Battles (London: SCM Press; Philadelphia: Westminster Press, 1961).

Defoe, Daniel, *Captain Singleton*, ed. Shiv K. Kumar (London: Oxford University Press, 1969).

Defoe, Daniel, *Colonel Jack*, ed. Samuel Holt Monk (London: Oxford University Press, 1965).

Defoe, Daniel, *The Farther Adventures of Robinson Crusoe* (Oxford: Shakespeare Head Press, 1927).

Defoe, Daniel, *The History of the Devil* (Totowa, NJ: Rowman & Littlefield, 1972).

Defoe, Daniel, *A Journal of the Plague Year*, ed. Louis A. Landa (London: Oxford University Press, 1969).

Defoe, Daniel, *The Life and Strange Surprizing Adventures of Robinson Crusoe*, ed. J. Donald Crowley (London: Oxford University Press, 1972).

Defoe, Daniel, *Moll Flanders*, ed. G. A. Starr (London: Oxford University Press, 1971).

Defoe, Daniel, *Roxana*, ed. Jane Jack (London: Oxford University Press, 1964).

Dent, Arthur, *The Opening of Heaven Gates* (London, 1617).

Dent, Arthur, *The Plaine Man's Path-Way to Heaven* (Amsterdam: Theatrum Orbis Terrarum; Norwood NJ: Walter J. Johnson, 1974).

Gildon, Charles, *The Life and Strange Surprizing Adventures of Mr D . . . De F . . ., of London, Hosier* (London, 1719).

Hardy, Thomas, *Tess of the D'Urbervilles*, ed. P. N. Furbank (London: Macmillan, 1974).

Heidegger, Martin, *Being and Time*, trans. John Macquarrie and Edward Robinson (London: SCM Press; New York: Harper, 1962).

Ionesco, Eugene, *Plays*, I, trans. Donald Watson (London: John Calder, 1958).

Locke, John, *Two Treatises of Government*, ed. Peter Laslett (Cambridge: Cambridge University Press, 1963).

Lukács, Georg, *The History of Class Consciousness*, trans. Rodney Livingstone (London: Merlin Press; Cambridge, Mass.: MIT Press, 1971).

Macherey, Pierre, *A Theory of Literary Production*, trans. Geoffrey Wall (London: Routledge & Kegan Paul, 1978).

Marx, Karl, *Capital*, trans. Eden and Cedar Paul (London: Dent; New York: Dutton, 1930, rev. 1972).

Nietzsche, Friedrich, *Thus Spake Zarathustra*, trans. R. J. Hollingdale (Harmondsworth: Penguin, 1961).

O'Connor, D. J., *Free Will* (London: Macmillan; Garden City, NY: Anchor Books, 1971).

Patrick, Simon, *The Parable of the Pilgrim* (London, 1668).

Ramus, Petrus, *Dialectica*, trans. R. F(age), Gent. (London, 1632).

Ramus, Petrus, *The Logike* (Menston: Scolar Press, 1970).

Rorty, Richard, *Consequences of Pragmatism* (Hemel Hempstead: Harvester Wheatsheaf; Minneapolis: University of Minnesota Press, 1982).

Rousseau, Jean-Jacques, *The Social Contract and Discourses*, trans. G. D. H. Cole, rev. J. H. Brumfitt and J. C. Hall (London: Dent, 1913, 1973).

Sartre, Jean-Paul, *Being and Nothingness*, trans. Hazel E. Barnes (London: Methuen; New York: Philosophical Library, 1958).

Sartre, Jean-Paul, *What is Literature?*, trans. Bernard Frechtman (London: Methuen, 1967; New York: Harper & Row, 1965).

Trusted, Jennifer, *Free Will and Responsibility* (Oxford: Oxford University Press, 1984).

Weber, Max, *The Protestant Ethic and the Spirit of Capitalism*, trans. Talcott Parsons (London: George Allen & Unwin, 1930; New York: Scribner, 1958).

SECONDARY SOURCES

Althusser, Louis and Etienne Balibar, *Reading Capital*, trans. Ben Brewster (London: NLB, 1972; New York: Pantheon, 1971).

Ashworth, E. J., *Language and Logic in the Post-medieval Period* (Dordrecht: D. Reidel, 1974).

Backscheider, Paula R., *A Being More Intense: A Study of the Prose Works of Bunyan, Swift and Defoe* (New York: AMS Press, 1984).

Backscheider, Paula R., *Daniel Defoe: Ambition and Innovation* (Lexington: University Press of Kentucky, 1986).

Bastian, F., *Defoe's Early Life* (London: Macmillan, 1981).

Batson, E. Beatrice, *John Bunyan, Allegory and Imagination* (London: Croom Helm; Totowa, NJ: Barnes & Noble, 1984).

Bell, Ian A., *Defoe's Fictions* (London: Croom Helm; Totowa, NJ: Barnes & Noble, 1985).

Bercovitch, Sacvan, *The Puritan Origins of the American Self* (New Haven: Yale University Press, 1975).

Birdsall, Virginia Ogden, *Defoe's Perpetual Seekers* (Cranbury, NJ: Associated University Presses, 1985).

Bottrall, Margaret, *Every Man a Phoenix: Studies in Seventeenth-century Autobiography* (London: John Murray, 1958; Freeport, NY: Books for Libraries Press, 1972).

Bouwsma, William J., *John Calvin: A Sixteenth-century Portrait* (Oxford: Oxford University Press, 1988).

Calder, John, ed., *Beckett at 60: A Festschrift* (London: Calder & Boyars, 1967).

Caldwell, Patricia, *The Puritan Conversion Narrative* (Cambridge: Cambridge University Press, 1983).

Curtis, Laura A., *The Elusive Daniel Defoe* (London: Vision; Totowa, NJ: Barnes & Noble, 1984).

Davies, Horton, *Worship and Theology in England*, i–v (London: Oxford University Press; Princeton, NJ: Princeton University Press, 1961–75).

Davis, Lennard, J., *Factual Fictions: The Origins of the English Novel* (New York: Columbia University Press, 1983).

Delany, Paul, *British Autobiography in the Seventeenth Century* (London: Routledge & Kegan Paul; New York: Columbia University Press, 1969).

Dijkstra, Bram, *Defoe and Economics* (London: Macmillan; New York: St Martin's Press, 1987).

Dobrée, Bonamy, *English Literature in the Early Eighteenth Century* (Oxford: Clarendon Press, 1959).

Donovan, Robert Alan, *The Shaping Vision: Imagination in the English Novel from Defoe to Dickens* (Ithaca, NY: Cornell University Press, 1966).

Dowey, Edward A., *The Knowledge of God in Calvin's Theology* (New York: Columbia University Press, 1952).

Ebner, Dean, *Autobiography in Seventeenth-century England* (The Hague: Mouton, 1971).

Elliott, Robert C., ed., *Twentieth-century Interpretations of Moll Flanders* (Englewood Cliffs, NJ: Prentice Hall, 1970).

Finlayson, Michael G., *Historians, Puritanism and the English Revolution* (Toronto: University of Toronto Press, 1983).

Fish, Stanley, *Self-consuming Artifacts* (Berkeley: University of California Press, 1972).

Froude, J. A., *John Bunyan* (London: Macmillan, 1880).

Greaves, Richard L., *John Bunyan* (Abingdon: Sutton Courtenay Press; Grand Rapids: Eerdmans, 1969).

Green, Martin, *Dreams of Adventure, Deeds of Empire* (New York: Basic Books, 1979; London: Routledge & Kegan Paul, 1980).

Haller, William, *The Rise of Puritanism* (New York: Columbia University Press, 1938).

Harding, Mary Esther, *Journey into Self* (New York: Longmans, Green, 1956; London: Vision Press, 1958).

Higman, Francis M., *The Style of John Calvin in his French Polemical Treatises* (London: Oxford University Press, 1967).

Hill, Christopher, *A Turbulent, Seditious, and Factious People* (Oxford: Clarendon Press, 1988).

Hunter, J. Paul, *The Reluctant Pilgrim* (Baltimore: Johns Hopkins University Press, 1966).

Iser, Wolfgang, *The Implied Reader: Patterns of Communication in Prose Fiction from Bunyan to Beckett* (Baltimore: Johns Hopkins University Press, 1974).

Kaufmann, U. Milo, *The Pilgrim's Progress and Traditions in Puritan Meditation* (New Haven: Yale University Press, 1966).

Keeble, N. H., ed., *John Bunyan: Conventicle and Parnassus* (Oxford: Clarendon Press, 1988).

Keeble, N. H., *The Literary Culture of Nonconformity in Later Seventeenth-century England* (Leicester: Leicester University Press; Athens, Ga.: University of Georgia Press, 1987).

Kendall, R. T., *Calvin and English Calvinism to 1649* (Oxford: Oxford University Press, 1979).

Macey, Samuel L., *Money and the Novel* (Victoria, BC: Sono Nis Press, 1983).

McKeon, Michael, *The Origins of the English Novel, 1600–1740* (Baltimore: Johns Hopkins University Press, 1987).

McKillop, A. D., *The Early Masters of English Fiction* (Lawrence: University of Kansas Press, 1956; London: Constable, 1962).

Macpherson, C. B., *The Political Theory of Possessive Individualism* (London: Oxford University Press, 1962).

McVeagh, John, *Tradefull Merchants: The Portrayal of the Capitalist in Literature* (London: Routledge & Kegan Paul, 1981).

Malament, Barbara C., ed., *After the Reformation: Essays in Honor of J. H. Hexter* (Manchester: Manchester University Press; Philadelphia: University of Pennsylvania Press, 1980).

Mason, Shirlene, *Daniel Defoe and the Status of Women* (St Albans, Vt.: Eden Press, 1978).

Miller, Perry, *The New England Mind: From Colony to Province* (Cambridge, Mass.: Harvard University Press, 1953).

Miller, Perry, *The New England Mind: The Seventeenth Century* (Cambridge, Mass.: Harvard University Press, 1954).

Miller, Perry and Thomas H. Johnson, eds, *The Puritans* (New York: American Book Co., 1938).

Mitchell, W. Fraser, *English Pulpit Oratory from Andrewes to Tillotson* (London: SPCK, 1932; New York: Russell & Russell, 1962).

Newey, Vincent, ed., *The Pilgrim's Progress: Critical and Historical*

Views (Liverpool: Liverpool University Press; Totowa, NJ: Barnes & Noble, 1980).

Novak, M. E., *Defoe and the Nature of Man* (London: Oxford University Press, 1963);.

Novak, M. E., *Economics and the Fiction of Daniel Defoe* (Berkeley: University of California Press, 1962).

Novak, M. E., *Eighteenth-century English Literature* (London: Macmillan, 1983).

Novak, M. E., ed., *English Literature in the Age of Disguise* (Berkeley: University of California Press, 1977).

Ong, Walter J., *Ramus, Method, and the Decay of Dialogue* (Cambridge, Mass.: Harvard University Press, 1958).

Preston, John, *The Created Self: The Reader's Role in Eighteenth-century Fiction* (London: Heinemann; New York: Barnes & Noble, 1970).

Richetti, John J., *Defoe's Narratives: Situations and Structures* (Oxford: Clarendon Press, 1975).

Rogers, Pat, *Eighteenth-century Encounters: Studies in Literature and Society in the Age of Walpole* (Brighton: Harvester; Totowa, NJ: Barnes & Noble, 1985).

Rogers, Pat, *Robinson Crusoe* (London: George Allen & Unwin, 1979).

Rupp, Gordon, *Six Makers of English Religion, 1500–1700* (London: Hodder & Stoughton; New York: Harper, 1957).

Salzman, Paul, *English Prose Fiction 1558–1700: A Critical History* (Oxford: Clarendon Press, 1985).

Sharrock, Roger, *John Bunyan* (London: Macmillan; New York: St Martin's Press, 1968).

Shinagel, Michael, *Daniel Defoe and Middle-class Gentility* (Cambridge, Mass.: Harvard University Press, 1968).

Sill, Geoffrey, M., *Defoe and the Idea of Fiction* (Newark, NJ & London: University of Delaware Press/Associated University Presses, 1983).

Simpson, Alan, *Puritanism in Old and New England* (Chicago: University of Chicago Press, 1955).

Spacks, Patricia Meyer, *Imagining a Self: Autobiography and Novel in Eighteenth-century England* (Cambridge, Mass.: Harvard University Press, 1976).

Starr, G. A., *Defoe and Casuistry* (Princeton, NJ: Princeton University Press, 1971).

Starr, G. A., *Defoe and Spiritual Autobiography* (Princeton, NJ: Princeton University Press, 1965).

Sutherland, James, *Daniel Defoe: A Critical Study* (Cambridge, Mass.: Harvard University Press, 1971).

Sutherland, James, *English Literature of the Late Seventeenth Century* (Oxford: Clarendon Press, 1969).

Talon, Henri, *John Bunyan: The Man and his Works*, trans. B. Wall (London: Rockliff, 1951; New York: Longmans, Green, 1956).

Tawney, R. H., *Religion and the Rise of Capitalism* (London: John Murray; New York: Harcourt, Brace, 1926).

Tillyard, E. M. W., *The English Epic and its Background* (London: Chatto & Windus, 1954; New York: Oxford University Press, 1966).

Tindall, W. Y., *John Bunyan, Mechanick Preacher* (New York: Columbia University Press, 1934).

Van Ghent, Dorothy, *The English Novel: Form and Function* (New York: Holt, Rinehart and Winston, 1953).

Venables, Edmund, *Life of John Bunyan* (London: Walter Scott; New York: Thomas Whittaker, 1888).

Watkins, Owen, *The Puritan Experience* (London: Routledge & Kegan Paul; New York: Schocken, 1972).

Watt, Ian, *The Rise of the Novel* (London: Chatto & Windus; Berkeley: University of California Press, 1957).

Webber, Joan, *The Eloquent 'I': Style and Self in Seventeenth-century Prose* (Madison: University of Wisconsin Press, 1968).

Wendel, François, *Calvin*, trans. Philip Mairet (London: William Collins; New York: Harper & Row, 1963).

West, Alick, *The Mountain in the Sunlight* (London: Lawrence & Wishart, 1958; Westport, Conn.: Greenwood Press, 1980).

Wharey, J. B., *A Study of the Sources of Bunyan's Allegories* (Baltimore: Furst, 1904).

Wright, Louis B., *Middle Class Culture in Elizabethan England* (Chapel Hill, NC: University of North Carolina Press, 1935).

Zimmerman, Everett, *Defoe and the Novel* (Berkeley: University of California Press, 1975).

ARTICLES

Borsay, Peter, 'The English urban renaissance: the development of provincial urban culture c.1680–1780', *SH*, 5 (1977), 581–603.

Brown, Homer O., 'The displaced self in the novels of Daniel Defoe', *ELH*, 38 (1971), 562–90.

Dugdale, Clarence Eugene, 'Bunyan's court scenes', *TSE*, 21 (1941), 64–78.

Greaves, Richard L., 'John Bunyan's *Holy War* and London Nonconformity', *BQ*, 26 (1975), 158–68.

Hussey, Maurice, 'Arthur Dent's *Plaine Man's Path-way to Heaven*', *MLR*, 44 (1949), 26–34.

Hussey, Maurice, 'Christian conduct in Bunyan and Baxter', *BQ*, 14 (1951), 75–83.

Keeble, N. H., '*The Pilgrim's Progress*: a Puritan fiction', *BQ*, 27 (1980), 321–36.

Keeble, N. H., 'The way and the ways of Puritan story', *English*, 33 (1984), 209–32.

Knott, John R., Jr, 'Bunyan's gospel day: a reading of *The Pilgrim's Progress*', *ELR*, 3 (1973), 443–61.

Koonce, Howard L., 'Moll's muddle: Defoe's use of irony in *Moll Flanders*', *ELH*, 30 (1963), 377–94.

Mullet, M., 'The internal politics of Bedford, 1660–1688', *PBHRS*, 59 (1980), 1–42.

Novak, M. E., 'Crusoe the king and the political evolution of his island', *SEL*, 2 (1962), 337–50.

Nussbaum, Felicity A., '"By these words I was sustained": Bunyan's *Grace Abounding*', *ELH*, 49 (1982), 18–34.

Royce, Josiah, 'The case of John Bunyan', *PR*, 1 (1894), 22–33, 134–51, 230–40.

Sharrock, Roger, '*The Life and Death of Mr Badman*: facts and problems', *MLR*, 82 (1987), 15–29.

Sharrock, Roger, 'Spiritual autobiography in *The Pilgrim's Progress*', *RES*, 24 (1948), 102–20.

Sharrock, Roger, 'The trial of vices in Puritan fiction', *BQ*, 14 (1951), 3–12.

Sim, Stuart, 'Bunyan's *Holy War* and the dialectics of long-drawn-outness', *Restoration*, 9 (1985), 93–8.

Sim Stuart, '"For some it driveth to dispaire": Calvinist soteriology and character models in Arthur Dent's *Plaine Man's Path-way to Heaven*', *ES*, 69 (1988), 238–48.

Sim, Stuart, 'Interrogating an ideology: Defoe's *Robinson Crusoe*', *BJECS*, 10 (1987), 163–73.

Sim, Stuart, 'Isolating the reprobate: paradox as a strategy for social critique in Bunyan's *Mr Badman*', *BS*, 1 (1988/9), 30–41.

Sim, Stuart, 'Opposing the unopposable: *Roxana* and the paradox of reprobation', *BJECS*, 8 (1985), 179–86.

Sim, Stuart, '"Vertuous mediocrity and Fanatick conventicle":

pilgrimage styles in Bishop Simon Patrick and John Bunyan',
ES, 68 (1987), 316–24.

Thickstun, Margaret Olofson, 'From Christiana to Steadfast:
subsuming the feminine in *The Pilgrim's Progress*', SEL, 26
(1986), 439–53.

West, Alick, '*The Holy War* and *The Pilgrim's Progress*', MQ, 8
(1953), 169–82.

Wharey, J. B., 'Bunyan's *Holy War* and the conflict-type of morality
play', *MLN*, 34 (1919), 65–73.

Wharey, J. B., 'Bunyan's *Mr Badman*', *MLN*, 36 (1921), 65–79.

INDEX

213